TALL TALI

HIGH TOWERS

SIMPLE IDEAS

'N STUFF

*A History of Greenville's First
All Country Music Radio Station*

WESC RADIO
1949-1991
WALLY MULLINAX, VP Retired

Library of Congress Control Number: 2003104978, April 2, 2003

ISBN 1-931600-35-X

Publisher: Wally Mullinax Communications Consultants, Inc.
        17 Hiawatha Drive
        Greenville, SC 29615
        Phone: (864) 244-4716

CONTENTS

INTRODUCTION

How many times have you heard someone say, "When I retire I'll write a book about this place!"

Well, I decided to do it. I hope you will find it interesting; from life on Main Street in the '40s to the development of Greenville's first 24-hour country music station, I hope you'll find within these pages a snapshot of some of the finest people in the world, the WESC staff. Through trial and error, good times and bad times, with good ideas — and some that were not so good — the WESC staff built a wonderful company. I've said WESC had the best and most loyal audience on radio. It's for all of these reasons there was never a day that I did not look forward to going to work. To these talented individuals and the people they served, I humbly present this book.

ACKNOWLEDGMENTS

My sincere thanks to all who encouraged me to write this account of my career at WESC.

To my friend and secretary, Connie Glennon, who corrected what the spell check missed and changed my poor punctuation. I'll pay you with love and admiration if the book doesn't sell. Thanks a bunch, Connie.

To my friend and legal counsel, Jay Bender, who read the manuscript at the cost of an "arm and a leg," a million thanks!

Thanks to the University of South Carolina and the South Carolina Broadcasters Association for the use of archival material. Also, to the others who contributed pictures.

DEDICATION

To my wife, Helen, who emphasized, sympathized and socialized with me through the years. Thanks!

And to the Listeners and Sponsors that supported us, thanks a zillion.

Finally to my readers, if you like it tell your friends and suggest they buy a book. If you don't like it ask them to buy one and burn it 'cause I want to get rid of the darn things.

Part I

The Beginning

Chapter 1

The Beginning Idea: Music! Music! Music!

WESC AM came on the air in Greenville, South Carolina, Sunday, March 16, 1947, with test programs. The regular broadcast schedule started the next day, St. Patrick's Day. The station colors were green on white. Some of the station printing had a touch of black accenting the green. The slogan was: "WESC, 5000 watts on clear channel — 660 in Dixie — Starting from Greenville." Georgia native Scott Russell, an attorney with the Commerce Department in Washington, D.C., came to Greenville to start the station, naming the corporation the Greenville Broadcasting Company, Inc. In addition to Mr. Russell, the stockholders were: Ben and Jim Russell (Mr. Russell's sons from his first marriage) and Greenville investors Fred Symmes and Sidney Bruce. Scott Russell was in the textile business in Macon, Georgia, before going to Washington, and no doubt already knew them.

Probably the shareholders were motivated more by friendship and civic pride than profit. Also, they perhaps wanted to help the Russell family get the frequency granted, because the FCC favored applications if local citizens were involved. While in Washington, Mr. Russell, a widower, married Christie Kennedy, secretary to U.S. Senator Walter F. George of Georgia. The couple had high hopes of eventually having an unlimited time station on 660 KC in Greenville. Many broadcasters believed the FCC would soon change the rules regulating the "daytime" stations assigned to the clear channels, such as 660 KC, to allow twenty-four hour operation. The FCC did not permit 660 KC to be used on a twenty-four hour basis in the continental United States except in New York City. That license was held by RCA, the parent company of the National Broadcasting Company. In the planning stage, there was discussion about switching WESC AM to 640 KC and moving 660 KC to Atlanta when the rules changed. Another option was to apply for 640 KC in the Charlotte or Greensboro, North Carolina, area if and when the FCC rules permitted 640 KC to be used in the eastern part of the country.

So, using the rules under which radio was regulated at the time, the Greenville Broadcasting Company, Inc., applied for and received an FCC grant for 660 KC, WESC AM 5000 watts daytime, "660 in Dixie — We Entertain South Carolina." The station was granted on August 9, 1946. Washington legal counsel for the application was Neville Miller. A.D. Ring and Associates, also of Washington, prepared the engineering.

A transmitter site was secured west of Greenville, on Farr's Bridge Road, at the White Horse Road intersection. A prominent Berea area property owner, Mr. Tom Jones, leased land to the corporation for the purpose of constructing the ground system and transmitter tower. The company chose a downtown site for its studios, so after some excavation, studios and offices were built in the basement of the Provost building, located at Main and College Streets. History buffs may be interested in real estate values in Greenville in 1946. As I recall, the studio rent was three hundred dollars per month and the transmitter property rent was seventy-five dollars per week. That would have been less than 50 cents per square foot for studio space and about $10 per acre a month for transmitter property. The leases ran for ten years. I suppose the Greenville Broadcasting Company constructed the studios at its own expense.

The studios located at Number One College Street were in an area of the city appealing to upscale shoppers. The stores offered fashionable merchandise — some of it a little more expensive than that sold in other Main Street shops. Two theatres, the Carolina and Fox, featured the latest movies. Within a few blocks the Center, Ritz and Bijou played reruns, westerns or whatever else the law or local mores allowed. The Ottaray Hotel was located across North Main Street from the Provost building. The hotel dining room was a popular eating place for shoppers and the business community. Often hotel patrons watched Greenvillians come and go while rocking in the large green chairs on the big white front porch that faced south on North Main Street. The sounds of the city were the honking of taxicabs and the whirl of electric motors powering the trolley cars. Often in the turn at College and Main the trolley cables jumped the overhead track, requiring the driver to get out of the trolley and reattach them. This gave the high school kids an opportunity to toss paper airplanes or sing. As hotel guests rocked to the sights and sounds of Main Street, the pleasant fragrances of petunias, dahlias and roses in the hotel porch planters added to their enjoyment.

A few doors down Main Street the soda fountain at Ashmore's Pharmacy was a popular meeting place for some of Greenville's teens. Many of the guys gathered on the sidewalk, talking about whatever young people talked about — probably girls, sports and cars. This was also a good spot for girl watching. Furman University coeds and the belles of Southern Bell strolled Main and College streets. Another meeting place, within a block of the WESC studios, was Sam's Lunch, located on College Street at the Townes Street intersection. Sam served mustard-laden hot dogs and hamburgers with chili, onions or other trimmings. Sam's quick service menu attracted people from nearby businesses, as well as young men and women from the Women's College of Furman University. The Furman women's campus was located in the three hundred block of College Street, now occupied by Heritage Green. Those with ties to the school affectionately called it "the zoo."

The Toastee Restaurant was located on North Main Street about a half a block south from the Ottaray Hotel. This restaurant was known for blue-plate lunches and hamburger steaks. The Toastee steaks were served piping hot with a plate full of french fries. A popular server at the Toastee was Bob Brown who had just returned from a POW camp in Germany. Bob now operates the University Shop in North Hills Shopping Center. The Deluxe Diner was located on North Main across from where the Daniel Building (BB&T Bank) now stands. Its attractions were scrambled eggs, grits and toast with a choice of bacon, sausage or ham. The hamburgers were very good: topped with lettuce, tomato and a thick slice of onion. The buns were toasted, adding a special flavor to the trimmings stacked neatly on the bun oozing with mustard, catsup and other spreads squeezed from plastic containers on the counter. The Deluxe fare also included cheeseburgers, roast pork sandwiches, pancakes and other short orders. One of the diner's enticements was chocolate icebox pie. The Deluxe Diner was a popular stop after high school and college athletic events for two reasons: the food was good and the owner of the Diner, the Tzouvelekas family, had sons involved in sports, so its patrons could always get the Greenville, Parker, Furman and Clemson scores when they stopped at the Deluxe Diner.

Nick's Diner was located about a block north on the left, across from Springwood Cemetery. Nick's seating was mostly arranged in booths where customers with more time and a bigger appetite, or seeking privacy, usually found it. Nick's menu featured fried chicken, steaks, chops, salads, pies and cakes.

The Waffle Shop was located in the YWCA building on West North Street near the Buncombe Street United Methodist Church. Some of its favorite dishes were homemade vegetable soup, cornbread, buttermilk, iced tea and mouth watering home-cooked pot roast, turkey, dressing, chicken with rice and gravy. Many traveling salesmen planned their stop in Greenville to include lunch at the Waffle Shop. One of the best-known steak houses in the state, Charlie's Steak House, was about three blocks away, over on East Coffee Street. Many Greenvillians, as well as out-of-town visitors, planned shopping and business trips around thoughts of a thick, juicy T-bone with steak fries and onion rings from Charlie's Steak House.

All of these eateries attracted patrons from throughout the county to the area where WESC's studios were to be constructed. While the studios were under construction some customers at the restaurants joined the "WESC Sidewalk Superintendents Club." After the station was built, WESC staff members and performing musicians were regular patrons at the restaurants.

Headquarters for the "Sidewalk Superintendents Club" was an area enclosed by a tall wooden fence which surrounded an opening in the Provost Building at the College Street level.

Behind the fence was a hole in the outside wall of the building through which the construction workers removed dirt from under the structure. This excavated space became the WESC studios. Christie and Gary Provost were the landlords. Splashed across the white fence were billboard size green letters with the announcement "Coming Soon — 5000 watts, WESC,.660 in Dixie — Starting from Greenville!" The message on the fence invited the passerby to peek into the peephole and become a member of the WESC Sidewalk Superintendents Club. WESC's Art Roberts and WMRC's Bob Poole obviously had some fun with that.

The Main and College Street intersection was a busy corner. The Chevrolet, Oldsmobile and Kaiser car dealerships were in the area, as well as tire dealerships, a record shop, a liquor store and saloon, complete with swinging doors, bar stools and shavings on the floor. In a couple of years, some of the saloon patrons, who were enjoying a Saturday snort, wandered into the radio station wanting to meet Hank Williams, Kitty Wells, Roy Acuff or Ernest Tubb. Most went away happy when they were told that the stars were in Nashville to perform for them on the Grand Ole Opry. We usually promised to play them a record and they went back across the street to wait for their request and name to be announced on the radio.

Occasionally, the bar and booze attracted street preachers with PA systems installed on their automobiles. These sidewalk orators parked in front of the station's College Street entrance and spread the word about the dangers of cigarettes, whiskey and wild, wild women. Usually the cops arrived just about the time the street preachers completed their message of hellfire and damnation. The delay was probably the city's way of controlling them without confronting them.

College Street in those days stopped at North Main, so

there was plenty of activity on the two corners. At the Pure Oil service station on the northwest corner the passerby could get directions to Asheville, a fill-up complete with bumper-to-bumper service and, if you wanted to take the time, a game of checkers. The checkerboard was all set up on a table erected with soft drink crates. Other empty crates provided seating.

On the south side of the Main and College corner, there was a good observation point for describing parades, as well as Man On The Street broadcasts. The Furman Homecoming Parade, the Armistice Parade and the Christmas Parade were regularly on the city calendar but sometimes St. Patrick's Day and Memorial Day parades were hastily organized by Mayor Kenneth Cass to appease WESC's Art Roberts and WMRC's Bob Poole.

WMRC — the second station to be built in Greenville — located its studio on the second floor of the Provost Building. So the morning guys became good friends and sometimes collaborated with each other as they went about their morning mischief. Sometimes Roberts and Poole were responding to criticism from new citizens — many of whom were stationed at the Greenville Army Air Base, later renamed Donaldson Air Force Base — who were accustomed to celebrating ALL the holidays.

Parades were not usually held in Greenville on July 4th or Labor Day, so Mayor Cass escaped a good-natured tongue lashing on these holidays. The textile mills shut down for July 4th, allowing many textile workers to be out of town fishing, eating watermelon at family reunions or attending textile baseball games. Labor Day wasn't celebrated much in Greenville County in the late '40s because the people were too busy. The farmers were picking and ginning cotton, textile workers were weaving and spinning it and vets on the G.I. Bill were rushing to finish college or vocational school. Many were establishing homes for the wave of babies born after the war. These kids were later labeled **Baby Boomers**. The business community was too busy supplying consumer items caused by the wartime shortages to get excited about an end of summer holiday. There just wasn't much time to observe Labor Day. Some in the power structure may have intentionally turned their backs on a union holiday in this nonunion cotton mill town but I think most people in Greenville labored on Labor Day because they were focused on whatever was important to them: providing for their families, preparing for their futures and making up for the time lost while in the military. A few people went to the beaches and they became the nucleus of the Southern 500 auto-racing crowd at Darlington.

An announcer and control operator reported the parades. The announcer was expected to describe the parade without a script: capturing the Furman spirit at the Homecoming Parade, stimulating national pride for the armed forces on November 11th and projecting the spirit of the season at Christmas. Art Roberts and Wayne Davis were always very good on these impromptu ad-lib assignments. They sometimes talked for more than an hour without notes.

When WESC signed on the air, Greenville's oldest station, WFBC AM (l330 KC), located in the Poinsett Hotel on South Main Street, produced a special program saluting their new competitor. The refrain in a song written especially for the show and heard throughout the broadcast, boasted of the business climate in Greenville:

"Greenville is growing and Greenville is fair — there's room for more stations to come on the air."

This WFBC program was written, produced and performed by most all of the WFBC staff. It turned out to be prophetic because the show featured country and gospel music.

The country music band heard on the special salute was **Lee Boswell and the Hi Neighbor Gang**. The gospel quartet was **The Melody Masters.**

After leaving Greenville the gospel singers became nationally known performers in the gospel music field. The members of the group were: Big Chief Weatherington, Jake Hess, Kat Freeman and Wally Varner. I was a part-time announcer at WFBC while a student at Furman University in 1947, and was assigned to be the announcer for **The Melody Masters** program. This gave me some valuable experience and established a rapport with gospel music fans. The relationship was helpful to me after I joined the staff of WESC in 1949.

WESC President Scott Russell set an example for the staff with his punctual work schedule: weekdays 9:00 a.m. to 5:00 p.m., Saturdays 9:00 a.m. to 1:00 p.m., lunch noon to 1:00 p.m. Although WESC subscribed to Western Union time service, its clocks probably could have been adjusted with Mr. Russell's arrival or departure. He also made a statement about himself in the way he traveled to and from work — in a chauffeur driven Patrician Packard. This was Scott Russell. He knew most of the movers and shakers in the first half of the 20th century. His friends included World War I flying ace Eddie Rickenbacker and other business and industrial pioneers. Having an impressive car with a driver was a mark of success. Incidentally, I had the privilege of meeting and chatting with Eddie Rickenbacker while he was visiting Mr. Russell at WESC. Mr. Russell was a World War I buddy of the aviator. I believe they were in the 94th Aero Squadron in World War I.

Eddie Rickenbacker was a national hero. As a First Lieutenant in the U.S. Army Air Corps in the First World War and while on voluntary patrol over the lines near Billy,

France, September 25th, 1918, Rickenbacker attacked seven German planes, shooting down two of them. For his gallantry above and beyond the call of duty Lt. Edward V. Rickenbacker was awarded the Congressional Medal of Honor. He received many other citations and honors from the United States and France for his valor and bravery. After the war he pioneered commercial aviation. At the beginning of World War II Rickenbacker survived an air crash at sea, catching seagulls, eating their raw flesh and using the entrails as fish bait. In today's jargon Captain Eddie Rickenbacker was a "hot topic." After I was introduced to him, I asked if he would grant me an interview. Mr. Rickenbacker told me he could not grant an interview because he was under contract to a national publication for articles already written for future publication. As I recall, Art Roberts or Wayne Davis did interview him but they were limited in their questioning. Rickenbacker hung around the station until it was time for Russell to go to lunch. Remember I said Mr. Russell was punctual? Lunchtime was twelve noon, so even with a national hero as his guest Scott Russell kept his schedule.

Perhaps it was because he had worked in Washington or maybe it was because he had a dispute with labor unions in Georgia, but for whatever reason, Scott Russell was a fair employer. WESC, from the day it went on the air, provided health insurance, vacations, holidays, good working conditions and opportunities for extra income through talent and production fees.

Mr. Russell wasn't like one of his Georgia contemporaries who opened a station in an upstate town and commuted from northeast Georgia to oversee the business located in a non-air-conditioned studio. The staff of that station always needed paper clips, rubber bands, pencils and other office supplies. When the staff complained about the lack of materials with which to accomplish their work "Mr. Tightwad's" reply was "We'll buy that when we get over the hill." One day he came into the station and announced to the staff that he had sold the station for a tidy profit. A staff member spoke up and said, "Now that you have all that money, maybe we can get some paper clips," to which he replied, "That's your problem; I'm going over the hill." And out the door he went.

WESC always, even in its darkest days, paid better than average wages and paychecks were on time. All during the 42 years I worked at the station I never missed a payday nor was my paycheck late.

In addition to president and general manager Scott Russell, among the members of WESC's first staff were: Caldwell Cline, program director, recruited from WBT, Charlotte, and Art Roberts, chief announcer, a graduate of the University of South Carolina and native of Boise, Idaho. Also on the staff were: Ken Keese, music director, and Wayne Davis, news director; announcers Ed Blair and Vernon Fox; chief engineer Lewis Elias and transmitter/studio technician Horace Morris. Also, part-time announcers Ken Heatherly, Joe Thomas, Hal Goller, Ben Howard, and Bob Edwards. The part-time announcers worked weekend or late afternoon shifts; some were assigned duties in the control room. Also, Heatherly and Howard may have been part-time salesmen. Office personnel included Betty McCowan, secretary to Mr. Russell; Betty Bell, traffic director; Helen Roberts, copy director; and Dot Slaughter, copywriter. Jimmy Little was commercial manager and Sam Hutchens, a salesman. A more complete list of station employees appears in Part II.

In the late '40s, the staff included Jay "Jake" Presson, who left Greenville and established his own chain of small radio stations in North Carolina, and Jim Brownell. Later, Mr. Brownell managed several small stations in the upstate before retiring from WCCP (l560 KC) in Clemson, S.C. He is now deceased. Audrey Hunt was one of the first women to have a regular program. The role of women in radio in those days was mostly to host a quarter hour program of music and feature material from the newswire. There was most always a recipe. Usually the commercials spotlighted women's fashions, new appliances or news appealing to homemakers. What these programs were called depended on the audience. In polite company they were usually "ladies' programs" but to the Southern adman it was "housewife time."

WESC's first women's director, Audrey Hunt, left WESC when her husband, a Southern Bell executive, was transferred to Columbia. She joined the staff at WIS (560 KC). After leaving WESC, Dot Slaughter married the chief of the Clemson College News Bureau, Ed Osborne. Later, the couple owned and operated WBCU (l460 KC) in Union, S.C., until their retirement. Mr. Osborne died in 2000.

Bob Edwards helped establish WFIS (l600 KC) in Fountain Inn, S.C. In the late '50s, Mr. Edwards and his investors sold WFIS to Wayne Davis, then station manager of WESC. At the time of this writing Mr. Davis serves as mayor of Fountain Inn, S.C. Bob Edwards is deceased. Betty McCowan became a media buyer for the Henderson Advertising Agency. Later, as the Leslie Advertising media director, Ms. McCowan earned a national reputation for buying advertising. When possible, she included radio in the client's advertising mix, probably because she observed the power of radio at WESC. Ms. McCowan is deceased. Ken Heatherly joined the sales staff at a local car dealership and eventually became a sales executive with the Chrysler Corporation in Detroit. He is retired in Florida. Hal Goller became a Greenville business and civic leader excelling as an agent with the MONY insurance company. He won 55

National Quality awards in his 50-year career. Mr. Goller died in 2000.

After leaving WESC, Joe Thomas worked for WMRC (1440 KC) before going into the United States Army during the Korean conflict. 1st Lt. Thomas was shot down and killed while piloting an artillery observation plane in Korea. It was a voluntary mission that occurred while Lt. Thomas was awaiting passage home after flying the required number of missions. Joe Thomas and his wife, Faye, were dinner guests in our home the night before he left Greenville to go to Korea. When it came time to leave, Joe and I walked to his car together. Out of earshot from Faye, he told me that he had a strange feeling he would never return. I tried to reassure him, saying that he had lived a Christian life and had been a good influence on all of us and surely if anyone came home it would be he. I believe Joe Thomas sacrificed his life for his comrades. World War II flyers tell me the odds of survival diminish sharply after a pilot reaches his required number of missions. Surely Joe Thomas knew the odds would be against him if he flew that last mission. He flew to knock out enemy artillery and save American lives.

"Greater love hath no man than this, that a man lay down his life for his friends" (St. John 15:13).

Vernon Fox established WCKI (1300 KC) in Greer, S.C. When Vernon started the station he came to me saying that he needed $1500 to purchase a used transmitter. He offered me 50% of the station if I would put up the money. That would have been a good investment had the FCC rules permitted me to remain at WESC. But they didn't and I didn't. Vernon Fox was a good man. He served in WWII and brought too many of those memories home with him. Vernon Fox is now deceased but his dream of a "home folks" radio station still lives. Vernon took it to the first level, then our ole friend

Marshall Pack, his son, Ronnie, and Ronnie's wife, Arleen, made it a gospel music lighthouse for Greer, Greenville and Spartanburg.

Horace Morris started Greenville's first industrial communications and paging service. Sam Hutchens left WESC to become the first general manager of WEAB (800 KC) in Greer, S.C. Later, Hutchens helped start stations at Myrtle Beach and some other Southeastern coastal cities. Ben Howard entered the automobile financing business. Jim Little became a restaurateur and motel owner. Mr. Little established the first Howard Johnson's restaurant in Greenville, located on Wade Hampton Boulevard; at the time of this writing the Red Lobster Restaurant occupies the building across the street from the Liberty Corporation headquarters.

After leaving Greenville, Art Roberts worked in St. Louis and perhaps some other stations in the Midwest before retiring in Idaho. Caldwell Cline joined his wife's family in the antiques business in North Carolina. Ed Blair went to work for WGST (920 KC), the Georgia Tech station in Atlanta. Ed was frequently heard on CBS network news reports. He eventually returned to Chattanooga, Tennessee, where he died at an early age.

Some of the other staff members in the late '40s were: Troy Bagwell, control operator; Ray Stanfield and Ron Clary, announcers; Jessie "Rudy" Dickerson, control operator; Charles Fletcher, janitor; Jacquelyn Keese, program assistant; Doris Moorehead, copywriter; and Boyd Staton, salesman. Some of the transmitter operators in the late '40s were: Charles Kirkwood, Robert Vogal, Paul Dick and William Gregory. The FCC required stations to have licensed first class radiotelephone operators on duty at the transmitter location whenever the transmitter was on the air. Since the WESC transmitter was located away from the studio, the transmitter operators rarely came in the studio, except to pick up their paycheck. Often a new hire would introduce himself to an after business hours studio employee only to discover they were already phone pals.

Some Greenvillians may want to know what happened to Ray Stanfield. Ray left WESC in 1950, and after a few months at WFBC (1330 KC) he joined the staff of WIS (560 KC) in Columbia working for radio pioneer G. Richard Shafto. Mr. Shafto saw management potential in Ray and encouraged him to move into the WIS management program. Ray eventually went to Charlotte to manage the Liberty Life (Cosmos) station in Charlotte, WIST (930 KC), until the station could be sold. Ray was a sharp programmer and a good salesman, always looking for ways to improve his station. So, he listened to distant clear channel stations at night while parked at drive-in restaurants or on trips. He discovered a rock-formatted station, convinced his superiors in Columbia that he should switch the programming on WIST. It became Charlotte's first rock station and was a huge success.

When the station was sold, for much more than the original half-million-dollar asking price, Ray was offered a job with a large radio rep firm in New York (PG&W). He eventually became its national sales manager. In 1964, I visited Ray Stanfield in his New York office located in a skyscraper with a picture window at his back overlooking the city of New York. It was an impressive sight. When station owners and advertising clients were seated in Ray's office negotiating contracts, I'm sure it would have been hard for them to argue over the little things with such a magnificent background.

After leaving PG&W, Ray Stanfield worked for stations in Denver and Los Angeles before going to work for Paul Chapman & Associates, a radio/TV brokerage firm headquartered in Atlanta. Ray represented the firm on the West

Coast. The owner of the firm, Paul Chapman, was a native of Greenville and former staff member with Ray Stanfield at WFBC. When Paul Chapman retired he sold the firm to Ray Stanfield, and Ray enjoyed a very successful career helping clients buy and sell radio and television stations all over America. In the 1980's, a story in **Broadcasting Magazine** reported on the activity of the radio/TV brokerage business for that year. Ray Stanfield had reported his personal sales at over one hundred million dollars for that one year. You can do the math at the customary 5% commission. I guess that WESC alumnus did right well for himself. Ray Stanfield is now deceased. Ray Stanfield married his Greenville High School sweetheart Pat McHugh, they remained together until she died in California. I was a pallbearer at Pat Stanfield's funeral. Her grave is in the Springwood Cemetery in Greenville. Ray's second wife, Evie, assisted him in his brokerage business, stood by him during his long bout with cancer and entombed his body in California.

WESC's first program format was music, news and sports. The programs were produced with phonograph records listed on the **Billboard** magazine and popular music charts, as well as the Lang-Worth and SESAC music libraries. The library services provided scripts for their programs, using music licensed and performed under their contracts. Sometimes the scripts instructed the local announcer to interview the artist, inserting the artist's transcribed comments. You might say the announcer had a conversation with a transcription. A skillful announcer made these programs sound "live" using music bridges, production aids and the voices of the big band leaders. Some of the other shows featured announcers who could play the organ or the piano, playing musical bridges as they introduced the transcribed or recorded music. Sometimes these announcers played the instruments, read poems or sang.

WESC boasted about its independence. That is, it did not have a network. The networks usually required their stations to broadcast a minimum number of "free" commercial hours each month-mostly speech and drama programs. Speech programs were considered to be counter-productive for music stations. Thus, even in 1947 the program gurus were promoting "More Music." Some hours were commercial free with limited speech. However, these music periods were not **promoted** as "commercial free" because management believed such comments projected a negative message.

Most of the time, the announcer simply announced the program, in a matter-of-fact voice, as "30 minutes of uninterrupted music." Station breaks were required on the hour and half hour but sometimes station breaks were omitted on the half hour if a long passage of classical music was to be interrupted. The FCC didn't want to upset the classical music crowd.

Chapter 2

The 1940's:
A Good Idea ~ Comedy,
Country and Cash!

In the late 1940's, a strong commercial manager usually set the agenda for new radio stations. Cliff Bowers believed in programming radio stations to generate revenue. He knew that country and gospel music programs produced results for advertisers. Also, Cliff knew that ball games were easy to sell. So, when Mr. Bowers came aboard as commercial manager, some of the popular music programs on WESC were replaced by country music, gospel music and sports events. In addition to Mr. Bowers' skill as a salesman, he was involved in the civic and religious life of Greenville. This community involvement made him and his product more attractive to the main street merchant in the '40s.

Cliff Bowers taught Sunday school at the Buncombe Street United Methodist Church, was active in the Boy Scouts, Rotary Club and participated in the activities of the Greenville Chamber of Commerce. He was a good representative of the company and a good recruiter. He soon brought

Edward L. Martin aboard as a salesman. A native of Greenville, Mr. Martin convinced many of his friends in the Greenville community to support the station. Soon revenues began to rise. Ed Martin made a significant contribution to the success of WESC during the short time he was on the staff but his stay at the station was cut short because he was recalled into the U.S. Navy during the Korean conflict. Ed Martin did not return to WESC after his discharge. Instead he became a manufacturer's representative and enjoyed a very successful sales career outside of radio.

Upon the arrival of Cliff Bowers as commercial manager, WESC began accepting paid religious programs. One of the most popular and successful was the Rev. Harold B. Sightler with **The Bright Spot Hour.** This program began on WMRC in 1944 and moved to WESC at the invitation of Bowers. The Reverend Sightler described Cliff as "a real friend of the old time Gospel." The Reverend Sightler's programs featured inspiring religious music, performed by musicians who, in addition to helping with his radio broadcast, often supplied special music for his revivals.

Among those assisting the Rev. Sightler, according to the "Bright Spot Hour" archives, were: Mrs. Preston Garrett, organ/piano; *The Bright Spot Hour Male Trio,* whose members were Horace Jones, Lloyd Jones, and the Reverend Wyatt Jones; and *The Bright Spot Hour Ladies Trio,* which included Grace Brookshire, Minnie Brewer and Nadine Brookshire. *The Harmony Trio* featured Hubert Kirby, Leon Southerland, J.B. Compton and Charles Carson. Organist for *The Bright Spot Hour* was Minnie Brewer. The first announcer for *The Bright Spot Hour* after it was moved to WESC was Wayne Davis and assisting in the control room was Troy Bagwell. A 1956 Nielsen Pulse Survey reported that the *Bright Spot Hour* was the most popular program on WESC. It attracted about

27% of the radio homes in 19 surrounding counties to WESC.

The Rev. Sightler was heard on WESC for about 16 years, during which time he established the Tabernacle Baptist Church in Greenville, and syndicated *The Bright Spot Hour* into other Southern states. In time, Mr. Sightler's ministry purchased a station on 1540 KC in Pickens, S.C., and changed the call letters to WTBI. When the FCC rules permitted, WTBI added the FM station (91.7 FM). These stations are now operated from studios at the Tabernacle Baptist Church campus on White Horse Road in Greenville. Dr. Sightler is deceased but his grandson, Evangelist Bennie Carper, continues the ministry. This is the oldest continuous local broadcast in Greenville. The Reverend Carper says the program uses current radio production technology but stays true to the King James Version of the Bible. At this writing, *The Bright Spot Hour* is heard on fifty U.S. radio stations. It is also heard in England and Australia by short wave radio.

Chapter 3

A High Frequency Idea

WESC FM (92.5 FM) went on the air in 1948, about a year after WESC AM signed on. The dial position 92.5 FM was selected because the listener could switch from WESC AM to WESC FM simply by turning the AM/FM selector switch. On most FM radios the dial position didn't have to be changed when WESC AM left the air. Later the FCC designated the station as a Class C station, a classification reserved for FM stations to cover a large area. Since the curvature of the earth has a lot to do with FM reception, I asked an engineer — about the time WESC FM was given its class C designation — why 92.5 was such a good frequency. He explained the transmitter site could be moved to the mountains, offering a better line of sight to more people. In the days of two and three dollar spots, moving a transmitter to a high mountain was the stuff dreams were made of.

As a "sign on" promotion for WESC FM, and as a gesture of goodwill from WSM (650 KC) in Nashville, Tennessee,

WESC FM was permitted to broadcast **The Grand Ole Opry** for a few months. This required WESC FM to install a special telephone line — they called it a balanced line — from Greenville to Nashville to insure good music transmission. The promotion was a success! Greenville area country music fans with access to FM receivers listened to *The Grand Ole Opry* on crystal clear FM without the uncertainty of weather and sky wave conditions. What a difference!

One of WESC FM's first regular programs was the nightly Bob Jones University program. Since BJU did not have a radio station at this time, the school used their WESC program as a public relations tool and outreach ministry. In the tradition of Bob Jones University the quality of the music and production was very good. Also, the religious speakers communicated with modulated voices. They were different from the run of the mill radio evangelist heard on most radio stations in those days. Some of them must have thought, "The louder I shout the farther I'll be heard." The Bob Jones programs featured messages by Dr. Bob Jones, Sr., Dr. Bob Jones, Jr., and guest speakers visiting the university. The programs were not political or controversial but focused on winning souls and friends for the university. The announcers were Dave Yearick and Jim Ryerson. I apologize if there were others, but these were the ones I remember. Dave Yearick became a successful pastor at the Hampton Park Baptist Church of Greenville and Jim Ryerson served the university for many years as general manager of WMUU AM/FM and later as a member of the faculty.

The airing of the Bob Jones University program and the success of Dr. Sightler's ministry may have set the course for WESC in the late '40s and '50s, because in a few years WESC presented **Back to the Bible** with Theodore Epps; **The Old Fashion Revival Hour** with Dr. Charles E. Fuller; **Evangelist**

Billy Graham; The Ole Preacher Man, Brother Maze Jackson with **Broadcasting for Jesus;** and Evangelist Oliver B. Greene with **The Gospel Hour**, to mention a few.

In the early '50s, the Rev. Maze Jackson originated the **Broadcasting for Jesus** program at WESC but later moved his headquarters to Atlanta, Ga., where he was heard on 50,000 watt WGUN (1010 KC). In those days, a young country singer by the name of Roy Drusky was a D.J. for WGUN. Drusky introduced Brother Maze to that vast radio audience before moving to Nashville where his mellow voice and smooth singing of country ballads brought him success as a country act.

In Greenville, Mr. Raymond Jennings was soloist and Mrs. Ruth Baker pianist on some of the **Broadcasting for Jesus** programs produced at WESC. Occasionally, Greenville area church choirs provided special music. The choirs came to the radio station usually at night, and transcribed several songs that were used from time to time. Also featured were some of the transcribed songs of *The Duncan Sisters*, a popular ladies group heard during the Greenville radio ministry of the Reverend J. Harold Smith, who founded **The Radio Bible Hour** on WFBC (1330 KC) in the 1930's. The members of the Duncan Sisters trio were: Lula Duncan (Mrs. Lake Ellis), Lena Duncan (Mrs. Jack Hambright) and Lamar Duncan (Mrs. Wayne Anderson).

I announced and produced the programs for the Reverend Jackson. He reserved Monday nights for this and often it took all night. Tuesday morning, the tape recordings were taken to the post office and mailed to WBSC (1050 KC) in Bennettsville, S.C., WCPS (760 KC) in Tarboro, N.C., and WJAT (800 KC) in Swainsboro, Ga. These stations may have duplicated the tapes and sent them to other stations, or perhaps used an FM relay system to expand the network from time to time. Inexpensive cassette recorders and the technology for high speed duplicating were not developed. Therefore, to form an inexpensive network the tape recordings were often duplicated by a station and forwarded to other stations on the minister's network, for later release. This process was called "bicycling." In addition to introducing and producing the programs, I also made the appeal for financial support, describing with as much persuasion as possible, and without being offensive, the joy the listener would receive from supporting the Lord's work.

Most every Monday night my new bride, Helen, slept on a couch in the WESC lobby while Brother Maze and I recorded six and sometimes twelve 30-minute programs. Since we could not use the station's facilities until after sign-off, it was almost an overnight task — every week! There were glitches. The early machines did not have a "fail safe" system indicating when the machine was recording. It was discouraging to discover in the middle of the night that the "record " switch had not been turned on or a tape came apart at a splice, requiring the program to be redone. Brother Maze was pleasant during these stressful times. He knew mistakes and equipment failures were unavoidable.

I mention these nightmares to inform younger generations about how our business evolved. We learned by experience that a special splicing tape was needed to ensure a dependable splice. Tape makers responded. Also, equipment manufacturers learned that it was necessary to build into the tape machines a warning system — a red light — indicating when the machine was recording. Manufacturers began to wire the machines so that the meter didn't peak unless the recorder was on "record." This helped. We could see the meter peaking and know we were recording the program. There were other frustrations that were corrected by experience.

Sometimes the tapes were returned with the "record" side turned over. We soon learned to check and erase all tapes before reusing them. Today's broadcasters are lucky to have disc recorders that allow bits and pieces to be lifted out of programs and dropped in electronically. Although we had magnetic tape recorders in the '50s, I remember the first tape in the middle '40s was carbon, then came wire, and the ultimate (so we thought), magnetic tape.

The Reverend Jackson was the first local evangelist to appear regularly on TV. He was seen on a thirty minute Sunday night telecast in the summer of 1953 or '54. The program was adjacent to Billy Graham on Greenville's first TV station, WGVL-TV, UHF channel 23. In those days, Mr. Graham was seen each week on ABC with a thirty-minute program about 10:30 p.m. So, being on the air before Billy Graham, even though there were few UHF sets, was a big plus.

There were no TV stations between Greenville and Atlanta, so many homes installed "bow ties" to receive the UHF signal. Some twenty years later, before the FCC required all TV sets to receive UHF, Greenville got another UHF station, WGGS-TV 16. By this time, some people had learned to make a homemade antenna with aluminum wrap. Since all sets must now have VHF and UHF, and local over the air signals must be on local cable, the UHF stations can compete with the VHF Station.

Channel 23, with studios in the Calhoun Towers, a high rise on North Main Street, originated studio programs with just one camera. So, Brother Maze basically produced the TV program with a filmed introduction, slide pictures, recorded music, a live prayer and a live message featuring *the young man with an old message,* Brother Maze Jackson and **Broadcasting for Jesus.** I made the appeals for financial support for TV, describing the books and other gifts that were sent to viewers upon request. This was before channel 4 went on the air and it was among the first programs in Greenville to use a local radio personality. The telecast was discontinued when Mr. Jackson moved to Atlanta. His radio ministry eventually targeted truckers. **The Truck Driver's Special** was heard during the overnight hours on some of the powerful 50,000 watt clear channel stations around the country. These stations, located in Tennessee, Texas and some other states in middle America, can get out there and stay with them on the road. Maze Jackson suffered several heart attacks, and after recovering from an attack suffered in his motel room while out preaching a revival, a friend asked him when he planned to retire. The young man with an old message replied that he would go out with his boots on. In a year or so, Maze Jackson was dead! Maze Jackson died in 1996. He was 76. Faithful 'til the end to his message and mission.

The Reverend Oliver B. Greene produced his programs in studios located on White Oak Road in Greenville. He came with WESC in, I think, 1951. **The Gospel Hour** was syndicated to a large network mostly in the South and Midwest. At the height of his ministry he was on 100 radio stations. In his autobiography he states the time charges were $1,000 a day. Although Dr. Greene rarely came to the station, a member of his staff, Ralph Horne, delivered the taped programs to WESC. Mr. Horne was prompt, met deadlines and was liked by WESC staff members. He was a good representative of **The Gospel Hour**. When tapes broke, the wrong program was broadcast, or some other mistake occurred, Mr. Horne always acted in a "Christ-like" manner and this made a positive impression on WESC staff members, causing them to vigorously defend Dr. Greene when some not-too-tolerant listener criticized the minister. The Reverend

Greene is deceased but his family continues his ministry.

Billy Graham distributed his program on the ABC radio network. Mr. Graham's song leader, The Rev. Cliff Barrows, who lived in Greenville, on a few occasions brought **The Hour of Decision** master program to WESC to be sent by special telephone line to the ABC Radio Network in New York for release the following Sunday. Although a very busy personality on the world stage of religious broadcasting, Cliff Barrows seemed never to be in a great hurry when he visited the station. He always took time to cultivate friendships. This persona paid off because the staff took great care to see that the **Hour of Decision** was transmitted to ABC without error. Also, the telephone company was cautious to be sure ABC received a quality program for retransmission. WESC usually assigned its chief engineer, Harold White, and later, Don Gowns, to this project. When cassette tapes became commonplace as a delivery system, Mr. John Lenning of the Graham Association team provided the tapes. Mr. Lenning died in 2002.

Among the churches WESC served in its first fifty years were the Washington Avenue Baptist Church with Dr. W. Daniel Greer and the Overbrook Baptist Church with Dr. Cooper Patrick. During the ministry of Dr. Hardy Clemons, Greenville First Baptist presented their Sunday worship service on WESC AM. Through the years we were pleased to serve the Pendleton Street Baptist Church with William R. West, Jr., pastor; the Laurel Baptist Church with its pastor, the Rev. Jessie Hill; and many others. WESC served groups outside the Baptist faith. The Rev. L.C. Heaston, Mrs. C.C. Shellnut and Dr. W. Norman Greenway were among the other ministers heard on the station.

WESC also allocated public service time for religious programs. The Greenville Ministerial Association provided speakers for a daily ten-minute program heard each afternoon at 4:45. Dr. E.F. Haight, head of the religion department at Furman University, was usually the featured speaker. On Sunday morning, Dr. C. Frank Pittman, pastor of the Central Baptist Church and a professor of religion at Furman University, taught **The International Sunday School Lesson.**

From time to time there were many religious programs representing other denominations: **The Methodist Men's Hour**, **The Wesleyan Hour, Forward in Faith**, **The Voice of Prophecy**, **The Lutheran Hour** and **The Baptist Hour**, just to mention a few.

By 1948, WESC started programming more live studio shows. Usually, they were heard in the mid-morning hours and for an hour at noon. **Chuck Pruit and the Dixie Partners**; **Bob and Jim Edwards and the Blue Ridge Rangers; Bonnie Lou and Buster**, **Don Reno and Red Smiley;** and **Carl Butler and Pearle** were among the country artists participating in live studio shows. Some of these bands stayed in the area only a few weeks while they worked public appearances at schools and community buildings in the WESC coverage area. Visitors were always welcome at the radio station during the studio shows. Both studio "A" and studio "B" were furnished with several rows of chairs to accommodate the audience. The studios were equipped with a baby grand piano. Also, Studio A was equipped with a Hammond organ.

The musicians practiced for about thirty minutes with a studio audience present before going on the air. This motivated the musicians and created a stage show atmosphere. They were singing to people, not an empty room in a basement uptown. However, there was a downside: the audience and band members were allowed to smoke in the studios. The hallways and office area filled with clouds of cigarette smoke. Some of the gospel singers complained about the odor in their concert clothes but not much was done about prohibiting smoking because most adults smoked. Too, the harmful effects of tobacco smoke were not proven. About the only people speaking out against tobacco were some preachers who warned: "You should not smoke or chew nor run around with people who do." Few, if any, foresaw "NO SMOKING" signs posted in public buildings. By the way, the office crew took their coffee and lunch breaks about the time the music started, and smoke began to curl around the corners and into the offices.

At least once, the great country singer Hank Williams appeared on WESC. While on tour, Hank Williams sang on a WESC broadcast from Mary's Record Shop on South Main Street. Bob Edwards was emcee of the program. Mary Mitchell, owner of the shop, remembers Hank sang two songs with Bob Edwards' group, **The Blue Ridge Rangers**. According to Mrs. Mitchell, it was unusual for a recording star to perform on an impromptu basis, but Hank, who had attended the broadcast to be interviewed about a personal appearance in Greenville, was enjoying the show and graciously accepted an invitation to join in the music making. Mrs. Mitchell does not remember the song Hank Williams performed; perhaps it was *My Bucket's Got a Hole in It* or *Why Don't You Love Me* because Bob's band used these songs a lot on their shows.

The surprise appearance by the Grand Ole Opry star pleased the quickly assembled crowd, many of whom had rushed to see him after hearing on their car radios that Hank Williams was at Mary's. By the way, people didn't listen to the radio in cars much in those days. Less than 30% of the cars had radios. Also, many of the old pre-war vacuum tube car radios had played out. Auto dealerships seldom ordered factory-installed radios because this added to the sticker price.

Seeing listeners respond immediately to something on the radio was thrilling. In a few years almost every car would have a radio and the WESC mobile mike would revolutionize the way Greenville car dealers sold cars. The transistor made radio listening mobile and added greatly to radio's resurgence after local television came on the scene.

The members of **The Blue Ridge Rangers** were: Bob Edwards, vocalist and emcee; Jim Edwards, steel guitar; Allan Riddle, vocalist; Ansel Garrett, guitar; Pee Wee Milton, guitar; Vernon Fox, piano; and Squeaky Davis, accordion. Some of the favorites of **The Blue Ridge Rangers** were *Goodnight Irene, Steel Guitar Rag* and *Move It on Over.* Their fans often requested Allen Riddle to sing the songs made popular by Eddie Arnold: *Any Time* and *Don't Rob Another Man's Castle* were favorites in the late '40s. Allen Riddle was a gifted singer and all the musicians were talented. "Duck" Daniel was an accomplished steel guitar player and often played and sang the Ernest Tubb hits. Any of them could have been a success in Nashville; however, they put the security of a regular paycheck above the risks associated with full-time country showbiz in Nashville.

Gospel music was scheduled on Sunday mornings on WESC. **The Gay Quartet** headed a list of local gospel music groups. Joe Brown, father of longtime Greenville County Sheriff Johnny Mack Brown, sang 2nd tenor; Grady Hall, 1st tenor; Seith Hall, lead; and Frank Hall, bass. Other members of the group from time to time were: Frank Hopkins, bass; Charles Welchel, lead; and William "Bill" Kirby. Bill Kirby's interest in radio led to a broadcast career, first with WESC AM as a salesman and later as the owner of WBBR (1580 KC) in Travelers Rest, S.C.

The Gay Quartet was named for its sponsor, the Gay Clothing Store that was located in the first block of East

Washington Street. In those days, the word "gay" did not define sexual orientation. However, by the time the Gay Clothing Store was sold, the use of the word "gay" was beginning to have sexual implications. The quartet changed its name to **The Paris Mountain Male Quartet.** Sheriff Brown says his father insisted on the change. Other gospel groups on WESC included duo Elmo and Francis Harmon, **The South Greenville Quartet** and Conner Hall with the **Homeland Harmony Quartet.**

The original **Melodyaires Quartet** was a popular Sunday morning feature. When tape recordings became commonplace the **Melodyaires** were often sponsored daily. The quartet featured: Bill Baker, baritone; Claude Hunter, tenor; Carl Whitman, lead; Charlie Baker, bass; and Mrs. Ruth Baker at the piano. Mrs. Ruth Baker is still playing gospel music. At the time of this writing she plays for **The Evangelaires Quartet,** a group headed by her son Terry Baker. Joining Ruth and Terry on the television show that is seen on WGGS TV 16 in Greenville are: David Stockton, lead singer; Phillip Dewease, tenor; Pat Turner, bass; and Terry, baritone. Johnny Williams is heard on guitar. The Baker family was and is very musical. When Bill Baker, founder of the **Melodyaires**, went into the ministry, his brother Charles stepped forward to keep the group going. Although Charles Baker is now deceased, his sons John and Tony and a grandson "Tater" keep the **Melodyaires** singing. There were other performers who provided WESC listeners with many hours of listening pleasure in the early years but their names have been lost in time. The singers developed their talent in the churches in the area and local radio provided them the opportunity to be heard.

From the very beginning, WESC received commercial support in the small towns in its coverage area. Itinerant time salesmen arranged for special public service programs to be aired. They went into the small towns and sold the commercials to the merchants. The program content promoted tourist attractions in or near the towns. Many of these shows were sold in Easley, Fountain Inn, Hendersonville, Tryon and other communities. These were places where enterprising merchants saw an opportunity to attract customers visiting the mountains and foothills. Then, as now, the mountains attracted vacationers from other parts of the country. These programs were an effort to inform them of the natural beauty and the historical sites in the area. Later, led by Senator Earl Morris of Pickens County and others, state lawmakers saw the value of promoting tourism in South Carolina. Today, it's the #2 industry. Tourism most certainly would have been developed without these radio shows; however, their importance cannot be underestimated.

In the 1980's, when Dick Riley became S.C. Governor, emphasis was placed on local festivals. The state provided seed money for local citizens to get involved in promoting themselves. Today, as in the '40s, these promotions such as the Catfish Festival, the Gold Rush Days, the Corn Festival and the Kudzu Festival, just to mention a few, provide an opportunity for hometown merchants to promote their communities and businesses. And just like the '40s, local radio receives a needed revenue stream while promoting itself in these communities.

The key to success, then as now, was to be honest in dealing with the people. WESC president and general manager Scott Russell was a good judge of character and picked the best independent time salesmen to represent WESC. One of these promoters was George Turpin, who came to Greenville annually to sell his promotions and renew his friendship with area merchants. Usually, his campaigns aired during January, February and March, when station inventories were unsold.

In fact, Turpin settled in Greenville for a while, joining the WESC sales staff. Turpin was a great salesman: as they say, a trash mover, a sell a ton guy — when motivated.

Turpin got motivated on a sunny March afternoon in the late '40s. He drove a sleek black Mercury convertible, which incidentally was the envy of the clerks staffing the stores along Greenville's Main Street. On this balmy early spring afternoon, when the clerks were out along the street enjoying the sunshine, Turpin decided to drive down Main Street with the top back, steering the car with his bare feet while seated on the back of the driver's seat. He got the notoriety he was looking for plus a little more. It just happened that the station president and general manager, Scott Russell, had walked down Main Street on personal business. Upon seeing Turpin's one-man acrobatic car show Russell promptly returned to the station. Of course, he requested a private audience with our star salesman and convertible clown. We never learned ALL that was said behind closed doors nor did Mr. Russell raise his voice but Turpin left the station in a hurry! He returned that afternoon turning in several new orders that totaled several thousand dollars. No doubt about it, Turpin could sell a ton when motivated!

Icy winters hit Greenville in the late forties and were too much for George Turpin, who liked to come to Greenville in the autumn, sell his promotions and retreat to the Florida sunshine. So it wasn't long before the balmy beaches of Florida beckoned.

WESC launched a special "home town salutes" promotion at "sign on" in 1947. A package of WESC souvenir clocks and commercials were sold to area merchants. One is still in operation and can be seen at Martha's Hardware in Travelers Rest, S.C. M.J. "Dolly" Cooper, owner of the Piedmont Economy Store in Piedmont, S.C., bought the promotion and proudly displayed his WESC clock for more than forty years. Mr. Cooper donated the clock to the S.C. Broadcasters Association Radio Exhibit at the State Museum in Columbia. Incidentally, M.J. "Dolly" Cooper represented Anderson County in the state legislature for many years and credited his first successful election campaign to his political advertising heard on WESC.

Another advertiser who supported WESC when it signed on the air was Mr. Clyde Jones, operator of a mercantile store in West Greenville named the Peerless Mart. Mr. Jones advertised this store on WESC, and later, the Welcome Family Shop, which was located on the Old Easley Bridge Road. Clyde Jones believed in radio and encouraged his two sons to make radio a career. They are Kenley Jones of NBC TV News and Mike Jones, who worked for WOWO, Ft. Wayne, Indiana, and WGST in Atlanta, Ga. After working at these stations, Mike Jones returned to Greenville and entered business with his father operating John Michael's, a men's shop at the intersection of the Old Easley Bridge Road and Washington Avenue. That stretch of road is now known as Shoeless Joe Jackson Boulevard. Kenley Jones worked for WQOK (1440 KC) during some of the summers he was home from his studies at Northwestern University. Greenville and WESC were proud of the "Jones Brothers."

About a year after WESC signed on the air, Caldwell Cline left the station and Art Roberts was named program director and morning personality. Art was a very funny man! His morning show with popular music, news and a-la-Roberts quickly attracted an upscale audience. The show, **Breakfast in Bedlam**, served advertisers on Main Street, Augusta Road and the downtown area. He attracted a large audience in the city of Greenville. A new voice with a quick wit, which was getting attention from listeners and advertisers that WFBC considered "their base," stirred things up! Shortly, WFBC began looking for someone to challenge WESC's Art Roberts. The names Clare Chadwell (WIS, 560 KC), Cliff Grey (WSPA, 950 KC) and others were rumored, but Allen Newcomb of WIS accepted the job.

"Greenville is growing and Greenville is fair; there's room for another station to come on the air."

Roberts was not the only morning man attracting attention. WMRC's Bob Poole had returned from the Army Air Force and quickly became the voice of the textile communities, mostly located in the Parker District, west of town. Roberts and Poole believed their shows appealed to different audiences. So, they double-teamed the opposition, playfully poking fun at each other, playing pranks on one another, appearing as guests on the other's show, and in an "offhanded way" promoted each other. Roberts and Poole also jointly promoted public service drives, the annual March of Dimes, Community Chest and other community charities. The strategy worked!! Roberts and Poole were the toast of Greenville in 1948 and 1949, Roberts with **Breakfast in Bedlam** and Bob Poole with **Poole's Party Line.**

Among the Jaycee leaders appearing on these programs was Nick Theodore. Later Mr. Theodore ran for public office serving in the South Carolina House of Representatives, South Carolina Senate and as Lt. Governor.

Bob Poole was assisted in the production of his show by his uncle, Buck Poole, whose duties included screening phone calls, taking requests, producing the show and allowing Bob to verbally abuse him whenever their opinions clashed — which was about every morning! The chemistry between them caused the audience to get emotionally involved — some sympathizing with Buck — others Bob — as their disagreements rippled throughout the community over fried eggs, grits, bacon, toast and coffee at Greenville's early morning cafés.

When WESC FM signed on in 1948, WESC AM/FM affiliated with the **Mutual Broadcasting System** and scheduled a lot of that network's programming. Among the daily programs were: **Ladies Be Seated** and **Queen for a Day**. These two popular audience participation shows provided WESC with an exciting afternoon lineup. The shows made WESC competitive with WMRC and WFBC. Obviously, **Breakfast in Bedlam** gave WESC a strong morning show. The mid-morning country and religious shows competed with WMRC, an ABC affiliate, airing the **Don McNeal Breakfast Club,** and later in the morning **Breakfast at Sardi's,** originating from the West Coast. WFBC did not concede the mid-morning hours. That station produced its own audience participation program, **Kitchen Mechanic,** a program emceed by WFBC General Manager Bevo Whitmire involving almost all the WFBC air staff. Weekday afternoons, WFBC aired the NBC soap operas.

Queen for a Day and **Ladies Be Seated,** the two MBS audience participation shows, originated in Chicago and aired in the 2:00 to 3:00 p.m. time slot. In the early afternoon WESC aired a program of concert music. Announced by Ray Stanfield, the show was scripted by RCA and featured that company's classical artists performing music available on the RCA-Red Seal label. In 1949, WESC listeners were exposed to just about every type of programming heard in the South: country, comedy/variety, religious, classical, news, sports, audience participation and popular. The only large group not being served with full-length programming was the black population. This changed in the 1950's.

During the '50s Sunday mornings were filled with The Southland Jubilee Singers, Old Ship of Zion, the Morning

Star Quartet and the Gospel Travelers. All were popular local black groups that sold their own commercials to merchants serving the black communities. Since I worked on Sunday morning, I was not only the announcer/control operator, but also the cashier. Before going on the air the groups paid me for their airtime and since I was the only station employee on duty, my instructions were to admit only four singers into the studio for each show. There was one exception to this rule. A personable young black man known only as "Ashmore" always insisted that he should be present during the time the shows were in progress. Once I challenged Ashmore demanding to know why he had to be in the studio since only four singers were needed for a quartet. Ashmore insisted that he had to be in the studio because he was the utility man. When I inquired just what the utility man did, Ashmore was ready with the answer. The utility man was available if and when one of the singers wasn't able to perform. Presumably, he sang all the parts. I didn't take that any further because a guy that talented deserved a little break. I grew fond of Ashmore but in time he stopped coming to the station. When I asked about him, I was told that he had been shot and killed. It's a sad commentary on the life and times in the South of the 1950's. People living in the black population were shot and killed but nobody outside those communities noticed it much.

WESC's affiliation with MBS enabled the station to feature several nightly mystery programs, news commentaries and other general audience shows. The MBS network provided local advertisers an opportunity to position commercials in programs with network quality. Among the newscasters were Gabriel Heater, Cedric Foster and Fulton Lewis, Jr. These quarter hour news commentaries usually consisted of about five minutes of news and ten minutes of commentary on the news. The commentator gave background information on the

41

news story to be discussed, followed by several minutes of commentary that led to the newsman's conclusion on the issue. Therefore, the programs reflected knowledge and thought, not just the unreasoned political bashing or wild opinions heard on most talk shows today. The audience respected the commentator's view even if it didn't agree. Today, the political talk shows just feed the bias of the faithful, producing a lot of heat but very little light. The general public — in my opinion — doesn't listen to them.

Some of the commentators had little catchy phrases that caused their audience to remember them. I think it was Gabriel Heater that came on the air with: "Ah yes, there's good news tonight!" So, the phrase became a common expression in the '40s.

Other MBS shows included the dramas: **I Love a Mystery, The Green Hornet,** and the panel show **Can You Top This,** which became the model for a TV show. **Hawaii Calling** had a large audience of South Pacific veterans. Presumably, the music of the islands provided a nostalgic link to the past.

Since the Mutual Broadcasting System acquired some of its programs from affiliates around the country, WESC presented a cross section of national opinion. **The National Farm and Home Hour** originated in Chicago and aired news for farmers. **Washington Week** reported from the capital. As a Mutual affiliate, WESC aired the Baseball World Series. Greenville didn't have local television, so the fall series introduced WESC to thousands of new listeners who otherwise might not have noticed Greenville's third station. Soon, WESC was GREENVILLE to out-of-town listeners. The man on the street in some of the towns thirty miles from Greenville said he listened to GREENVILLE meaning WESC.

The Vice President for Affiliate Relations at MBS was Robert A. Schmid. About ten years later, Bob Schmid remembered "660 in Dixie" with its popularity and large coverage area. He became interested in purchasing the station.

In 1949 WESC affiliated with the Dallas based **Liberty Broadcasting System** to secure their daily broadcasts of major league baseball recreated from Western Union wire reports. Faced with reduced time clearances, MBS decided to affiliate with Greenville's fifth station, WAKE (1490 KC). (The Bob Jones University station WMUU AM, (1260 KC) was the fourth.) The LBS affiliation enabled WESC to offer its listeners **The LBS Game of the Day** and **Musical Bingo.** Among the other network shows were: **Musical Scoreboard** and newscaster Westbrook Van Voorhees. WESC listeners instantly recognized the Voorhees voice because he was heard on most of the newsreels shown in area theaters.

During football and basketball season LBS offered a wide choice of college football and basketball games. These programs were available for local sponsorship. The LBS president, Gordon McClendon, recreated most of the baseball broadcasts from his Dallas studios. He sent a crew on the road in 1951 but it wasn't enough to save his network. He said the business practices of the baseball owners; they say competition from MBS — caused him to fold in 1951. After LBS folded, Gordon McClendon concentrated on his radio stations in the Southwest. He developed a rock format using music, news, time, weather, temperature, jingles and D.J.'s with rapid speech patterns.

Later, when stations started copying the McClendon success, some stations used a metronome to establish the speech rate of their D.J.'s. This programming — **the rock and roll format** — earned McClendon fame and increased his fortune, but baseball must have been a disappointment. In a very emotional conference call to the affiliates in 1951, McClendon folded the network, blaming the business tactics of Major League Baseball and other circumstances for his network's demise. The successful survivor was the Mutual Broadcasting System, which had started broadcasting a **Game of the Day** live from the ballparks, featuring Al Helfer. The irony of it was that WESC gave up the Mutual Network to join LBS to bring major league baseball to Greenville — EVERY DAY — but eventually lost MLB because it had given up its MBS affiliation. By the way, the MBS sports announcer assigned to the west coast was Bob Fulton, the voice of the South Carolina Gamecocks. The reader can get a "behind the scenes" look at Al Helfer and some of the other sportscasters in Bob Fulton's book **Hi Everybody! This Is Bob Fulton,** written by Bob Fulton with Don Barton and published by Summerhouse Press in Columbia in 1996.

When WESC FM signed on the air in 1948, sports played a big part in the program schedule. Wayne Davis used a Western Union baseball wire service to recreate the Greenville Spinners' Sally League baseball games. Wayne described the out of town Spinners games while sitting in a WESC studio in Greenville. He used special reports filed by a Western Union reporter at ballparks around the league. Wayne's knowledge of the game and his imaginative accounts were very entertaining. One game made this history book — not because a player hit the longest home run, but because the ticker tape stopped. Wayne Davis kept talking. He described the batter fouling off pitches, the pitcher stepping off the mound, the batter stepping out of the batter's box, a pitcher-catcher conference at the mound, a manager's visit to the mound, and everything else he could think to do to fill the time until the Western Union service was restored. Perhaps the ticker started again in a couple of minutes; however, for years, every time the story was told, the Western Union "down time" increased. As the tale is spun today, that broadcast may have set a record for the longest "at bat" in baseball.

The prevailing attitude was "The show must go on!" Radio was a theatre of the mind! Informing listeners about the failure of Western Union did not serve or entertain listeners and would perhaps spoil their fantasy. Wayne wasn't about to admit the Western Union wire service failure. FCC rules required the station to make an announcement at the beginning and the end of each broadcast to inform the audience the program was a "re-creation" of a baseball game, presented by WESC for the purpose of <u>entertaining</u> and informing its audience.

Baseball re-creation was easy to sell because it was the only baseball on the air around Greenville. A skillful announcer such as Gordon McClendon in Texas, Wayne Poucher in Columbia or Wayne Davis could create a baseball game from Western Union reports that would put the listener in a seat at the ballpark. About the only thing the listener missed was the smell of mustard on hot dogs.

I think most people agreed "The Old Scotsman," as McClendon called himself, was the best in the business. In the beginning, he originated the broadcasts from his station, KLIF (ll90 KC) in Dallas, Texas. As the broadcasts moved around the league he talked about the "Happy Hungarian" serenading a buxom blond. The couple showed up at most of the ballparks, especially if the city had a large Hungarian population. THAT "Happy Hungarian" was the producer of McClendon's broadcast, Dick Uray. Mr. Uray took great delight in slipping a little Hungarian serenade into the game for all the Hungarian fans. Richard Uray eventually became a college professor and was the first chairman of the Broadcast Sequence at the University of South Carolina. Many former USC College of Journalism students have achieved success — some well known throughout America, names like Leeza Gibbons, Rita Crosby and Vanna White. Dr. Uray perhaps never told his students about <u>his</u> coast to coast "Happy Hungarian Serenades."

The thousands of baseball fans who enjoyed the ballpark banter would never know the REAL "Happy Hungarian." After Dr. Uray's death it was learned that he assisted many deserving students in completing their college studies after their funds were exhausted. He never had natural children but he sure had a large adopted family.

Rick Uray was also a producer for **Musical Bingo** on L.B.S. This musical game was played just like bingo. Listeners obtained bingo cards at local Greenville merchants or wherever WESC chose to distribute them. During the program, the Dallas based announcer called out bingo numbers and played records — usually the popular tunes of the day. Bingo players competed for a variety of prizes including toys, household appliances and money.

Dr. Uray's experience in commercial radio gave him a good background for teaching. During his years at USC, Dr. Richard Uray also served as executive manager of the South Carolina Broadcasters Association. Perhaps this story will help people who never knew Dr. Uray appreciate him. One evening while on an SCBA Washington trip — it was during the Watergate hearings, as I recall — Dr. Uray and I were having dinner with South Carolina 4th District Congressman James R. Mann at a Ruston, Va., restaurant. Congressman Mann, you remember, played a major role in the Watergate crisis, which many say was a test of the U.S. Constitution. Our dining table was beside a picture window with a panoramic night view of the capital. Congressman Mann excused himself to make a phone call, and during <u>his absence I</u> observed tears coming into Dr. Uray's eyes. I asked him what was wrong; he said he felt OK but the occasion was overwhelming. He shared with me the story of his parents coming to America from

Hungary. They settled in Chicago, worked and sacrificed to earn citizenship, giving him opportunity and freedom that America offers to all who embrace its values. He said the night view of the capital, the monuments and dinner with a U.S. Congressman caused him to be overcome with gratitude. Dr. Richard Uray loved America and its people. He was proud of his citizenship and proud to be a South Carolina broadcaster.

As I look back on that evening and my memories of Dr. Uray, THAT was what made him a great teacher and broadcaster. He appreciated the United States with its representative form of government; he cared for America and devoted his life to educating its young people to serve the American people through broadcasting. He gave his money, earned from teaching the broadcasting arts, to students who needed a boost in order to become broadcasters. It was his way of saying, "Thank you, America, for the freedom and opportunity you offer to all people." Dr. Richard Uray's career and money trained broadcast professionals so that they in turn could keep the dream of opportunity and freedom alive in America.

All who knew Dr. Uray respected him, and as executive manager of SCBA, he brought the association instant credibility among the nation's broadcasters, educators and lawmakers. Dr. Richard Uray was inducted into the SCBA Hall of Fame in 1995.

One of the most prestigious awards given each year by SCBA is the Richard Uray Award to the South Carolina radio or television station demonstrating the best public service record for the previous year.

Although the Liberty Broadcasting System wasn't on the radio landscape very long, there's a story about how the sports world discovered legendary sports announcer Lindsey Nelson. The Liberty Broadcasting System aired numerous college football games every weekend. Some of them included the University of Tennessee. One Saturday the weather prevented Gordon McClendon's plane from landing in Knoxville, so he asked the Tennessee Vols announcer, Lindsey Nelson, to send his account of the game to LBS. Based on Mr. Nelson's description of that game, he was invited to come to the network. It had hundreds of affiliates at the time and he received national exposure. Soon, Lindsey Nelson was heard and hired by the nation's major networks. He became one of America's most popular radio and television football announcers. WESC aired many of the sports events that Lindsey Nelson described on the Liberty Broadcasting System.

During the late forties amateur boxing was popular in Greenville. The Greenville YMCA, some of the textile communities and several military installations entered teams in the Golden Gloves Tournaments held annually in Greenville. WESC FM aired the championship fights for a few years. Greenville Police Sergeant Harry Ward, himself an amateur boxer, voiced these broadcasts. Some of the Greenville fighters were Guido Capri, Joe Snyder, Marion Campbell and Bob Wade. Our local fighters were competitive and generated a lot of interest in amateur boxing.

Speaking of boxing, I met the great Jack Dempsey when he came through Greenville on a promotional tour in the '50s. **Greenville News-Piedmont** publisher Roger C. Peace gave a small luncheon for "the champ" at the Poinsett Hotel and invited me. I felt honored just to have received an invitation to have lunch with the champ, but a luncheon hosted by the publisher of the Greenville newspapers and attended by some of the outstanding news professionals of that day made it extra special.

The WFBC (1330 KC) veteran sportscaster Verner Tate was out of town on assignment, so there I was, the only radio guy with a bunch of newspaper pros including the legendary Carter "Scoop" Latimer, sports editor of the **Greenville News,** talking boxing over country ham and eggs, red eye gravy, grits, jam, jelly, homemade biscuits, black coffee and all that good stuff. It was quite an experience to interact, one on one, with the "Champ" and these newspaper pioneers. Once during the meal someone mentioned that I aired a record show targeted to the black population. This seemed to impress Jack Dempsey and he launched into a review of the great fighters he knew who were black. I asked him why there were so many good black boxers while the number of good white fighters seemed to be declining. His explanation was that good fighters come from segments of the population where people have to do physical labor, construction work, that sort of thing.

When we ordered lunch, the "Champ" ordered first, choosing country ham and eggs and saying he remembered staying at the Poinsett Hotel when he came through Greenville on his way to Hendersonville, N.C., to train for a fight in the late '20s. He said throughout all those years he wanted to return to the Poinsett for country ham, eggs, grits and the rest, along with the hotel's southern hospitality. He also remembered that the Poinsett circulated new currency and washed its coins.

When WESC FM came on the air in 1948 it was licensed for twenty-four hour service but it would be years before the station operated twenty-four hours.

Here is how the FM station was programmed in the early days. Bob Edwards signed on the FM station at 5:00 a.m. and played country music until 7:30 a.m., when Art Roberts came on the air with **Breakfast in Bedlam.** The AM station signed on when the sun came up. As you can see, Roberts had a consistent time slot with AM and FM coverage. After WWII the country returned to standard time so during the summer months Bob Edwards was heard on AM and FM with country music until 7:30 a.m. In the late afternoon the same simulcast routine was followed with Ray Stanfield. He called the program **Stanfield's Showcase**. Ray Stanfield was an announcer at WFBC before enlisting in the U.S. Navy. When he returned to Greenville in the late '40s, he joined the staff of WESC and rapidly established himself as a football announcer, classical music announcer and afternoon drive-time personality. Stanfield was a favorite in the front office and often its chief prankster.

One story circulated for years about Stanfield's pranks. When the WESC studios were built, the office area was painted but the studios were left unpainted because some believed unpainted studios improved acoustics. One afternoon while Mr. Russell and most of the office staff were at lunch, Ray Stanfield completed announcing a music program from a small, unpainted announcer booth which was located next to the painted office area. As Ray left for lunch he turned to the porter, Willie Garrett, whom the staff affectionately called "Lightning" and said, "Lightning, get some paint and paint this d — ugly studio." When Mr. Russell returned, he found "Lightning" obediently following Stanfield's command. He had taken the remark as an order. Needless to say, the painting stopped! Garrett was not reprimanded but Stanfield, who was Mr. Russell's "fair haired boy," was called on the carpet. Ray was in the doghouse for about a week. A week was equivalent to a life sentence with Scott Russell, who was even tempered and didn't carry grudges.

Wayne Davis, as some of my readers know, has a deep voice. In those days he was bothered a lot by laryngitis. Now folks, when a fellow with the pipes that Wayne Davis has gets laryngitis, he can barely be understood. One day Wayne Davis finished the news and walked out into the office and was greeted by Scott Russell, who had been listening. Mr. Russell said: "Wayne, go on home and come back when you're well — there's nothing as useless around a radio station as an announcer that can't talk."

In those days, local colleges didn't market their football games on an exclusive basis. Stations wanting to broadcast Clemson or Furman football usually paid a small fee, reserved their space in the press box and showed up. Parker and Greenville high schools also welcomed all broadcasters. These games were easy to sell, so Stanfield and Commercial Manager Cliff Bowers took advantage of the income streams.

Sterling High, Greenville High and Furman University played their home games at Sirrine Stadium. Using feeds from other stations and originating from the stadium, WESC FM sometimes aired football games on Wednesday, Thursday, Friday nights and Saturday afternoons. Frequently Saturday night games were on the schedule. All of this without leaving Greenville.

Many of the college games were a rebroadcast of another station's signal. This was "copying" a signal and it was not permitted by the FCC rules unless a station received permission from the other station to do so. The FM stations did not stay on frequency very well, so it was almost a full time job to tune and retune an incoming station to insure a clear broadcast. It was part of the announcer's duty to "ride herd" on the incoming signal and be ready to cut away on cue and drop in the local commercial. The cutaways had to be clean and the commercials timed to the second. In order to accomplish this the announcer listened to the incoming station on earphones while reading a live local commercial. Now, I can hear someone saying, You idiot, why didn't you use tape? Can you believe the sponsors almost always insisted on "live commercials"? What, a recorded commercial? Are you kidding? I want a live human being announcing my copy, not something canned and counterfeit!

A Sterling High teacher, Wilfred J. Walker, broadcast the home games for Sterling, Greenville's public high school for African-Americans. He was very entertaining and was heard simultaneously on WESC FM radio and the stadium public address system. His description of a game sounded like this: "Rabbit Johnson is down at the 30 yard line. Uh-oh, there goes that red rag again; the man in the striped pants is taking L O N G, long steps. ...Hey, Mr. Ref, S L O W down! REF! You're going the WRONG way. The Tigers want you to go the other way.... Woo, Mr. Ref. S T O P! That's ENOUGH!" The fans in the stadium and the radio audience roared their approval. WESC listeners loved Wilfred J. Walker and he developed a large following among people of both races. Some folks tuned in just to hear his commentary. He had a winsome personality and the audience enjoyed his humor.

Wilfred J. Walker was also the first African American in the upstate to host a record show bearing his name.

In 1949, a WESC broadcast crew originated the South Carolina Gamecock home games. In those days the out-of-town games of most of the colleges were not heard on radio, probably because of the expense involved. WIS (560 KC) in Columbia was probably the flagship station but Ray Stanfield of WESC was the Gamecock play-by-play announcer. I was hired by WESC program director Art Roberts to announce the commercials and color on the USC/UNC game on October 8, 1949. It was my first assignment for WESC.

Frankly, after some fifty years I do not remember much about the game, so I checked the microfilm of the **GREENVILLE NEWS** story at the Greenville public library. My ole friend Alderman Duncan covered the game for the Greenville paper. Fifteen years later, I was to establish a friendship with Alderman at South Carolina Broadcasters Association meetings.

Brother Duncan reported that the great All American Charlie "Choo Choo" Justice — a triple threat player — played for the Tar Heels and legendary football coach Carl Snavely directed the Carolina Blue. Rex Enright was the head football coach for South Carolina. There was a lot of interest in the Southern Conference game because the Tar Heels were undefeated. South Carolina was expected to put up a good fight with its ground and passing attack. The game was played before a shirtsleeve crowd of about 28,000 fans. Ray Stanfield interviewed a newspaper reporter at halftime and my best guess is that it was Alderman Duncan. At the half the score was 7-7. However, North Carolina won 28-13. Alderman Duncan wrote that Charlie Justice put on a show: running, passing and punting the football. Carolina fans did not go away disappointed because Wadiak, Boyle, Strickland, Fagan and the other Gamecocks kept the score close into the third quarter.

At the conclusion of the broadcast someone I did not know stuck his head in the broadcast booth and reported that he thought there were about 25 stations on the network. That many stations would have delivered a big audience considering there were no television stations to air football and Clemson played a rare Saturday night game with Mississippi State.

In addition to my announcing duties on college football that fall, I also operated the remote unit for the Sterling High School games. A friendship with Wilfred J. Walker began during these broadcasts and this exposure prepared me for an opportunity that came along in the spring of 1950.

The makers of Royal Crown Hair Dressing bought a fifteen-minute program of rhythm and blues music. The show was to be broadcast each weekday afternoon at 3:00, about the time the school day ended. The company sponsored fifteen minutes and supplied prospects for WESC's representative in Atlanta to sell another quarter hour on a participation basis. Therefore, the program was to be heard for thirty minutes. Competitive auditions to choose the emcee were recorded by staff members and sent to the Royal Crown Company in Memphis. To my surprise, I won the audition! It was a break for me because this assured me I would have a regular job. Also, the $5 per program talent fee supplemented my $57.50 weekly salary. My exposure on Sterling football carried over to the new program, helping me to be accepted by the black community. In fact, many people believed me to be an African-American and I didn't correct them. Race wasn't an issue; we were there to entertain.

Recently I was asked if racial bias was involved in my selection. The inquirer said Columbia had Mike Rast as Dr. Jive and Spartanburg had Al Smith as Prince Albert, both white guys. Well, I don't know about the other stations but I do know how I was selected. All of the announcers on the staff auditioned for the show and I was picked because the sponsors thought I could sell Royal Crown hair Dressing. Perhaps if there had been a minority on the staff my career would have gone in another direction. You might say if WESC had been an equal opportunity employer I may not have gotten the opportunity to build a forty-two year career with one station.

Chapter 4

A Better Idea: R-R-R

We named the rhythm and blues show **The Ebony Swing Club** and I called myself the Bee Bop King. Who came up with "Bee Bop King" I don't remember. Perhaps Mary Mitchell at Mary's Record Shop, WESC Program Director Art Roberts or someone else. After picking up a few R&B hits at Mary's Record Shop on the South Main Street Bridge, I came on the air using the theme song *Page Boy Shuffle* by Joe Thomas. Beginning with that loud, wonderful saxophone, after about 15 seconds the music was faded, the mike opened and I began with a machine gun delivery saying:

From Charlotte, North Carolina — to — Atlanta, G-A!
And — Knoxville, Tennessee. To the sea!
We're with it. And ain't gonna quit it! —
Here — in the chicken shack!
The shack's a-shaking, the joint's a-rocking,
The fillies and chickens are dancin'.

> We're in the groove — REAL groovy. And —
> Mel-oo-rooney.
> Get set for 30 minutes of gutbucket jazz on **The
> Ebony Swing Club**
> With… the ole Bee Bop King.

The music was turned up as loud as the transmitter would transmit the sound for about two or three blasts. Then I continued:

> We'll do the bee bop. And the Lindy hop.
> Maybe do the shag. And — The ole rag mop.
> We'll boogie and woogie and have a ball, y'all!

After four years or so, all that chicken shack stuff at the opening of the show caused the audience to call it **The Chicken Shack** and instead of "Bee Bop King" I was nicknamed the "Chicken Shack." I'll explain how that came about later, so stay tuned, neighbors.

They say a good radio program is like a good speech. It has an impressive opening and closing and a lot of bull in between. If that is so, we may have qualified because we had an impressive close. On the reverse side of *Page Boy Shuffle* was *Teardrops*. Now, that's about the saddest wailing tune I've ever heard. We used it to leave the air, expressing how great it was to have been together and how sad we were to have to part, leaving the air by saying, "We'll be back tomorrow with Ruth Brown, the Platters, Ole Piano Red and Fats Domino singing the right string, baby, but the wrong yo-yo on Yo' Radio."

I tried to vary the "sign off" by rhyming whatever I said with a song title or artist.

Up until this time, Curt Webster out of WBT (1110 KC) in Charlotte had been the only personality in the Carolinas strongly identified with a theme. Curt attracted national attention by going back a decade or so and picking *Heartaches* by Ted Weems as a theme and riding it to national prominence on his late night show. When Mary and Bill Mitchell suggested *Page Boy Shuffle* for my show, they predicted it could become as strong a signature for me as *Heartaches* had been for Webster. That seemed farfetched at the time but they were right! Judging by the comments I hear from people who listened to the show when they were teenagers, *Page Boy Shuffle* surpassed *Heartaches* as an identifiable program theme.

As recently as the 1990's, I was asked by two former listeners to my **Chicken Shack Show** — one in Hendersonville and the other in Spartanburg — to prepare about a minute of this introduction to be played at their high school reunions. I was flattered and happily obliged after Leighton Grantham of Easley, South Carolina, supplied me with a copy of the record. It was reported to me that when the tape played on the speakers in the dining room in Spartanburg, the audience rose out of their seats to see if I would walk into the room. That's pretty darn good for a show that had not been on the air in about forty-five years.

The chatter used in opening the program didn't make a lot of sense to adult audiences in the '50s; however, teens related to it. This was "their" chatter and "their" music. At last! Somebody on the radio was playing different music and they embraced it. Some of my friends listened to the teenagers and gave me feedback. You might call this the first focus group. If teenagers came up with new slang expressions, we used them. In a few years teenagers, black and white, invented a word for the dance they did to the music: "Shagging."

Upstate South Carolina grew up with the **Ebony Swing Club** or **Chicken Shack,** a nickname given to me by Bill Young, the Furman head football coach. One afternoon in 1954, during practice, Coach Young blew his whistle, called the team over and said, "This is Wally Mullinax, the *Chicken Shack;* he'll be our play-by-play announcer this year." The name stuck! Coach Young's brother, Jim, who worked at WESC as a salesman/announcer started calling me *"Chicken Shack"* around the station and on the air so the name stuck. I became the *Chicken Shack* to thousands of young people. The program was heard from the country clubs to the greasy pubs and from the pool halls to learning halls of ivy.

Among **The Chicken Shack** fans were Greenville High students Dick Riley and Carroll Campbell, who became governors of South Carolina. Johnny Mack Brown became sheriff of Greenville County. Furman football player Don Garrison became president of Tri-County Technical College at Pendleton, S.C. In Pelzer, a teenager named "Shag" Barnett listened when he wasn't shagging flies at the baseball park. He studied social work at Furman University, where a favorite professor of a lot of Furman alums, Laura Smith Ebaugh, told some of her classes the lyrics in the songs played on the *Chicken Shack* were "shocking" but Greenville needed to be shocked! She said Greenville needed to become more aware of a subculture that existed in the city.

Wayne "Shag" Barnett became a parole officer in the South Carolina court system. Mr. Barnett performed his duty with fairness and mercy. Wayne "Shag" Barnett befriended many young men who were in trouble with the law. The odds are that Mr. Barnett learned a lot about life outside of upstate textile communities by listening to the lyrics of some of the records he heard on **The Chicken Shack.**

R&B music brought lifetime pleasure to some youngsters. Randy Methena grew up in a Bob Jones University family; as a young lad he listened to the show and loved it. Methena graduated from Furman University and became a successful businessman. He purchased a radio station — WPCI 1490

AM — and programmed his station with some of that ole gutbucket blues.

With apologies to many D.J.'s I may have forgotten, or did not know about, here are some of the familiar radio names in the Greenville/Spartanburg/Anderson area that later enjoyed success playing R&B music. I think of them as the next generation of D.J.'s to spin the records. They took it, improved it and it lives today. Leighton Grantham, Ken Rodgers, Harry Turner, Johnny Batson, Max Mace, Jerry Peeler, Bill Pittman, Jack Moore, Dan Scott, Scott Shannon, Perry Woods, Jr., and Mal Harrison. Radio stations all across America programmed R&B music, helping its devotees become what many describe as a cult. They meet annually at the beach to reminisce and shag 'til they drop.

The Chicken Shack program attracted young adults who were not in school. Fred Collins, Jr., in the "piccolo" business with his father, describes himself as a big fan of the music. He says he listened to **The Chicken Shack** and **The Old Lazy Man** — Frank Cope. Frank Cope was heard on WMRC (1440 KC) each evening about 5:00 to 7:00 p.m. Although the **Old Lazy Man** show didn't play R&B, it had a large drive time audience of upscale Greenvillians devoted to big bands and ballads. Frank Cope was a special air talent.

Fred Collins, Jr., says his father insisted the coin music machines be called "piccolos" because "juke box" had connotations of "juke joints" — considered undesirable places in the cotton mill towns that were the buckle of the Bible Belt. Fred tells me his father did not own pinball machines when these machines became popular because pinball machines were controversial — some people thought they were evil. Fred Collins, Jr., continued his interest in the entertainment business, moving from piccolos to pinball machines to video poker. When video poker machines were ruled illegal in South Carolina, Fred Collins, Jr., was the largest operator in the state.

Fred Collins, Jr., became a mover and shaker in South Carolina. He has been severely criticized while not being given credit for his positive contributions. Examples are 911 emergency service and Crimestoppers. The first time I ever heard of 911 emergency service was when Mr. Collins asked me to promote it on WESC. Fred found out about it in his travels and thought it was a good idea — especially for the elderly — and took it upon himself to lobby for it. He talked to members of the legislature, telephone officials and whoever would listen. Today, 911 service is a necessity. Give Fred Collins credit.

Crimestoppers was another public service Fred Collins promoted. He knew that I was active in the state broadcasters association and had contacts among its members. He gave me a standing offer. He would provide seed money to any of my friends who wanted to start a Crimestoppers program in their city. There are other causes that got Fred Collins' attention and he has responded!

Although Fred Collins marches to a different drummer than some of his critics, he was my radio friend in the '50s when he and other young people were movin' and groovin' to rhythm and blues music, and Fred Collins, Jr., is my friend today.

A more detailed account of R&B music and the artists that gripped teens of the '50s can be found in a book authored by Harry Turner entitled *This Magic Moment — Musical Reflections of a Generation.*

On **The Chicken Shack** we pushed the envelope by picking up words and phrases from songs such as *Sixty Minute Man* by Billy Ward and the Dominoes, *Little Mama* by the Clovers, *One Mint Julip* by the Clovers, *Right String Baby*

But the Wrong Yo-Yo by Piano Red, *Wine Spo Dee O Dee* by Sticks McGee, *You'll Never Walk Alone* by Roy Hamilton, *Earth Angel* by the Penguins, *Lawdy Miss Clawdy* by Lloyd Price, *Long Tall Sally* and *Tutti Fruitty* by Little Richard, *Little Red Rooster* and all the rest. I guess you might accuse me of being the first "Shock Jock" because the words, phrases, and voice inflections did not fit the radio industry mold for "proper radio speech." Also, the chatter and the personality were different from other shows but the program was never-ever dirty or off-color. Neither the FCC nor the industry tolerated profanity. In fact, the use of vulgarity was considered by the industry to show that a personality didn't have much talent. We were a little risqué, perhaps, but not dirty.

In 1950, appealing to Greenville teenagers produced listeners but not much revenue because the buying power of teens wasn't documented. The commercial appeal of rhythm and blues programs was to the black adult population. To attract black adults we included black gospel music on the play list. Some of the black gospel artists were: **Sister Rosetta Thorpe, The Five Blind Boys From Alabama**, **Sarah Vaughn**, **Clara Ward and The Ward Singers, The Dixie Hummingbirds** and many others. The young people accepted the spiritual songs in order to hear rhythm and blues. Soon teens were using lines from both spiritual and rhythm and blues songs as colloquial expressions. *Lawdy Miss Clawdy* and *Strange Things Happening Every Day* found their way into the everyday language of young people.

Lloyd Price, who sang *Lawdy Miss Clawdy,* has been inducted into the S.C. Music and Entertainment Hall of Fame.

Rhythm and blues programs such as **The Chicken Shack** were heard in every city with a large African-American population. There was not a political agenda but it's believed these radio shows helped break down the walls of segregation and promoted race relations. The R&B artists appeared at dances held at Textile Hall on West Washington Street next door to Saint Mary's Catholic Church. Both black and white teens attended. The black teens danced or listened on the main floor while the white teens watched, listened and sometimes danced in the balcony. The dances were enjoyed by both races and eventually became a part of South Carolina's heritage.

The Shag, South Carolina's official dance, was one of the dances associated with rhythm and blues. This music later became known as **Beach Music.** As I have said, we listened to the teens to learn about their new expressions of "jive talk" and with the help of Mary and Bill Mitchell, at Mary's Record Shop, learned which records were being played on the juke boxes at Atlantic Beach and North Myrtle Beach. The information was usually available from the record distributors in Charlotte on Monday or Tuesday. Mary Mitchell and her husband, Bill, went to Charlotte the first of every week to buy records and we anxiously waited for them to return to learn what was getting the most plays at the Grand Strand. They also brought with them a copy of the latest records provided by the record companies. Most of the complimentary records were identified on the label as "complimentary — not for sale." This was before record companies employed representatives and assigned them to the task of promoting records at the stations. If copies of the new releases were not available through the record companies, Mary Mitchell usually gave us a copy. Mary and Bill Mitchell were a great source of information and music. We were fortunate to have had their assistance in making our programs successful and I'm sure we contributed to the success of their business.

It's unfortunate that some D.J.'s in large markets corrupted their relationship with the record stores and labels bringing on the payola scandals. The aftermath was a code of ethics that all D.J.'s were required to adhere to. The rules became so stringent we had to explain to the audience that the record was given to us — naming the donor — for promotional purposes. Eventually, the Washington lawyers came up with a disclaimer requiring all the names of donors to be announced at the beginning and end of the shows. This was not as time consuming or commercialized as was first required. Can you imagine listening to an introduction of Little Richard's record *Long Tall Sally* with a credit line that required that we say something like: "This record was given to me by Mary Mitchell at Mary's Record Shop to be played on WESC. In playing the record at this time I must tell you that I have not received any other compensation for playing it. Now here's Little Richard and *Long Tall Sally*." This payola disclaimer was ridiculous. Luckily some legal beagle convinced the FCC that radio is show biz. Wading through that legal requirement destroyed the illusion in the theatre of the mind.

Here's how we made decisions about what records to put on **The Chicken Shack** play list. We asked listeners to write or telephone requests. The Mitchells contacted two coin operators, Case Music and B.N.W. Music, to find out what was being played on juke boxes at black businesses in town. We read trade magazines: **Billboard** and **Cash Box** reported record sales and popularity charts. Probably the most influential sources were: what the public was buying at Mary's and what Gene Noble was playing on WLAC (1540 KC). We had to stay ahead of the curve to be the leader.

The R&B audience was quick to accept new songs. It was necessary to monitor all of these sources and be FIRST with the LATEST because a fast breaking song could peak before it appeared in the trade magazines. After other stations in the WESC coverage area developed their R&B shows, being the **first D.J.** to play a new record was very important. If we played the records <u>first</u> we reaped the "street talk." In other words, if you ain't first, you're last!

The Ebony Swing Club or **Chicken Shack** began with thirty minutes Monday through Friday but by 1959, it aired three hours a day, six days a week. A 1956 Nielsen Pulse study reported 23% of the radio homes in a 19 county area were tuned in. That translated to about 50,000 listeners. So folks, there was a whole lot of shackin' going on.

I was encouraged to take the show to New York, and later offered a time slot on a suburban Atlanta station, even turned down an opportunity to go to Mexico and pitch direct mail advertising on a 500,000-watt station aimed at the Mississippi Delta. However, we stayed in Greenville, and by doing so, followed the advice of Lewis Rowen, an NBC announcer, who advised our radio class at Northwestern University, in the summer of 1949, to go home, get a job at a local station and build a name for yourself in your hometown. The community service we were able to do by staying in Greenville leads me to believe the Lord had a hand in the decisions.

During the **Ebony Swing Club** days when I was sick or on vacation, other staff members took turns spinning the records. One of these guest D.J.'s was Hugh Jarrett, an announcer we found from an ad in **Broadcasting** magazine. Hugh had just graduated from a broadcasting career school — one of many that sprang up around the country to meet the need for employees in the radio and television industry as it exploded in the '50s. Spinning records was Jarrett's second career choice — his dream was to be a singer like Hugh Cherry, one of the rising pop singers in Nashville. When Hugh Jarrett wasn't talking on the radio he was singing! Miss Helen Jenkins, who later became Mrs. Wally Mullinax, accompanied him for hours on the WESC studio piano while I worked a 3:00 to 11:00 p.m. shift. Hugh Jarrett dreamed of becoming a solo performer but achieved success as a member of the **Jordanaires Quartet.** The Jordanaires accompanied Elvis Presley on his early recordings, TV appearances and concerts. Today, some of the cable channels show Elvis' appearances on the **Ed Sullivan Show**. Hugh Jarrett is right there! Jarrett left the Jordanaires to become the overnight D.J. at WLAC (1540 KC) in Nashville, Tennessee, a 50,000 watt clear channel station with a potential audience of millions. He called himself **Big Hugh Baby**. So, Big Hugh Baby got his first D.J. and R&B experience on WESC in **The Chicken Shack**.

It's been reported that Elvis was influenced by rhythm and blues music. There is no evidence Elvis Presley ever heard **The Chicken Shack**; however, movie theater manager Paul Cook says Presley did make a theatre appearance in Spartanburg early in his career. According to Hub Sellers, a bluegrass musician living in the Greenville area, Elvis sang *Blue Moon of Kentucky* on the show. Mr. Sellers attended the show to see some of the pure country artists appearing with Elvis. Hub says appearing in Spartanburg with Elvis were: Charlie and Ira — The Louvin Brothers; Bennie Martin and the Carter Family. So, pure country music and its fans helped launch Elvis.

Blue Moon of Kentucky was Elvis' first record and I was the first D.J. in Greenville to play it. Mr. Clayton Powell, who now lives in the Inman, S.C., area, was a regular WESC listener in those days. Mr. Powell grew up in the Slater-Marietta area. He told me he was listening to **The Chicken Shack** one afternoon and heard me say, "Here's a young colored boy from Mississippi — Elvis Presley — singing a Bill Monroe song: *Blue Moon of Kentucky.*"

I can tell you, the phones went wild! Everybody wanted to hear the record again. At least one called to correct the mistake. I remember **that** record introduction as if it were yesterday — it was an historic moment: the artist made contact with the audience. There was something about the way Elvis sang the song that "grabbed you"!

Now, everybody who has ever selected a play list knows that a song has to "grab you" to get attention.

In spite of the audience reaction, when it was verified that Elvis was a white artist, we designated his records to be played on the **Country Earl Show,** which was WESC's popular morning show. The WESC format in the early '50s was blocked with the "3 R's" — Race, Rural and Religion. So the R&B was confined to one segment, country to another and religion had its designated time. Perhaps if we had <u>known</u> we were witnessing the birth of "country rock" we would have relaxed the rules.

In retrospect, I believe the record promoters misled me and perhaps other D.J.'s around the country, telling us Elvis was "colored" just to get the record played on the R&B shows. In my speech habits I did not use the term "colored." I was taught by sociology professors at Furman University to say "Negro," the accepted term for African Americans in those days. One wonders how many other R&B D.J.'s around the country made the same "mistake" while announcing Elvis' first record.

This suspicion seems to be confirmed by Country Earl's account of how the record was introduced in Greenville. He recalls a record salesman, remembered only as Pete, asked Earl if he would play a record by a thirteen year old "colored boy" named Elvis Presley. The title of the record: *Blue Moon of Kentucky,* written by Bill Monroe. Earl says he was the first to play the record. I'm OK with that just as long as Country Earl tells his listeners to buy my book.

Some of the listeners who tuned to WESC for the country programs stayed around for the R&B music because there wasn't much music on the radio in those days. The air was filled with soap dramas, baseball and audience participation but not much music. However, country music listeners soon got into the spirit of the "chittlin' music" and accepted it.

When mobile mike broadcasts became popular I had a comedy routine using the Carter Family's recording of *The Wildwood Flower.* Usually from a portable stage, during remote broadcasts, dressed in overalls, denim shirt, bandanna handkerchief, long wig and brogan shoes with horn rim glasses, I sang along with the record, crying with heart rending pathos about the hard-hearted scoundrel leaving his precious "wildwood flower." The audience loved it! Years later at the **Country Shindigs** held at the Memorial Auditorium, many people remembered the wildwood flower routine and jokingly asked me to sing *The Wildwood Flower.*

Chapter 5

Changing Minds/Changing Times

The spring of 1950 was a time of change at WESC. The president, founder and general manager of the Greenville Broadcasting Company, Scott Russell, died suddenly on April 21, 1950. Since Mr. Russell had not established a chain of command, his widow, Christie Kennedy Russell, tried to maintain the "status quo" by assuming the general manager's position. She believed this would avoid a power struggle between the program and sales departments, helping the station to continue to be successful without much change. In retrospect, it was unwise because within a few months, two key people left the station. Program Director/morning personality Art Roberts departed for St. Louis and Cliff Bowers, commercial manager, accepted a job away from Greenville.

I suspect some folks out there in radio land knew that without these key people WESC's fortunes would diminish. Maybe they helped a little by suggesting to station managers around the country where two good people might be available. If the suspicion is true, it's not unusual. Stations have been known to solve a program or sales problem by finding competing employees a better job out of town. I must admit I have helped some of my friendly competitors get a raise or find higher paychecks.

The departure of Roberts and Bowers did cause business to go south. So, in a few months, Christie turned to a friend in Atlanta for advice.

Mrs. Russell's Atlanta confidant — I won't identify him other than to say he was a soft drink pioneer — put her in touch with newspaper publisher Wilton Hall, owner of WAIM in Anderson, S.C. Mr. Hall was invited to invest in WESC. I do not know if the stock sale was ever completed but Glenn Warnock, general manager of WAIM (1230 KC), was named general manager of WESC, splitting his work week between Greenville and Anderson. The Warnock tenure lasted about a year in which the station continued to decline in popularity and revenues. However, there was one positive element in the Anderson experience. Warnock brought into the company John Y. Davenport of Anderson, S.C. Mr. Davenport came to WESC as its bookkeeper, remained with the station 40 years and retired as president of the company in 1990. He was a key player in making the station one of the most popular country music stations in America. Davenport died in 1998.

Christie Kennedy Russell believed in and understood the importance of community service. Her great interest was the Greenville General Hospital on Mallard Street, where she spent many hours as a volunteer. She enlisted the women of Greenville to serve in the hospital auxiliary, an organization dedicated to improving the Greenville General Hospital. Mrs. Russell worked extremely hard for the hospital. Rallying public support, she assigned newsman Charlie Spears the task of gathering, writing and producing a weekly quarter-hour program of hospital news. It was scheduled in prime time. In the pre-NFL TV days, prime time for daytime broadcasters was Sunday afternoon.

Mrs. Russell also lobbied the movers and shakers of Greenville, many of whom she knew socially, for hospital support. Perhaps Mrs. Russell's greatest legacy was the gift shop. She led the auxiliary to begin a coffee and gift shop at the Mallard Street facility. Although the Memorial Hospital campus has replaced the General Hospital, the gift shop continues to be operated. The Auxiliary to the Greenville Hospital System now operates gift shops at Greenville Memorial, Hillcrest and Allen Bennett Hospitals. The coffee shop/gift shop concept is gone, but the gift shops are operated with volunteer help, just as Christie Kennedy Russell envisioned them over fifty years ago. Today, there's a NEW look! A lot of MEN serve as volunteers!

In 1950, WESC initiated Greenville's first female D.J. program with beauty queen Jean Neal. While Miss Neal made the circuit competing for beauty titles Christie Russell was her chaperone. Mrs. Russell discharged this responsibility with grace and Southern charm, qualities that made her a favorite with Georgians visiting Senator George's office before her marriage to Scott Russell. Christie accompanied Miss Neal to Atlantic City for the Miss America Pageant and reported on the progress of Carolyn Fowler, Miss South Carolina, who was a native of Lyman, South Carolina. The people in the upstate were excited about Miss Fowler being in the contest and interested in her effort to bring back the crown, so there was a lot of interest in the pageant. Jean Neal and Mrs. Russell telephoned WESC every day reporting on the trip. In the days before satellites and localized network news feeds, this was unusual local news coverage. To our disappointment,

Carolyn Fowler did not bring back the title — that honor went to Miss Alabama. When the receptionist position came open at WESC, Jean Neal was given the opportunity to join the staff full time. She worked for WESC through 1951 and the first few months of '52 before winning a more important title: **Mrs.**

During the WAIM relationship, WESC became an affiliate of the **Palmetto Broadcasting System**, a company established by WAIM to syndicate the Clemson football games, **The Jack O'Connor Morning Show,** which was successful on WAIM, **Uncle Remus** with Jimmy Scribner, **Doc Durham and the Hi Neighbor Quartet,** and the **Progressive Network.** The two networks were distributed by WAIM on its FM station WCAC (l0l.1 FM).

The **Progressive Network** began on the West Coast. It was financed by some Hollywood investors and featured voice tracks supplied on transcription. Using these transcribed voice tracks and phonograph records, the **Palmetto Network** produced the programs and marketed them. It sounded like a good plan but there were glitches! Sometimes the format called for commercial records that were not available locally. Also, there were times when records were "lost" or broken, making it necessary to substitute. This required some ingenuity when the programs were produced; however, for the most part things went smoothly. WESC produced most of the programs for Palmetto Network syndication, aired them on WESC FM where they were picked up by WCAC (101.1 FM) for rebroadcast. The business plan was to sell advertising on WESC/WCAC and market the network programs to other stations in the upstate and Georgia for barter or cash. Good idea? Yes! BUT, it was ahead of its time. America wasn't ready for a fifth network. Some regional networks were successful in other areas of the country; however, the Southern economy needed to grow before there would be a market for a regional network in the South. Also, programmers needed to get the target RIGHT. The FM relay network was successful with Clemson football but 1950 was too early for a Southern regional network offering popular music.

If the **Palmetto Network** had been a full-time country music network in 1950, would it have succeeded? Was there enough advertising support for a **full-time** country music station in Greenville in 1950? The answers will never be known. Many broadcasters say the growth of Southern paychecks in the '60s provided the advertising revenues necessary to bring about the explosion of country music. In the 1950's, full-time country music stations had been tried but they failed in Atlanta and Charlotte. In the '50s, most stations programming country music — in markets the size of Greenville — added other types of musical programs to attract enough listeners and advertising dollars to pay the bills. Most programmers believed the population base in the Greenville area was too small in 1950 to support a full-time country station.

The Jack O'Connor Morning Show on WAIM featured tunes from the pop charts and the CBS transcription library. Jack O'Connor was popular in Anderson and Glenn Warnock thought it would be accepted in Greenville. So it became a part of the Palmetto Network experiment. The show was cancelled on WESC soon after it began, because O'Connor abruptly left WAIM, reportedly in a dispute over what he was to be paid for syndication. Next, WESC employed Chris Harwell as morning man. Chris had several character voices he used on his show but Greenville didn't listen. He returned to Philadelphia, Pa.

Cary Cox, the only football player in the history of Carolina and Clemson football to captain both teams, voiced the Clemson football games on the Palmetto Network in 1950. Mr. Cox was a Navy V-12 student at Carolina when he was captain for the Gamecocks. After his discharge from the Navy he played for the Clemson Tigers and served as captain, graduating in 1947. Competing stations around the state aired Clemson football, some using their own play-by-play crews; therefore, it was assumed that Tiger fans would be loyal to Cary Cox and listen to PBS. Also, his knowledge of football and his close friendships at Clemson projected an insider image. The Cary Cox version of Clemson football was accepted by the WESC audience but by the next year, 1951, WESC elected to originate its own games.

The 1950 U.S. Senate campaign of Senator Olin D. Johnston was advertised frequently on WESC. His challenger was Governor J. Strom Thurmond. This was the first statewide political campaign, to my knowledge, in which a candidate used a lot of radio. The buzzword today is "saturation" — they called it "blitzing" in those days. The Johnston campaign aired a catchy jingle to attract voters. It featured a gospel quartet with an up-tempo beat. The message was "Let's roll in with Olin…He's tried and true…Let's roll in with Olin. He's the one for you!" The song hit the target! Textile workers, farmers and government workers went to the polls and "rolled in with Olin."

Wilton E. Hall, Jr., whose father was publisher of the **INDEPENDENT/MAIL** in Anderson and a strong supporter of the Senator, informed me that Senator Johnston defeated Governor Thurmond by about 54% of the vote. He says it was the only time Senator Thurmond lost an election. I had forgotten the details of the election so I checked it out. Wilton is right. The July 12, 1950, edition of the **Greenville News** reported Johnston winning by 24,500 votes. In a Thurmond documentary aired on SCETV, Thurmond's former aide and political ally Harry Dent confirmed that the 1950 U.S. Senate race was the only political contest J. Strom Thurmond ever lost except, of course, his third Party run for President in 1948.

One wonders what the outcome would have been if Governor Thurmond had blitzed the WESC audience about six weeks before the July primary. In those days the Democratic primary was tantamount to election in South Carolina.

During the Glenn Warnock term as WESC general manager, a search was made for a frequency other than 660 KC. Greenville did not have a CBS station and Warnock believed he could secure a CBS affiliation if WESC was a full-time station. CBS programs were very popular: Jack Benny, Red Skelton, Amos n' Andy and the rest. The CBS news programs were among the best: Edward R. Murrow, Lowell Thomas and a host of CBS newsmen who had won the hearts of Mr. and Mrs. America with news reports from World War II battlefronts. The Korean conflict had just begun and Warnock believed it would be necessary to provide full-time AM network news service to compete. A frequency search revealed that 910 KC could be used in Greenville with a four-tower configuration. There was discussion about making an application for 1000 watts on 910 KC. However, after Christie Russell discussed the proposal with her Washington advisors and some of the ministers who were using the station, she opposed the idea. Obviously, 1000 watts on 910 KC could not match the daytime coverage of 5000 watts on 660 KC. She believed WESC's local programs and larger coverage area, even if it were just a daytime station, provided the competitive edge WESC needed.

This was an important decision because fifteen years later, when WESC installed an all day country music format, the extra power helped WESC to reach thousands of people in northeast Georgia, east Tennessee and the Carolinas that could not have been reached with 1000 watts on 910 KC. Also, remaining on 660 KC in the daytime kept WESC AM just one channel away from WSM on 650 KC, the 50,000 watt clear channel station from Nashville, Tennessee, that offered country music all night long including the Grand Ole Opry on Friday and Saturday nights. In the days when there wasn't much country music on the radio and the public listened to AM radio more than FM, some people — mostly country music fans — listened to WESC 660 AM during the day and WSM 650 AM at night.

Incidentally, 910 KC was eventually granted to Spartanburg, S.C.

Among the staff members during the early '50s were Bob McClure, salesman: Mr. McClure left WESC and in time, started a group of religious stations. Bill Bochman, sales manager: After leaving WESC, Mr. Bochman returned to Columbia. As sales manager of WNOK radio he was a member of the management team that brought Bob Fulton to Columbia. Bill told me that he and Moody McElveen, the WNOK general manager, listened to auditions from sports announcers throughout the country before they selected Bob Fulton to become the voice of the South Carolina Gamecocks. Later, Bill Bochman established WDXY (1240 KC) in Sumter, S.C. He served as SCBA president in 1968.

Dick Richards, salesman: Mr. Richards left Greenville to pursue a career in TV photojournalism. Much of his reporting was done in Central and South America. Jim Waldrop, news announcer, and Felton "Bill" Bailey, engineer: Mr. Waldrop had been a network announcer in New York during World War II. He soon departed for the Big Apple. Mr. Bailey went into industrial electronics. When Greenville Technical College was established, Mr. William F. Bailey was its first electronics instructor. As electronics grew in importance to the textile industry, Mr. Bailey's star rose at Greenville Tech. He eventually headed a large department of electronics specialists. One of the freelance personalities about this time was Greenville policeman Skip Shelton. Skip must have needed a little extra cash for his flying lessons because he stopped his program after completing flight training. He eventually became a corporate pilot and flew jets everywhere. At the time his program was heard on WESC, Skip partnered with another policeman, Joe Jordan, to escort VIPs around town. Skip and Joe appear with Gene Autry in Part III. By the way, Skip Shelton is an artist. I have a couple of his drawings, so you folks promote Skip.

Ellen D. Gattis, sales representative, left radio for another opportunity. Hubert Blankenship, Sr., whose air name was "Hub Terry," left Greenville, worked in media in Columbia and later became part owner of WJOT (1260 KC), Lake City, S.C. After selling his interest in WJOT, Mr. Blankenship became manager of WSPA (950 KC) in Spartanburg. He later became a Spartanburg realtor. Hub Terry (Blankenship) was president of SCBA in 1965.

Another popular announcer during the early '50s, was "Cactus" Jack Strong, alias Jon Husky. Strong aired a two-hour midmorning show as **Cactus Jack**. His Cactus Jack character sounded as if he was at a campfire spinning yarns and playing the country hits. He was really quite good as "Cactus Jack" and he also did professional air work using the name Jon Husky.

Around noon, Jack Strong returned as Jon Husky, playing pop tunes. Often Strong used both voices and most listeners never knew it was one person. Developing multiple talents offered job security.

On June 25, 1950, North Korea invaded South Korea.

President Harry S. Truman called it a "police action" and sent American troops to Korea in support of the United Nations effort to maintain the status quo. WESC reported the progress of the war with the Mutual Broadcasting System and the Progressive Network and later, the Liberty Broadcasting System. Also, WESC listeners followed the progress of the war through Associated Press reports read by the WESC staff. The WESC country boys could handle words like Pork Chop Ridge, General Douglas MacArthur and General Matthew B. Ridgway. But the Yalu River, Chosin Reservoir or Chinese General Lin Piao required practice. Unfortunately, time restraints required most newscasts to be read without practice time. Now you know why we didn't keep air checks of these newscasts.

Obviously, a good newsreader was in demand during the Korean War years. The undisputed chief among Greenville newscasters was WFBC's Norvin C. Duncan — who holds a national record for his ESSO REPORTERS — using the United Press news, but Fred Heckman, Bob Way, Charlie Spears, Sterling Wright and Wayne Davis kept WESC competitive with the AP wire service.

Chapter 6

A Greenville Idea:
Keep It Local!

When Mrs. Russell decided an alliance with WAIM was
not in her best interest, she invited Greenville businessman
Alester G. Furman, Jr., to participate in a reorganization of
the company. In October 1951, Mr. Furman paid $44,000 for
44% of the company with Christie Kennedy Russell retaining
56%. Investing in WESC demonstrated Mr. Furman's faith
in the Greenville community to support the station, as well as
helping Christie Russell settle her deceased husband's estate.
Although he did not take an active role in the operation of the
station, Mr. Furman's business experience, personal charm
and reputation in the Greenville community added credibility
to the business.

In the early '50s, WESC survived some dark days —
competition was fierce! The two market leaders, WFBC and
WMRC, were entrenched with good local ownership,
management, staff and programs. Also, Greenville's growth
did not come until the late '50s; therefore, many potential

advertisers believed the town was just too small for the number of radio stations on the air. In addition to WESC AM and WESC FM there were WFBC AM, WFBC FM, WMRC AM, WMRC FM, WAKE AM and WMUU AM all wanting a piece of the pie. So, having a prominent citizen like Mr. Alester G. Furman, Jr., as part owner of the station helped a lot.

In 1951, Ennis Bray was named general manager of WESC. About a year later, in 1952, Bray was elevated to vice president and general manager. Mr. Bray's experience as manager of WAIM (1230 KC) in Anderson, WMRC (1490 KC) in Greenville and WEGO (1410 KC) in Concord, N.C., equipped him for the job. He was an experienced salesman and a sports fan. Also, his background as a drummer with a dance band provided him with the connections needed for pop radio. He knew most of the musicians during the big band era. His musical taste and interest in sports were soon reflected in WESC's programs. Bray thought he had commitments from three WMRC staff members to join him at WESC; however, only two made the switch. Margaret Bennett and Jimmy Simpson came aboard.

Margaret Bennett was a good worker, an excellent typist with great telephone skills, and a pleasant receptionist. Her people skills equipped her for almost any special project. These characteristics were necessary for a person at a front desk in the 1950's because they had a lot of contact with the public. The receptionist was the first and last staff member to see visitors in the station and handled every telephone call. So, a good receptionist was worth more than some stations could afford to pay them. I guess that's why machines eventually took over these jobs in a lot of businesses.

How important is a good receptionist? The good ones are worth their weight in gold. When I telephone Channel 4 in Greenville, which isn't very often, Mary Ann Snyder answers the phone and as soon as I speak she recognizes my voice and calls me by name. She listened to me on the radio and remembers my voice. Mary Ann usually has something good to say about the days when she listened to me on WESC. Does that little extra touch mean anything to me? You bet it does!

Margaret Bennett was THAT kind of receptionist. Also, Maggie was counted on to make WESC FM's reports of election returns accurate and competitive. She developed her own election exit poll long before the news pros figured out how to do it. Ms. Bennett made a few phone calls and predicted the outcome of most local elections before the polls closed.

Also, "Aunt Margaret" was emcee of a kiddies record program she called **Tiny Tot Time.**

Jimmy Simpson was multi-talented. He played the piano and organ, sometimes singing along with the records. Simpson was a very good disc jockey as well as sports announcer. In bringing Jimmy Simpson aboard, Mr. Bray hoped to lock up the sports audience and its associated advertising dollars, but to Bray's disappointment Jimmy Simpson was offered a bigger job in Raleigh, North Carolina. It was a dream job: announcing N.C. State sports and the Raleigh baseball team in the Carolina League. He departed for Raleigh. Eventually, Jimmy Simpson left the radio business to operate a restaurant in eastern North Carolina.

In the summer of 1951, WESC FM aired textile baseball games almost every night except Wednesday and Sunday. Just about every textile community fielded a team, competing in the Western Carolina League or the Greenville Textile League. The station served as many communities as possible by selecting games from both leagues. This exposure helped WESC to build its influence in the mill communities. Hub Terry (Blankenship) was a key in this effort. He selected the games, gathered information about the players and described the games. It was a privilege for me to work with Hub on these broadcasts and he taught me the basics of broadcasting baseball. Legendary textile players, former minor leaguers and outstanding college athletes played on the textile teams. The games were usually played before large crowds at the community ballparks.

The textile teams were able to attract good players because the companies paid well. The promise of a regular paycheck, without the hardship of minor league travel, appealed to the players. Some of them were seeing their major league dreams turn to nightmares because their family responsibilities were increasing.

Another source for players was the colleges. Most were legitimately employed for the summer and invited to play for the community team.

The textile baseball season of '51 helped WESC establish lasting relationships with some of these players. It turned out to be a building block for the future. Several of them became big WESC boosters; others were to become sponsors when WESC hit the jackpot with country music.

The WESC staff during Mr. Bray's tenure as general manager included Ray Woodard, a former Carolina League umpire and announcer. After a few months Woodard returned to eastern North Carolina. Dave Moss: a program director with excellent basketball announcing skills, described the Furman basketball games during the early college careers of Frank Selvy and Nield Gordon. Also, Moss aired some of the Clemson basketball games. Upon leaving WESC, Dave Moss joined the staff of WCRS (l450 KC) in Greenwood, S.C., where he originated the Furman Basketball Network for one season. Before leaving South Carolina, Moss announced the University of South Carolina basketball games while he was on the staff of WIS (560 KC) in Columbia. The Moss philosophy was to land a job and immediately start looking for a better one. His career goal focused on college basketball. He returned to New Jersey, a hotbed for sports, acquired ownership in a station at Camden, New Jersey, and operated it as a sports station. That was probably one of the first all sports stations in the country.

Dave eventually settled in Princeton, N.J., where he associated himself with a firm marketing a test designed to discover the potential success of sales applicants. In the 1970's, Dave Moss helped me evaluate the sales skills of the WESC sales staff. Using his test and his advice, he helped me make some important sales management decisions resulting in significant sales gains. I am grateful to Dave Moss for his assistance in discovering the strengths of WESC's sales staff. Mr. Moss is now deceased.

Here's an example of how we used the Sales Personality Dynamics test that Dave Moss recommended. We discovered through the test that Allan Jenkins, one of our salesmen, was a very detail-oriented person. If you asked him what time it was he would tell you all about the parts in the watch, so to speak. Dave Moss advised us to assign Allan to advertising agencies. It was a perfect fit! Allan Jenkins became very successful working with advertising agencies. He became a member of the American Advertising Federation, holding offices on the local, regional and national level. It is hard to believe that one of our guys sat on the national Advertising Federation board with the giants of the industry. I'm proud of Allan Jenkins and grateful to him for his friendship and good work at WESC. Allan now owns his own agency: Altamont Marketing Communications, Inc.

Now back to the staff of the '50s. Fred Heckman, newsman: Heckman's talents were in news and audience participation.

One popular WESC program during Heckman's year at WESC was **Heckman's House Party,** an early afternoon audience participation/variety show. The show featured Greenville musicians. Staff members Bob Way and Hugh Jarrett were regular singers on **Heckman's House Party**. Helen Herring, a very gifted pianist and organist, was a valued member of the cast. After leaving WESC, Fred Heckman worked for WCRS (1450 KC) in Greenwood, then left South Carolina. Fred Heckman had a distinguished career as news director for WIBC (1070 KC), a 50,000-watt station in Indianapolis, Indiana. One of the sales reps at WESC in 1952 was Johnny Croft. He became sales manager at WIBC. Heckman and Croft, as far as I know, finished their careers at WIBC.

Robert "Bob" Way was program director during the Bray years. It was Bob Way who mentored "Country Earl" Baughman. Way encouraged Baughman to learn how to operate the control board, to practice reading aloud and occasionally permitted him to announce station breaks. This experience prepared Earl Baughman to join the staff at WESC when he got the opportunity.

When general manager Ennis Bray resigned to start WJAN (1400 KC) in Spartanburg, S.C., he took Way with him. Way soon returned to Ohio, where he became news director for a large radio/TV operation owned by the Taft family.

Hugh Jarrett, another Bray recruit, was successful with the Jordanaires and WLAC (1510 KC) in Nashville, Tennessee. Later, Jarrett was a D.J. and promoter in the Atlanta area.

Charlie Spears came to WESC in 1953 from Spartanburg, where he had worked for WSPA (950 KC) and WORD (1400 KC, later 910 KC). During the short time he was at WESC, Spears commuted from Spartanburg to Greenville by bus. He never learned to drive a car nor did he ever marry. Spears and his mother, a retired teacher, lived in Spartanburg just a few blocks from both WSPA and WORD. He had a house full of cats and returned to Spartanburg where he could care for his cats and walk to work. Traveling by any means frightened him. Eccentric? Perhaps; however, Charlie Spears had one of the best voices in the business and great writing skills. He could read anything without practice and studied the dictionary constantly. All of this, plus the fact he was never late or absent from work made him a jewel. Charlie Spears was a rare talent and could have gone to New York or any big city BUT unfortunately he would have had to leave Spartanburg and his cats and commute to work. Spears is deceased.

Sterling Wright: Mr. Wright also worked for the stations in Spartanburg before coming to WESC. After leaving WESC, Sterling Wright went to Charlotte, where he worked for WSOC Radio and TV. He is probably best known in the Carolinas for his association with the Shrine Bowl of the Carolinas high school all-star football game. WESC aired the game for many years and at the request of Mr. Wright we supplied FM radio receivers to the children at the Shriners Hospital in Greenville so they could listen to the game. The play-by-play announcers were usually chosen from around the Carolinas after the death of Lee Kirby, the legendary WBT sports announcer who helped start the series. The announcers always greeted the children at the Shriners Hospital by announcing each patient's name on the air.

Sterling Wright was a true professional who fondly remembered his WESC days. Sometimes he called just to stay in touch with his friends at WESC. In passing, I want to express my thanks to Joe Sessoms, general manager of WASC (1530 KC) in Spartanburg for his good work on the Shrine Bowl network after Sterling Wright retired. Joe has been assisted by Ron Owenby of WAGI (105.3 FM) in Gaffney, S.C.

Joe was a fellow Shriner, a former president of SCBA and a good friend. We had some wonderful golf matches during SCBA summer meetings at the beach. During one tournament — not an SCBA event — Joe's opponent thought he was fudging too much and complained saying, "Joe, you are cheating!" Joe replied, "I have to cheat to keep up with you." What a compliment!

Now, back to WESC in the early '50s. Among the members of the staff: Ralph Petty, Jr., who came to WESC from Pittsburgh, Pa. His duties were program director and news announcer; however, after a stay of about eight months he returned to Pittsburgh. Johnny James, salesman: Although a very good salesman, Mr. James' first love was furniture. He returned to that business. Some of the other salesmen during the early '50s were: Charles "Buzz" Goodyear, Gordon Anderson and Johnny Kuykendall.

WESC general manager Ennis Bray was a visionary who left his mark on Carolina radio. He believed in FM and thought the quality of FM reception would revolutionize radio listening. He was right but his timing was wrong.

Although WESC FM was already on the air when Ennis Bray arrived, he diversified and revitalized programming, boosting sponsor interest. Mr. Bray initiated a WESC application for Channel 4 TV; however, the application was dropped when one of the WESC principal stockholders, Alester G. Furman, Jr., opted to join the efforts of newspaper publisher Roger C. Peace (WFBC) and businessman Robert A. Jolley (WMRC) to establish VHF TV Channel 4 in Greenville. Many observers believed the competing applications, which were largely financed by these three leading Greenville businessmen, would require years of litigation.

The merger of WFBC and WMRC cleared the way for

Channel 4 to be granted following the VHF TV thaw in the '50s. Mr. Furman told me the principals in the three applications were in a Washington hotel waiting for an FCC hearing to begin the next day. The hearing would decide which company was to be awarded the station. Mr. Furman said he called the parties together and suggested they merge. Instead of going into FCC hearings the next day, they worked out the details of a merger and Greenville got its first and only VHF TV station. However, there was a casualty. Greenville's first local TV outlet, a UHF channel, WGVL Channel 23, returned its license to the FCC. Ben McKinnon, the general manager of WGVL, eventually became executive director of the Alabama Broadcasters Association. No doubt his experience with the early days of UHF television in Greenville and his earlier days at WBTV in Charlotte helped shape the industry.

WESC's next manager was Buddy Starcher, the Columbia recording artist, who came to the station in 1953. A country singer, Starcher experienced the power of country radio as an entertainer, and he was not about to sell it cheap. Starcher didn't go on the street to make sales calls nor did he call businesses on the phone. He believed airtime on country music programs was worth more than the merchants were willing to pay. When retailers were paying ten to fifteen dollars a quarter hour, Starcher was billing thirty to fifty dollars a quarter hour selling baby chicks, guitar and piano courses, high school home study courses, patent medicines and other items by direct mail. He set a goal of fifty dollars for each quarter hour of air time used for a program. He expected this goal to be reached by mail order sales, and more often than not, the goal was met.

Starcher judged WESC announcers — he called them air salesmen — by the number of mail orders they received. He developed air salesmen out of Country Earl Baughman and me. He taught us how to get listeners to respond. The keys were **urgency, availability, pride, envy** and **personal service.** Writing copy to sell rose bushes, he persuasively wrote: "Send your order now because this offer isn't going to last long …if you wait you'll be too late! [*urgency*] When you see these beautiful roses in your neighbor's yard, you'll say, 'Why didn't I listen to ole Country Earl and get my order in the mail?' [*envy*] Remember: send no money...Just pay the postman $3.98 plus COD charges when he brings your rosebushes to your door…and wait until the mailman sees your beautiful roses! [*pride*] He'll surely want some of your roses to take home to his wife. Now, if you don't have beautiful roses that are the envy of the neighborhood you need to go to the phone right now and call me at XXX XXXX or send me a penny postcard to XXXXXX. I'm waiting for your call OR I'll be looking for your card in the mail. I'll see to it that you are among the first to get these beautiful, hardy rosebushes." [*Personal service*]

This was valuable experience for us because after Starcher moved on, WESC returned to the street with its "results oriented" advertising. Using airtime to **sell** rather than **selling** airtime. Buddy Starcher stayed in Greenville for one season, departing in 1954 to pursue other opportunities. He always left the air by saying, "Good-bye, and may the angels sleep on your pillow tonight." For a while it became a staff farewell when staff members left the office. We didn't say, "So long" or "Good night." We said, "Good-bye, and may the angels sleep on your pillow tonight."

After a few years of grieving over the death of Scott Russell, a man she truly loved, Christie Kennedy Russell married former Furman University Athletics Director James G. Meade in 1953. When Buddy Starcher departed, she named her husband sales manager and she assumed the title of general manager. Bookkeeper John Davenport was promoted to assistant manager.

Buddy Starcher left his footprint on WESC programs. He acquired several religious programs, helping WESC to become a better radio station: **The Hour of Decision** with Billy Graham, **The Old Fashion Revival Hour** with Charles E. Fuller and **Back to the Bible** with Theodore Epps as its speaker. These programs were added to a schedule which already included **The Gospel Hour** featuring evangelist Oliver B. Greene and **The Bright Spot Hour** with the Rev. Harold B. Sightler. These programs anchored WESC's 3-R's format: Religion-Rural-Race.

In a few years, Country Earl with his early morning **Country Earl Show** and mid-morning **Gospel Train**, Floyd Edge as **Uncle Dudley,** and **The Chicken Shack** helped make WESC a very successful radio station. In the last half of the fabulous fifties, WESC had a firm grip on a large segment of the population in the Carolinas and northeast Georgia. One person out of four who listened to the radio in a 19 county area depended on WESC for music, news and sports. There were no peaks and valleys in the audience. WESC could claim a block of one-fourth of the population as its audience. Remember also, local television was in its infancy. More importantly, when WESC advertised a product the audience responded. Used car dealers, mobile home dealers and all sorts of independent businessmen depended on two advertising vehicles to sell their merchandise: WESC and their local newspaper. The 3-R's format provided a needed service to nineteen counties.

WESC did not duck controversial issues. *The Pastor's Study* was a venue in which the Reverend Frank Pickney, rector of the Christ Episcopal Church of Greenville, answered Bible questions called in to the program. This Sunday afternoon quarter hour was lengthened to thirty minutes, providing time to explore the issue of a burning hell. The program aired for a few months but was canceled after it became mired in the "burning hell" controversy, leaving little time for other discussion. From this experience I learned you can not make friends for yourself or your station with religious controversy.

WESC provided a forum for labor issues. Both sides were given access to the airwaves. Alston Calhoun, a newspaper editor turned radio commentator, was heard each Sunday afternoon during the early '50s. He expounded an anti-union view on *Americanism Preferred.* Spokesmen for the unions were allowed to present their side. They did so, mostly during periods leading up to labor elections. The union elections at the fiberglass plant in Anderson and the Duke Power plant at Pharr Shoals are two examples. Although most of the broadcasters in the South opposed unions the FCC required them to make time available without charge for opposing views. WESC provided time for discussion and sold them spots.

It is my opinion the "Equal Time" requirement was in the public interest. If the FCC reinstated the Equal Time requirement, we wouldn't have so many "nuts" expounding their lunatic fringe ideas without rebuttal on the nation's airwaves.

WESC opened its mikes for local news commentary. Newspaper columnist/insurance agent Charlie Garrison aired the radio version of his weekly newspaper column, *Caught on the Wing,* which ran in the **INDEPENDENT-MAIL** in Anderson.

In 1955, Christie Kennedy Russell Meade appointed her husband, Jim Meade, general manager of WESC. His experience as a Washington Redskins professional football player, a college athletic director and football coach provided an excellent background for promoting and selling radio. Jim Meade managed like he coached. Commanding, demanding and praising. Meade was tough but fair. A man for the time.

Meade was also tough in the military. A lot of stories circulated about his "macho persona" in the military. He was an officer in the paratroopers, serving in both the European and Pacific theatres.

One of my Meade favorites is about a parachute jump. Being the ranking officer on a mission, he rose to give the jump order and told the troops if anyone failed to jump he would kick them out. While making the threat he realized he was the ranking officer and remembered he was to jump FIRST!

Jim Meade recognized that some of the talents of staff members were not utilized. For example: Wayne Davis looked and sounded like a radio executive. His deep voice, executive appearance, patience and people skills equipped him to train new people. They were impressed with Wayne — he sounded like he knew what he was talking about, and he usually did, so new hires had confidence in what he said. As PD, some of his responsibility was to recruit and train the air staff.

As has been said, Wayne was one of the first WESC employees but left after Mr. Russell died. He helped establish Greenville's fifth station, WAKE (1490 KC), in 1950. He returned when Jim Meade came to the station and Meade hired him as program director, later promoting him to assistant station manager. When John Davenport became general manager, Wayne was made station manager.

Jim Meade believed in hiring people without previous radio experience and teaching them the business. He said new people didn't have anything to "unlearn." Meade employed Jim Young, the brother of Furman University Head Football

Coach Bill Young, as a salesman/announcer, and Bill Ingram to manage sales.

Mr. Ingram was an experienced salesman, trained by Fred Mathews at Harper Brothers' Office Supply Company. The Greenville business community recognized Harper Brothers as a company with a good sales training program. Ingram learned his lessons well; therefore, all he needed to be effective in his job as a radio salesman was product knowledge. John Davenport supplied this and soon Ingram was producing business.

Meade and Ingram recruited a sales staff: W.H. "Bill" Kirby came to WESC from law enforcement and Carlyle Huff from the dairy business. Also, Earl Baughman (Country Earl) and I were encouraged to sell, assigned accounts and trained by Bill Ingram. Bill Ingram was a good sales trainer in the Fred Mathews mold. Bill Ingram died in Charleston in 2002. I learned a lot from Bill Ingram and Jim Meade.

Years before the Army adopted the slogan "Be All You Can Be," Jim Meade was encouraging every member of the WESC staff to be: <u>ALL YOU CAN BE.</u>

Challenging the tough Main Street "newspaper/one station mentality," Meade insisted on WESC's SHARE of the business. He never identified "WESC's share of the business" but he was effective in demanding it anyway.

More than once, Meade called merchants insisting that he get "his share" of the business, after a sales event had been announced in the newspaper or on another station. He was tough on the WESC salesman who did not make regular sales calls. When a promotion was announced by a store and WESC didn't have an order he wanted to know why. Meade would call the merchant to find out if they were being called upon. Woe unto the salesman who didn't make regular sales calls to the businesses on his list.

Sales manager Bill Ingram appealed to the merchants to be "fair." Thus, WESC established the street slogan: "Go get WESC's FAIR SHARE."

WESC was successful under the management of Jim Meade. Using his promotional skills he increased the station's popularity by advertising the personalities in the newspaper, on city buses, taxicabs and on movie trailers. This was a departure from the Russell philosophy. Mr. Russell didn't believe in buying advertising that was more expensive than his own. Now, I can almost hear promotion directors laughing. But before you have too much fun with that one, remember, Scott Russell was a successful corporate lawyer and ran a successful textile company before going to Washington. He was a man with a strong will. Radio station promotion was new to him. Had he lived, you can bet that he would have learned the ropes and made a fortune as the industry developed.

Recognizing outstanding performance, Jim Meade promoted John Davenport to station manager and later to assistant general manager. When Meade left John was promoted to general manager. Meade and Davenport used newspaper, movie trailers, billboards, city buses and taxicabs to promote **WESC — 660 in Dixie — First in Greenville.** The slogan was splashed everywhere. It advertised the WESC dial position but, obviously, there were implied meanings. Some competing salesmen, who raved and ranted to retailers about "WESC's preachers and hayseed music" now spent their time giving their version of why WESC was not "First in Greenville."

Meade rewarded our sales effort with steak suppers and cash bonuses to build team spirit. WESC became a competitive force in the Greenville advertising community. However, Jim and Christie's marriage failed. He left WESC and managed WQOK (1440 KC) for a few months before returning to his native Maryland, where he had been an outstanding football player for the University of Maryland. Jim Meade is deceased.

Some of the other employees who gave service and moral support to WESC in the period between 1950 and 1955 were: Charlie Dubose, salesman; transmitter operators Ed Healy, Billy Baldwin and Fred Bryan; Women's Director Betté Battle; copywriter Julie Fuggerson; and Julius Anderson, janitor.

When Jim and Christie Meade parted ways, Christie Meade left Greenville to live with her sister, Mamie Kennedy, in Atlanta. John Davenport was promoted to general manager. Wayne Davis was named station manager, Bill Ingram continued as commercial manager, Country Earl Baughman, a morning personality/salesman, and I continued as personality/salesman. Jim Young left WESC to become a manufacturer's representative and Floyd Edge (Uncle Dudley) was hired as a personality/salesman. By this time, WESC's 3-R format had become popular around the country — "3-R's" was a marketing term to help advertisers understand the station's programming: "3-R's" stood for Rural, Religion and Race.

The year 1955 was a good one for WESC, if for no other reason than Dan Greer, pastor of the Washington Avenue Baptist Church of Greenville, started airing his Sunday morning messages. The ministry of Rev. Greer was matched perfectly with WESC's audience. Today's advertising gurus call it demographics and psychographics. Rev. Greer was a textile baseball player, a country musician and textile worker before his conversion. Deeply spiritual and totally committed, Dan Greer went back to school to prepare for the ministry. First he completed his high school work with the help of a private tutor, and then he continued his education at North Greenville College and Furman University. Finally, Dan Greer

94

finished his formal education at the Southeastern Baptist Theological Seminary at Wake Forest, North Carolina.

While attending school Rev. Greer continued to work in textiles but later he served as a church pastor while he continued to study. Dan Greer was uniquely prepared for the ministry. After Rev. Greer had been pastor of Washington Avenue Baptist for about a year, several Christian laymen — led by a deacon of the church, Malcolm Carter saw an opportunity to use Rev. Greer to reach more people for Christ by radio. They asked me to arrange for the Sunday worship service to be broadcast on WESC. Arranging for these broadcasts and supervising their taping was a source of personal satisfaction for me.

When Rev. Greer spoke to the WESC audience from the Washington Avenue Baptist Church pulpit about **commitment**, he spoke from personal experience. The worshipers in the church and those listening on the radio related to his message. Mr. Greer was a tireless worker and wherever he went, he asked people to listen to the Washington Avenue Baptist Church service on WESC. He believed a radio program enabled church prospects to get an overview of the service before attending and nonbelievers were reached effectively by radio. Also, he saw the broadcast as a motivational tool for the music program of the church. He recognized the personal relationship that was established with the audience. People listen while they're alone. It's a **one** on **one** medium. Thus, the Washington Avenue Baptist Church service was more than the broadcast of a worship service — it **connected** the worshiper in the pew and the listener in radio land with Dan Greer's persuasive presentation of the Gospel. The choir, pastor and people labored to present an appealing broadcast to reach new people for Christ. Also, it provided a worship service for members who were not present.

Mr. Paul Dickerson and other members of the church learned to operate the broadcast equipment and relayed the service to the station by telephone line where it was recorded. The tape of the Washington Avenue Baptist Church ll:00 a.m. service was broadcast at 1:30 p.m. the same afternoon. Assisting with the music were: Claude Turner, choir director; Terry Morgan, organist; Kathleen Ayers, pianist; Bobby Ebberhart, soloist; and Joan Wyatt, soloist. It was my pleasure to have been asked by The Rev. Greer to participate in the services of Washington Avenue Baptist Church on several occasions. I found the opening announcement of their program to be true. The program came on the air with this line: "THIS IS THE END OF YOUR SEARCH FOR A FRIENDLY CHURCH."

Dan Greer rarely missed being in the pulpit on Sunday mornings. He knew how important it was to be consistent. I can't say it enough: the power of radio lies in the listener's imagination — a theatre of the mind. Rev. Greer's presentation of the Gospel, humble spirit and pulpit skills connected with radio listeners and attracted them to WESC. On the other hand many radio listeners who were not regular in church attendance started going to WABC or listening to Dan on the radio. After more than twenty-five years as pastor of the Washington Avenue Baptist Church, Rev. Greer's health forced him to retire. The church called the Reverend Eddie Greene as pastor. Dr. Greer died in 1993. Some audiotapes of Dr. Greer's sermons are on file in the Library at North Greenville College.

Some of the WESC staff members in the middle and late '50s were: John Lewis Kuykendall, salesman. Mr. Kuykendall left to become a dairy farmer. Ralph Gordon, weekend announcer; Miss Judd Moore, copywriter; Don Bailey, announcer/copywriter. Mr. Bailey left WESC upon graduation from Bob Jones University to pursue his career goal with the

Billy Graham Evangelistic Association. Don Bailey was successful with the Billy Graham Ministry, serving in several capacities: in the film ministry, as an administrator in Minneapolis, and director of the Cove Retreat near Asheville, N.C. Don Bailey's voice was heard often on **The Hour of Decision** broadcast on ABC radio. Those who knew Don Bailey were not surprised with his success. He did splendid work and was a special staff member.

Office personnel in the middle '50s included: Ben and Betty Jo McGuire. Ben McGuire eventually became a minister in the Methodist Church.

Jim Pitts worked as a copywriter at WESC in 1959, while attending Furman University. After graduation and the completion of his seminary studies at Southern and Southeastern seminaries, Mr. Pitts joined the staff at Furman University, eventually becoming a university chaplain. Today, Furman University Chaplain Jim Pitts jokingly tells people about his radio days writing commercials for the **Chicken Shack.** Speaking at a Scottish Rite Maundy Thursday observance at which former Furman University President John Johns had introduced him, Chaplain Pitts said that he had good qualifications for the position of chaplain at Furman: he had been in Wally Mullinax's **Chicken Shack** and Dr. John John's Woodshed!

In the '50s, Allen Riddle served WESC as announcer and program director. Later, Mr. Riddle left WESC to help Bill Kirby establish WBBR (1580 KC) in Travelers Rest, S.C. Bill Krieger (Bernhard A. Krieger) started as an announcer and later was promoted to program director. When Mr. Krieger joined WESC in 1955, if I remember correctly, he had never been into a radio station. He just showed up asking for an audition. After Wayne Davis heard Krieger read a couple of announcements he asked me to sit in on the audition. My reaction was: Where is this guy working? When Wayne responded that he just walked in off the street asking for a job, I couldn't believe it. As they say in the business, he was a "natural." Of course, he was hired on the spot. It turned out, Bill Krieger's brother-in-law, Pee Wee Milton, was a guitarist associated with WESC through one of the bands. Unbeknownst to us, Bill might have gotten some coaching. Mr. Krieger later worked at WSPA (950 KC) and WMRB (1490 KC).

A key technician in the '50s was Harold White, who came from Iowa. He brought with him a knowledge of the business learned while on the staff of several midwest radio stations. He contributed to the development of the station by overseeing the construction of the first MOBILE MIKE and rewiring the station.

Engineers tell me that copper wire loses some of its value as a conductor of electrical current after about ten years. Harold White rewired the station and installed a new ground system. This improved the sound and coverage of the station. Mr. White also made some improvements in the FM signal. Thus, WESC was a better radio station because of Harold White's service to the company. Harold White is deceased.

The first remote vehicle in which Mr. White installed broadcast equipment was a mobile studio in the shape of a microphone. The mike, built on a trailer chassis by Shelton Rimer, a mobile home manufacturer, was pulled by a Chevy station wagon. It was the first of its kind in the nation. And very successful! The demand for this service made it necessary to build a second mobile mike, one that could be moved quickly to other broadcast sites. Harold White's Mobile Mike #2 was built on the back of a Ford Ranchero pick up truck but kept the microphone shape. We called it MOBILE MIKE-ERO. WESC sold the first unit to WCOS (1400 KC) in

Columbia, and while it was in use near the state capitol, a *Life Magazine* photographer took a picture of it. Later the picture appeared in an article in *Life* to illustrate how radio was reinventing itself. New ideas were necessary for the survival of the radio industry after TV replaced the radio set in the family living room.

WESC Radio WAS reinventing itself! We aired live remotes from MOBILE MIKE, producing country and gospel music shows on location. We broadcast live shows from the back of a flatbed truck. The trucks used to transport bales of cotton to the textile plants provided the best portable stages because we could set up the country show instruments on one end and the gospel show gear on the other end. During the broadcast we could switch the entertainment without interrupting the show.

WESC created an advertising package for grand openings, anniversaries and other special sales events. Our goal was to have at least five promotions from each used car or mobile home dealership a year. Merchants could buy turnkey promotions including live entertainment, a radio broadcast, commercials before and after the event, balloons for the kids, candy, ice cream — everything! We arranged for all the expenses to be billed to WESC and the advertiser had to write only one check. This simplification helped us sell the promotions. We rented the vehicles from a rental company when we were unable to arrange for a cotton truck at one of the plants. Actually, the broadcasts became so popular that some of the textile plants considered it a good public relations gesture to provide a truck when they had one available. This was before the days of the Marti remote transmitters, so WESC arranged for special telephone and electrical lines to be dropped at the remote sites. We said to the advertiser: "You pay one bill…WESC handles the details."

Sometimes advertisers created their own package. We said to the advertiser: "Just tell us what you want; WESC has a plan for every man. If we don't have one for your business we'll make one." Making the sale simple put us a leg up on our competition. We could get John Davenport on the phone, approve the deal and, bingo! The deal was done. After a few promotions we learned the boundaries that John would approve. Also, we knew the advertiser's credit history.

"Greenville is growing and Greenville is fair...there's room for more stations to come on the air."

WESC generated a lot of sales success stories with these special events and told other sales prospects about them. All staff members were informed about the sales results WESC produced for its clients. Thus, we inspired the staff and motivated our clients to buy more.

One such success occurred at a used car dealership located on the Old Easley Bridge Road near the intersection of White Horse Road. The dealer purchased a live one-hour country show and a one-hour gospel music show, airing them back-to-back. If he had ordered the Greenville Symphony we would have thrown that in too, if available! The show was complete: guitar pickers, pianos, singers, multiple mike setups, all on the back of a flatbed cotton truck. And there was free food: ice cream, hot dogs and soft drinks. Before the live show started we aired records from MOBILE MIKE to attract the crowd. After about two hours of the three-hour promotion, a Georgia listener came on the car lot, went directly to an almost-new Cadillac being advertised, took a test drive and purchased the car at the advertised price — paying cash! That one purchase paid for the promotion. The dealer asked us to stay on the air for another hour that afternoon and purchased a promotion the following week.

During these remotes, soft drink bottlers Coke, Pepsi and Royal Crown were really cooperative. They had a special party-dispensing unit they brought out for remotes. Joe Buckner, sales manager of Pet Dairy, brought a special freezer unit that Pet maintained for the purpose. The client paid for the ice cream item selected for the promotion and furnished the pop. John Gregory at Pepsi and Jim Cooksey at Coke had their own party truck. R.C. Cola was also popular. The bottlers furnished an attendant to pour the selected soft drink throughout the broadcast. Usually, a restaurateur doing business in the neighborhood of the car dealership came and served the hot dogs.

We did a lot of remotes at the D.B. Carter car lots, LeRoy Cannon, Snyder's Auto Sales, Harbin Brothers and others. Space will not permit me to tell ALL of the stories.

WESC and WMRB teamed up to advertise a joint promotion for the Buncombe Street car dealerships. In those days, Kash and Karry Super Glider Store was the largest grocery store under one roof in the state. Their low prices and large selection of groceries attracted people from all over the tri-state area. A high traffic area close to uptown shopping was ideal for car dealerships. In two blocks shoppers could find about 1000 cars for sale. That's not much inventory at today's mega dealerships but in the '50s it was a large selection.

During the two weeks before the 4th of July — before going on vacation — car buyers got the itch to trade. WESC and WMRB combined to advertise for the Buncombe Street dealers: Wes Snyder, LeRoy Cannon, Malcolm Carter, Bill Burgin and some others. As I remember, we broadcast for most of three days, the dealerships remained open and we sold hundreds of used cars. In addition to radio, the dealers used newspaper. And we rented spotlights — heaven knows where we found them — to pan the skies. All of this attracted a lot of attention in Greenville in the '50s. The advertisers formed a pool to pay the bills. Wes Snyder was one of the key players in making that idea work. So, you could say this promotion was Greenville's first joint dealership promotion and its first "radio station group."

During the '50s, most of WESC's automotive business came from used car dealers. As foreign cars came into the market, WESC earned a reputation as the station that could sell cars. We sold all the nameplates: Renault, Fiat, Volkswagen, Peugeot and the rest. As Greenville grew it attracted large volume dealers such as Mike Persia Chevrolet and Dixie Ford. Since most of them had their own marketing plan we became less involved in the planning and executing of sales events. We just mostly sold them the airtime.

Sponsors were very special to members of the WESC staff and we worked hard to make all their promotions successful. WESC was a link between the client and his customer and the client was WESC's link with its listener. The remotes helped us get out among the people. An enterprising D.J. who relates to the visitors and sponsors at a remote will make his client and station much more money. And eventually it will find its way into his paycheck.

There are many businessmen who helped WESC succeed and they need to know WESC and country radio could not have succeeded in Greenville without them. A lot of these businessmen are now deceased and most of the others have retired. Those who are still with us, and the families of those who are gone, should be proud of the part they played in developing a great source of entertainment and information for the upstate. The names Burgin, Carter, Snyder, Cannon, Harbin, Osteen, Martin, Powers, Minyard, Williamson, McKissick and many others helped build WESC. I know I speak for all of the WESC employees who were around during the early years: We could not have succeeded without the loyalty of the advertisers. THANK YOU!

By 1955, James F. Coggins of WKDK (1240 KC) in Newberry was describing the Clemson football games on a growing network. Before buying the Newberry station, Mr. Coggins established himself in the Anderson area as a Tiger broadcaster in the late '30s and '40s. In 1951 and 1952, he voiced the South Carolina Gamecock Network for WIS (560 KC) in Columbia. So, his name recognition — which was developed through this work — helped Jimmie Coggins, Clemson Athletic Director Frank Howard and others establish the **Clemson Football Network** in 1953. These pooled broadcasts made the Clemson games available to a statewide audience. WESC joined the network in 1955 and served as its flagship station for ten years. Mr. Coggins was the play-by-play announcer and Ed Osborne of WBCU (1460 KC) in Union, S.C., was the color and game analyst. Clemson Athletic Publicist Bob Bradley — they were not called sports information directors in those days — handled the administrative details of the network. This proved to be a big plus for WESC because it provided a quality low cost broadcast, freeing up WESC personnel to handle sales and other income producing duties without having to spend several days a week preparing to originate football games.

Many stations in the upstate received the WESC FM signal for the Clemson games, inserted their commercials and retransmitted it. Using WESC-FM as a relay station resulted in substantial savings to the network, and since the network was a "pool effort" Clemson football became affordable to stations all over South Carolina. Radio stations in the midlands, the Pee Dee and low country could join the Clemson Football Network, pay into the line charge pool and have Clemson football available for their listeners at affordable advertising rates. It was a first! ALL of the Clemson football games could be heard in every home in the state for the first time EVER! Except for winning football games, these radio broadcasts probably did more than anything else up to this time to increase the public's awareness of Clemson football. Coggins, Osborne, and Bradley gave Clemson football a GIANT step forward with the Clemson Football Network, but this would not have happened without the foresight and unselfishness of Clemson Athletics Director and Head Football Coach Frank Howard. Coach Howard wanted as much publicity for Clemson as he could get and wisely put his own financial interests aside to get more stations to carry the games.

The reasonable broadcast fees rippled throughout the system. Small town stations could afford to broadcast the games and sell their advertising at a price their hometown businesses could afford. The network was successful because everybody — the university, the stations along the network and the sponsors — cooperated to make it happen. Availability and affordability were the keys. Stations and sponsors were agreeable to some "overlap" as long as the cost was low, and since most people had this attitude the games were available to most everybody who wanted to be connected with Clemson football. We made listener surveys and learned that Clemson football fans listened to their local station. It was a win-win situation.

Mr. Coggins served as SCBA president in 1956 and Mr. Osborne in 1960. The South Carolina Broadcasters Association has honored both Mr. Coggins and Mr. Osborne for this and other service to the industry. Mr. Osborne was awarded a life membership in the association in 1990 and "Jimmie" Coggins was inducted into the SCBA Hall of Fame in 2000. Ed Osborne and James F. Coggins were exceptional broadcasters. Their legacy for future broadcasters included: public service, community involvement and commitment to their families.

It wasn't until James F. Coggins' funeral that I learned he was <u>Jimmie,</u> not <u>Jimmy,</u> Coggins. Sadly, Jimmie Coggins, Ed Osborne and Frank Cope — three people who were instrumental in the success of Clemson football on WESC and WMRB, died in 2000, just a few months apart.

WESC and WMRB (1490 KC) cooperated with each other to simulcast Clemson football. It was the first time in Greenville, that I know of, when competitive stations combined programs. The two stations agreed to air the Clemson football games, sell them as a package and the commercials were heard on WESC AM/FM and WMRB. This was a novel idea. The general managers of these stations, John Davenport of WESC and Frank Cope of WMRB, were futuristic. By having WESC AM/FM and WMRB cooperate to present the games they served the public interest, client interest and their own self-interest. It was an unusual example of cooperation between competing stations. Incidentally, salesmen selling the simulcast were careful to explain that a single station purchase was available. Of course, clients bought both stations because they wanted their commercials to be heard by everybody interested in the games. In today's radio climate, station reps sell station groups routinely because the rules have changed, but in the 1950's an alliance between competing stations was against FCC rules unless the salesman walked a fine line during the sale. We were required to explain to the prospective advertiser the stations could be bought separately.

WESC FM and WMRB (1490 KC) also simulcast the Greenville High School football games in the late fifties and early sixties. Merchants welcomed the opportunity to purchase both stations with one advertising buy. I voiced the play-by-play and through most of those years Max Mace was the color announcer. We used Greenville High journalism students as spotters.

We had many fine young men work with our broadcast team as spotters. I'm sure most of them became outstanding citizens. I want to share with my readers the story of one of them. Max Mulhman became a distinguished businessman and sports figure. Max was a talented writer and sports editor of the **Hi News**, The Greenville High student newspaper, and became a reporter for the **Greenville Piedmont**. Max Mace and I — and surely there were others — encouraged Max Mulhman to specialize in auto racing. He established a friendship with Curtis Turner, one of Charlotte's NASCAR pioneers, and through the contacts he made at that track, he became one of the most respected NASCAR reporters. He worked for a motor sports magazine on the West Coast before returning to Charlotte to open an advertising/promotional firm. It was Max Mulhman who developed the marketing plan and a lot of the promotional material that resulted in the Hornets and Panthers locating in Charlotte.

My friendship with Max Mace helped Mace decide to come to WESC. In 1959 when I was promoted to the position of sales manager at WESC, John Davenport, the general manager, asked me to pick my successor for **The Chicken Shack** program. Max had a popular R&B nighttime program on WMRB (1490 KC). I recommended Max for the job. When Max Mace came aboard he changed the music and patter to fit his style and personality. But I think the show had run its course, so we tried to make an early morning guy out of Max without success.

By 1960, the rock and roll format developed by Gordon McClendon at KLIF in Dallas had reached just about every town in America. Skimming off the teens, the rock and roll stations, as they were called, fragmented the audience. Today, we have "niche" programming. **The Chicken Shack** playlist had black gospel and rhythm and blues. That's the core group for several formats. By the way, we experimented with Dixieland, jazz and some of the black artists of the big band era without success.

In a few months Max moved on to WFBC (1330 KC) but his stay with us in 1959 and 1960 paved the way for him to be available when WESC made the plunge into all country music in 1965.

Friendships in the radio business helped fill staff positions and build alliances among broadcasters in other cities. *Friendships,* fostered and strengthened at South Carolina Broadcasters Association meetings, played a major role in the establishing of the broadcast sequence at the College of Journalism at USC. A broadcasting school in the state had been discussed at association meetings in the '50s and '60s but nobody stepped forward to say, "Let's do it." The South Carolina Broadcasters Association decided to do something about it during the presidency of WESC general manager John Davenport. The SCBA Education Committee approached the USC College of Journalism with the idea of beginning a school for broadcasting. The Education Committee chairman at the time was Richard Laughridge, who is now a retired vice president of WLTX TV in Columbia.

Mr. Laughridge remembers that officials at the state's only journalism school were less than enthusiastic about training electronic journalists. USC had a great reputation for training print journalists but there was a reluctance to jump into a field that depended on wires, cameras and microphones to tell the news story. Messrs. Davenport, Laughridge, Cleatus Brazzell (WELP 1360 KC) and some other SCBA members who also had a relationship with the Clemson Football Network visited with Dr. Robert C. Edwards, president of Clemson University, about beginning a broadcast school there. Dr. Edwards advised the group to present the idea to

Dr. Thomas Jones, president of the University of South Carolina, with the message: "If Carolina doesn't begin a broadcasting school, Clemson will!" The school was started at USC with the strong support of Dr. Jones and the new dean at the College of Journalism, Dr. Albert T. Scroggins. Later, Frank Harden, general manager of Channel 10 in Columbia, represented SCBA on a university search committee that recommended Dr. Richard Uray to be the first director of the broadcast sequence.

Uray, the Happy Hungarian, had fifteen years earlier assisted Gordon McClendon on his baseball network in Texas. Under an agreement with USC, SCBA supplemented Dr. Uray's salary until the new broadcast school grew into a full-fledged electronic media training center. Dean Albert Scroggins was a real friend of SCBA and the strong ties between Scroggins and the association continue. Now retired, Dean Scroggins has been awarded an Honorary Life Membership in SCBA.

The success of the school is due to strong support of many interested broadcasters, legislators and educators. Among them was WESC's John Davenport, who got the broadcasters going on one of their ideas, an idea that was just talk before the Davenport SCBA presidential year.

The graduates of the broadcasting sequence at the University of South Carolina can be found in radio, television, government agencies and public relations jobs all over the state. WESC has had a couple of good news people from USC, Bob Rightsell and Kim Deal. WESC and the Greenville community have also benefited from the services of Connie (Mrs. P.T.) Glennon and Dale Gilbert, who are also USC Journalism alums.

An effective promotion WESC used in the '50s was originating remote broadcasts at swimming pools. There were public lakes on just about every side of town but we always selected the pools that helped pay some of the expenses incurred in producing the remote. Wayne Davis usually was WESC's man poolside. He was assisted by his wife, Louise. Their children, Becky and Roger helped entertain the kids. We originated programs from Chick Springs Lake near Taylors and Pine Grove Lake on East North Street. There may have been others, such as Woods Lake, which was near the downtown airport.

At the risk of repeating myself — and I hope it will not be boring, I want to discuss the high school football broadcasts some more because they were such an important link in the chain that bound us to the community. I continue to believe covering high school sports is essential for low power radio stations to serve their community.

As has been said WESC and WMRB aired Greenville High. However in the '50s Wade Hampton High was built to serve the growing eastside of Greenville and it became clear that we could better serve the public by going our separate ways. In 1961 WESC FM served Wade Hampton and WMRB served Greenville High. Johnny Wright, a radio/TV personality who a few years previously left the business to enter the insurance field, joined the WESC staff and began broadcasting Wade Hampton High School football, first by tape delay, then live on WESC FM. Many of the families moving into the Wade Hampton area were newcomers to the city and since their children were attending Wade Hampton, broadcasting these football games gave this area of the city a sense of community. The broadcasts were successful in attracting an audience to WESC FM's Adult Contemporary album format and the Wade Hampton merchants supported the effort but as the '60s rolled on Johnny Wright left WESC to purchase a station in Florida. After Mr. Wright's departure, I continued to broadcast the Wade Hampton High games for a couple of years, but it was determined the station could serve more people by playing music.

I did the play-by-play or shared it with whoever else might be on the staff. In the '50s and '60s, there were Bill Bochman, Dave Moss, Ralph Petty and Johnny Wright. Bill Bochman taught me how to organize a play-by-play broadcast and held my hand while I learned to announce the games. Some other voices heard on the games were Paul Long, Reggie Long and Jim Young.

In the early fifties, I did play-by-play on some college games for WESC; however, this was about the time the colleges began to organize their own networks. I could make more money for the station and myself by buying a game from a college network, airing it on WESC, collecting my commissions and resting on the weekend. Although I enjoyed doing play-by-play and other sports programs, this was not my long suit. I discovered my forte was emceeing record programs and selling the advertising space on them. So, I concentrated my efforts in that area.

The biggest high school game of the year was played on Thanksgiving Day at Sirrine Stadium located at 100 Cleveland Street in Greenville. It matched the two largest high schools in the county — Parker and Greenville. The game always attracted a capacity crowd but when the two teams seemed to be evenly matched, the stadium was overflowing. All the radio stations in town turned out for this annual grudge match and the game was usually networked to some of the other stations in the upstate. The big Turkey Day match-up of the purple and gold and the red and white always determined "bragging rights" and just who would rule the roost for the next twelve months. Many of the players in the Greenville-Parker game had successful college football careers and significant lifetime careers. Who they are and what they accomplished might be material for another book.

WESC used the high school football games to promote the Clemson broadcasts, as well as other programs on the station. One night when Greenville High was playing an important game at Greenwood it was decided to take Country Earl to the game and introduce him to the football audience during the halftime break. Hopefully, we could attract some new listeners to Country Earl in the morning. He was in the mold of Will Rogers but unpolished and, to say the least, didn't win any PTA awards for his English. The lights went out at the stadium while the game was in progress and Country Earl was thrust into the spotlight or should I say moonlight. The stadium was dark and with no activity to describe, Country Earl was called upon to fill in. It was the best ad-lib performance of his career. His English was perfect and his description of what he had seen before the stadium went dark was very good. After the game, during the trip home, Country Earl was asked why he wasn't "Country Earl" on the broadcast. He replied, "I don't want the football fans to think I'm dumb."

Country Earl was a fine piece of work. He was heard first on WESC when he was a student at Mauldin High School. His band was known as "The Blue Steel Boys." The musical group — all Mauldin students — was given permission to leave school during the lunch hour to go to WESC for the radio program but required to return promptly after the show.

In the group were: Luther Fowler, emcee and guitar; Bobby Jones, guitar; Carl Wilson, mandolin; Raymond Hembree, guitar; and Earl Baughman, steel guitar. In addition to playing the steel guitar, Earl read the fan mail for the program, which was heard live from 12:30 to 1:00 p.m. daily. During the announcing of "mail call," Earl started attracting attention with his homespun humor. W.D. Reynolds, a champion fiddler bandleader, recognized Earl's talent and asked him to come to WESC on Saturday and emcee Reynolds' weekly program. Bob Way, WESC program director, encouraged Earl to learn the control board and permitted him to announce some public service announcements. When Buddy Starcher, himself a country recording artist, was employed as general manager he gave Earl a full-time job. I named him the "Earl of Country Music." Sometimes, other WESC announcers advertised his show by saying, "Country Squire"; thereafter Earl used the line *The Country Squire is on the wire — The Earl of Country Music.*

Country Earl (Earl Baughman) was heard on WESC for most of the fifties and into the sixties when he resigned to take a job with the John D. Hollingsworth Company. Earl was a favorite of Mr. Hollingsworth, who encouraged him to learn to play golf. Earl says Mr. Hollingsworth — although not a golfer himself — wanted employees to play golf to establish business relationships. Earl did the morning show and a mid-morning *Gospel Train* show. Given the expected morning audience turnover and the loyalty of the gospel music fans, Earl probably reached more people than anyone in upstate radio in the late fifties. Nielson Pulse in 1956 reported 23,212 listeners to the *Gospel Train* at 10:15 a.m. and 17,897 to his morning show at 8:30 a.m. in a 19 county area. Of course, some of these were duplicated listeners, but folks, it was a BIG audience for the time. Earl delighted the crowds by riding a mule in the Christmas parades.

The WESC janitors — we called them porters because they were furnished with crisp, starched uniforms — were very special people. In addition to keeping the place clean their duties included going to the post office on East Washington Street to get the mail in the morning. Upon returning to the station they sorted it into each staff member's mailbox. WESC air personalities received lots of fan mail, sometimes maybe 1000 cards and letters a week. So, including the mail orders, news releases, minister's mail, record promotions and normal business correspondence we probably should have given them the title of "mailman."

The porters also provided a courier service for whatever needed to be delivered in a hurry. At about 10:30 a.m. and 3:00 p.m. the porter took the staff orders for snacks. We didn't have a scheduled "break time." Staff members usually snacked at their workstations. Among those who performed these tasks in the '50s were John Griggs, Willie Moore and Haskell Shumate. By the way, the bathrooms were stocked about twice a week by a linen service with clean white hand towels. The bathrooms were kept spotlessly clean, perfumed and the floors buffed daily. These were trappings of companies that stressed service in the '40s and '50s. All the radio stations in Greenville sparkled! This was a statement about their ownership.

There are many Country Earl stories. This one is shared with Earl's permission.

The Rev. Dr. B. B. Caldwell, "The Ole Preacher Man," was heard daily on WESC for several years. Dr. Caldwell came into the studio one morning when Country Earl was at the height of his popularity and asked, "Where's this fellow you call Country Earl?" After having Earl pointed out to him, he observed the country boy in action through a studio window, listening on a studio monitor for maybe three minutes; then the wise ole preacher turned and said, "Don't educate him; you will ruin him." Someone else said, "If Earl packaged ignorance and sold it **all** America could stop work."

Country Earl is a smart fellow. John Vest, a beloved Mason and Shriner, coached Earl when he was taking his Masonic degrees. John Vest says he saw Earl about 40 years after the coaching sessions and Earl called him by name, even though they had not seen each other during the intervening years.

Earl wrote over a hundred songs, two of which were recorded and published. *Say Mama* was recorded by Gene Vinson and published by BMI. *God Is My Shepherd* was published by SESAC and recorded by Ed Enoch with the Statesmen Quartet. The Harvesters Quartet also recorded the song. At the time of this writing, he airs **Country Earl Classics** every Saturday morning on station WAGI FM (105.3) in Gaffney, South Carolina. WAGI covers a vast area in the Carolinas and Georgia so Earl hears regularly from his WESC listeners as well as new fans he is picking up in the Charlotte-Rock Hill area. In May of 2002, Earl closed his restaurant in Mauldin, S.C. When I visited him to discuss this book, I asked Earl how he felt about closing his restaurant. He said something like this: "It's time for me to stop working and start playing. I've got a lot of memories in this ole building; I was married here four times."

I mentioned the "Ole Preacher Man," Dr. B.B. Caldwell. In 1951, before Country Earl began his morning show on WESC, Hub Terry (Hubert Blankenship) was the morning announcer. Hub got the scare of his life one morning about the time he opened the station at 6:00 a.m. Dr. B.B. Caldwell was heard on tape each morning at 6:45 a.m. Hub Terry announced the opening and closing of the program. It was customary for the religious speaker to express a word of thanks to the announcers for their participation. This helped the announcers to become a part of the minister's program. At this time, Dr. Caldwell was teaching a series of very deep messages. I never knew the subject matter; however, a listener got the idea that Hub Terry was her dead son, reincarnated! She came to the studio and when Hub would not allow her to enter the control room area, she used a chair to smash up a studio. After that incident, Hub Terry didn't have to be reminded to keep the front door locked early in the morning when he was alone. By the way, the woman's family repaired the studio and obtained psychiatric treatment for her.

In the '60s a young Furman student, Wayne Seale, who later became Dr. Caldwell's son-in-law, worked for a while as a part-time announcer for WESC. After graduation Mr. Seale became a TV newsman at several Carolina stations. Wayne Seale lost his life in an airplane crash in Charlotte, N.C. At the time of the accident, Mr. Seale was news director at WCIV Channel 4 in Charleston and, according to a close friend, was en route to Washington, D.C., for two job interviews, both of which were lucrative anchor positions. The news of the crash and Wayne Seale's death came while a group of broadcasters from around the state were meeting in Columbia to plan a fundraiser to purchase furniture for the SCBA archives room at the university. Frank Harden (WIS 560 KC) was presiding and excused himself to accept an emergency phone call. When Frank came back into the room we knew by the look on his face that something dreadful had happened. He then broke the news to us. That was a sad day because Wayne was known and respected by broadcasters around the state. They admired him because of his fine work.

Chapter 7

Ideas Make $ & Sense

In the mid-fifties, WESC aired "pop/country" programs at noon and during afternoon drive. These programs and **Community Club Awards,** a franchised promotion, helped us to reach a broader listening base. The CCA promotion enlisted the club and church women of Greenville to do some unusual things to support their organizations. WESC organized the women with a series of coffee klatches. The participating women could earn money for their club's treasury by going to the station's CCA sponsors and taking demonstration drives at sponsoring auto dealerships, getting appliance demonstrations, saving bottle caps, sales slips, signing CCA in-store registration books, etc. The women working at it were able to earn a significant amount of money for their club or church group.

This promotion was good for WESC as well as its sponsors but required a commitment of about six months from everybody involved. CCA helped the station attract listeners, sponsors and community support — and for about three months out of the year, thousands of Greenville women shopped with a WESC "CCA promotional book" in their purses. The station gave away thousands of dollars! In the six or seven campaigns, held over as many years, the women probably earned $100,000. In those days, THAT was a tidy sum of money for one radio station to give away, especially in a town the size of Greenville.

The CCA campaigns helped WESC sales reps to sharpen their selling skills, too. A master salesman, Marty White of Augusta, Ga., came to Greenville several times a year to assist with the CCA campaigns. Marty had been a street fighter (slang for a tough shoe leather radio salesman) in Atlanta before he found Jess Willard of WGAC (580 KC) in Augusta, Ga. They teamed up to put Community Club Awards promotions pretty much throughout the Southeast, working with radio, television and newspapers.

Marty White was a very aggressive salesman and a good teacher. I learned a lot about selling radio from him and used some of my Marty White stories to train WESC sales reps for 30 years.

The key to **Community Club Awards** was its director. WESC had several good ones. "Cousin" Alma Hamil, Doris Ashley and Agnes Ivester are three that come to mind. Some other staff members who worked beyond the call of duty to make CCA successful were: Bill Krieger, Allen Riddle, Buddy Womack and Bill Ingram. And there was always John Davenport, supervising everything to be sure the sponsors, CCA women and listeners were happy with the campaign. Mr. Davenport wanted CCA to be a win-win situation for everybody and worked tirelessly to insure that everybody got what he or she expected out of the promotion. The fact that sponsors and community clubs continued year after year was

118

evidence of their satisfaction. Marty White often told me that WESC was one of his best stations because of the gross sales we produced and the organizational ability of John Davenport. This made me feel good about our company because Marty always had some of the top stations in the South on his CCA list. Three that come to mind are WCOS (1400 KC) in Columbia, WGAC (580 KC) in Augusta and WSOC (1260 KC) in Charlotte. He also said WESC listeners collected as much "CCA junk" as television and newspapers. You better believe I used that statement in my sales pitches.

CCA helped WESC to attract some of the larger advertisers. WHO could not include WESC in their budget after seeing the picture of a studio full of empty bread wrappers or potato chip bags? Some of the ladies saved cigarette packages by the pound, causing some of the Pentecostal church groups to complain that their members didn't smoke, and this put them at a disadvantage. However, a good CCA director could boost the church ladies' efforts by offering extra bonuses on items the ladies bought every week such as gasoline or bread. There was one sponsor category that was off limits in South Carolina. That was milk! You could not offer a premium to sell milk in South Carolina. Think of it. We could offer a premium to sell cigarettes but not milk. I'm told that law is no longer on the books.

Community Club Awards helped crumble the walls of sales resistance in the Greenville radio market. Soft drinks, department stores, auto dealers, furniture stores, appliance stores, supermarkets and other big accounts became WESC/CCA advertisers, and after enjoying success with their WESC/CCA campaigns, many of them made WESC a part of their regular advertising mix. As WESC salesmen, we included the CCA success stories in our sales talks throughout the year and it no doubt helped many businesses to decide to buy

WESC. The annual CCA organizational meeting was held in August. We invited the ladies to a coffee and Danish brunch at the Poinsett Hotel. This became an annual event for the club women, who used the CCA kickoff meeting to get their new club year off to a fast start. This was great public relations. The Greenville club women organized for a new club year at a WESC/CCA party.

Some of the other employees in the 1950's were: Maryann Taylor, bookkeeper; Olive Mobley, secretary; Francis Dean Whitted, copywriter; and Jim Thomas, announcer.

Chapter 8

A Fast Idea

In l958, WESC started broadcasting NASCAR auto races. C.D. and Enos Bishop — the Bishop brothers — had been suggesting that we broadcast the Darlington race but I couldn't think of a way to package and sell it. We got the idea about how to sell a stock car race from a broadcaster in Florida but the moral support to broadcast races came mostly from the Bishop brothers and other Greenville businessmen.

The manager of WNDB (1150 KC) in Daytona Beach, Fla., offered WESC FM an opportunity to broadcast the Daytona 500 in February 1958. At this time the stock cars ran up the flat sands at Daytona Beach and returned via the beach highway, US 1-A. The Daytona broadcaster wanted WESC FM to air the race to complete an FM relay link to a Martinsville, Virginia, station. The project was given to me because I had a track record for selling special events. Our guideline was simple: "If it can't be sold, it can't be broadcast." Without getting into a philosophical discussion, the conventional wisdom of the '50s dictated that a program must be sold before going on the air. It should have enough public interest to attract a sponsor or the idea was nixed. Otherwise, airing it would be a waste of station time, taking broadcast hours away from programs that might have more advertiser interest. Right or wrong, that was sound station management in those days, and as they say, you can't argue with success.

By the way, if you're in the radio business and your sales staff is making a lot of sales calls but you are not making money, put something on the radio the **advertisers** will buy. How do you do that? Call me and I'll tell you, FOR A FEE!

Today, the success of NASCAR racing on the radio is a sure bet. But in 1958, except for limited coverage of the Darlington 500, there were no car races on the radio in Greenville. There wasn't a marketing plan or a known list of advertisers interested in sponsoring NASCAR racing. Most broadcasters believed the Southern 500 was about all the business community would underwrite. In Greenville WFBC was airing segments of the Southern 500 but they left the race to air some regular programs: news, network and local commitments, etc. In fact, some broadcasters, advertisers and sportswriters debated the issue of whether stock car racing **was a sport.** Some believed stock car racing was just a daredevil show staged by ex-bootleggers. Local promoters, as well as those at Darlington, found it difficult to get much airtime on the radio sports shows or space on the sports pages of daily newspapers. Every year — usually in late spring or summer — the Darlington promoters came to the Cotton Club located in Greer and gave a media party to drum up support for the Southern 500. Usually, the Greenville and Spartanburg newspapers and radio sports reporters attended. At this time, TV applications were frozen and there were no TV stations between Charlotte and Atlanta.

Local track promoters made their rounds to the stations at the beginning of each racing year soliciting support. Nobody knocked the doors down to put car races on the air. Greenvillians were interested in listening to: Clemson, Furman and South Carolina football; Parker, Greenville and Sterling high school football; Greenville Spinner and textile baseball; and championship boxing matches. Some of the basketball games attracted an audience — and sponsors — but five hours of speech describing stock cars running around a track...Are you kidding? Stock car interest came in dead last, OR SO WE THOUGHT!

So you can see, clearing the program schedule for several hours to broadcast stock car racing was a challenge. However, after talking with the Bishop brothers, Lester Hunter, W.T. Kellett and several other businessmen who were also race fans, I decided this might be successful. Success, by the way, was defined as making some money. WESC accepted the Florida broadcaster's offer. In interviewing the business owners — mostly car related businesses — we learned there was a large, growing fan base out there. People who loved the sport saw it for what it was: a good way to reach people who made their living selling, servicing and repairing cars. This was a new income stream for the station.

We had a simple game plan. By using rates already established by the station, we took a weekend package of 36 commercials, scheduled six of the announcements during the race and 30 commercials in other day-parts throughout the weekend. This provided a weekend of advertising on a special event and coverage of the other WESC programs. It was cost effective for advertisers and justified the station's sales effort. Also, we believed even if the racing audience was small, we could deliver a good advertising value with the commercials scheduled on the other programs. In terms the advertiser could understand the racing package cost less than a quarter page in the daily newspaper. It worked! February 1958 was the first profitable February in the station's history!

Super speedways started springing up around the South and race fans demanded more races on the radio. At first, my attitude when tracks called offering a broadcast was, "Oh my gosh, not another stock car race!" But after a year or two the MRN network offered most of the races and we had accumulated a customer list, so we developed a package for the season. WESC FM became the NASCAR racing station for Greenville. There have been challenges! Some have tried to wrestle the broadcast rights away from WESC FM but their efforts have not been very successful.

In the '70s we had a challenge from WQOK (1440 KC). That station was successful in luring away the network operated out of Winston-Salem — about half of the races — with the promise of AM coverage. Our choice was to put them on AM or lose them. In fact, I received a call from a popular newspaper sports editor threatening to use the power of his newspaper to force us to either put the races on AM or he would see to it that we lost them. I don't know if his call was linked in any way to the effort by WQOK to obtain the races but it did cause us some concern because daily newspaper coverage is important to the tracks. In order to program the races on AM we would have had to switch some very popular religious programs to FM. They were: *Sunday Singing Time*, *The Washington Avenue Baptist Church*, *The Old Fashion Revival Hour*, *The Overbrook Baptist Church Service* and *The Hour of Decision* with Billy Graham.

Since so many religious listeners were loyal to WESC AM and race fans were loyal to WESC FM, we believed flip-flopping the programming would have made everybody angry. So we stayed the course. Since the other races were networked by the Motor Sports Network in Daytona Beach, Fla., where Mr. Bill France, Sr., made the decisions, we appealed to him to continue that network's relationship with WESC FM. Mr. France said something like "WESC FM started stock car racing on the radio in Greenville and we wouldn't think of switching the broadcasts to another station." This was a critical decision for us. It kept us in the racing business. Also, it spoke volumes as to just how influential WESC FM was in the world of auto racing. The WESC FM signal served race fans that could not hear WQOK or any of the other stations broadcasting the races. Also, since the network was not on a satellite WESC FM was used to help network the race broadcasts, making the races available to many other stations and their listeners.

After going through that year — I think it was 1972 — with just half the schedule, the network operator in Winston-Salem called to apologize for his mistake. He said that he had been looking at the Greenville market as just the city of Greenville but had learned that WESC FM had attracted a racing audience in South Carolina, North Carolina and Georgia. He had complaints from WESC FM listeners all over the tri-state area. Now folks, that is BRAND loyalty.

I hope it says something about WESC's business relationships. While we might have felt like telling the humbled program supplier to "go fly a kite" when he called to eat crow, that attitude wouldn't have benefited anybody. We accepted his apology and everybody won: our listeners, our sponsors and ourselves.

There was a year or so in the '80s when WESC FM did not have the races. By this time, all of the races were networked out of Daytona; Mr. Bill France, Sr., was no longer making the decisions; and WSSL FM had come to town. WESC FM would have had to break into its weekday country music service to meet the network requirement. THAT made it a country music or NASCAR decision, so we decided on country music.

Except for these interruptions, WESC FM has presented the races since 1958. So, WESC FM is Greenville's pioneer NASCAR racing station. It all began on the beach at Daytona and WESC FM was a link in the FM relay network stretching from Daytona Beach, Florida, to Martinsville, Virginia. Why an FM relay? Why didn't they just order phone lines or use satellites? The answer is simple: telephone lines were too costly and there were no satellites in the sky.

There's an interesting story about how WESC FM came to have broadcast rights to the two Darlington races. The broadcast rights for Greenville were assigned to WFBC (1330 KC) before that station gave them up in the middle '70s. It was almost an annual ritual for me to ask Paul Benson, who ran the Darlington radio network from his station, WJMX (970 KC) in Florence, S.C, for the two Darlington races. His answer was always the same: "You can have them when WFBC gives them up."

One year WFBC was late returning its contract to Mr. Benson and Paul called informing me he was issuing WESC FM a contract. I returned the executed agreement to him, along with a check for payment. A few days later, Paul Benson called to say WFBC did not return the contract because their general manager, Bruce Buchanan, was out of town on business. He asked me to nullify the contract and gave me a promise that WESC would have first refusal if and when WFBC gave them up.

Several years later, after Mr. Benson sold the network to a company in Winston-Salem, I received a call from the new owner, whom I did not know, telling me that WFBC had decided to discontinue broadcasting the Darlington races and that Paul Benson had made a notation in the records of the network specifying WESC was to have first refusal in the Greenville market when it became available. This is a wonderful example of how pioneer broadcasters such as Paul Benson built their businesses and reputations on trust with a handshake. Their word was their bond.

Paul Benson told me this story about how the Southern 500 radio network began. When the Labor Day race first started in the late '40s, the racetracks did not charge for broadcast rights. They wanted the publicity. Paul Benson and his WJMX crew went to Darlington to broadcast the race for the Florence station. While the WJMX crew was preparing for the broadcast, Doug Youngblood, general manager of WFIG (1490 KC) in Sumter, showed up with his crew. Paul Benson and Doug Youngblood began to discuss how unnecessary it was for both radio stations to "knock themselves out" competing for the press box space, interviews and other things needed to produce the broadcast. As I recall the story, Paul suggested to Doug Youngblood that WFIG just feed WJMX the race at no charge and WJMX would pack up and go home. Youngblood's reply was for WJMX to feed WFIG the race and WFIG would go home. Paul Benson accepted the offer and the Southern 500 radio network was born. It would be 25 years before WESC FM would join the Southern 500 network.

After our success with that first Daytona stock car race WESC experimented with other races — motorcycles, sports cars and Indy types — but we didn't have much luck except for the Indy 500. That race was aired successfully. Remember, success means to make some money so we broadcast the Indianapolis race until it was rescheduled, causing a conflict with NASCAR.

Chapter 9

The Idea Man

WESC AM/FM was profitable, attracting listeners and upgrading its equipment in 1958. We could sell a client five commercials a day for seven days of the week for about $200 and document almost a half million impressions. Of course, we didn't sell it that way because there wasn't that much interest in cost per thousand. Retailers wanted <u>results</u> and WESC produced results. However, our sales strategy was about to change.

Christie Russell Meade married W.E. "Bill" Mitchell, a retired Atlanta businessman and former chairman of the Georgia Power Company. At the annual Christmas party in 1957, Mrs. Christie Mitchell informed the staff that several people wanted to buy the station, but it was not for sale. That was before Mr. Mitchell, a man with great foresight who had turned the lights on in Atlanta, persuaded her that she should sell the station and invest the money in a tourist attraction at Stone Mountain, Georgia. The state of Georgia was offering several million dollars in grant money to an entrepreneur who would create an attraction to bring tourists to Georgia's Stone Mountain. Christie's idea was to build a miniature Georgia plantation with a farmhouse and a Southern mansion complete with cotton and cornfields. She envisioned a family's rise through several generations from virtual poverty after the Civil War, to prosperity. So with this dream and the timely appearance of Robert A. Schmid, Christie decided to sell.

Bob Schmid was a former vice president at the Mutual Broadcasting System who negotiated the WESC affiliation for MBS in the late '40s. After he relocated in Tryon, North Carolina, WESC came to Schmid's attention when his teenage daughter, Heidi, began listening to **The Chicken Shack.** He remembered the special frequency, the slogan "660 in Dixie" and the 5000 watts. After Messrs. Schmid and Mitchell convinced Christie to sell, she offered the station to the employees; however, we were not able to find financing for a purchase plan we had devised among ourselves. Christie sold the station to Bob and his wife, Jarrett Schmid, and invested the proceeds in her tourist dream at Stone Mountain.

For years, Butterfly McQueen, the black actress who played Prissy in **Gone With the Wind,** greeted visitors at Stone Mountain, Georgia. Christie Kennedy Mitchell offered me an opportunity to work at Stone Mountain and freelance **The Chicken Shack** from her tourist complex. She suggested that I make Prissy a part of the show. She insisted that she could find an Atlanta station to air the show. I was not interested in the tourist industry. In retrospect, Christie's idea had a lot of merit. The team of Prissy and **The Chicken Shack** may have been a big hit. Prissy certainly had national name recognition and the show was a proven winner in upstate South Carolina. Who knows — maybe we could have been big CNN stars.

The sale of WESC AM/FM to Bob and Jarrett Schmid turned out to be a good move for the station employees because Bob Schmid brought insight and skills to the station that were not available in-house. If we needed special program, production or promotional skills he brought in the best in the business to teach us. He opened doors we could not open for ourselves. It was a win-win situation for all of us: Christie moved on to pioneer Georgia tourism and WESC welcomed another president, one who knew his way around the concrete canyons of New York.

Bob and Jarrett Schmid were friends of radio pioneer Walter Brown, president of WSPA in Spartanburg, S.C. Sometime before the Schmids bought WESC, Mr. Brown encouraged them to purchase a farm near Tryon, North Carolina, on which to train horses. So, the Schmids bought a place between Tryon and Landrum and began renovating the house. They called it Saxon Woods Farms. Bob continued to work and live in New York, representing major market radio/ TV and newspaper properties, and Jarrett followed the horse circuit from Florida to New York. While the farmhouse was being renovated, the Schmids spent weekends and holidays there. It was located in South Carolina near the state line, a fact which Bob Schmid was quick to point out made him a South Carolina resident. When Jarrett wasn't on the horse circuit she divided her time between Tryon and New York.

As has been said, the Schmids' teenage daughter, Heidi, listened to WESC and **The Chicken Shack** when they came to Tryon. So, it wasn't long before Bob and Jarrett Schmid developed an interest in buying WESC. Eventually, Bob Schmid came to the station unannounced to inquire if WESC was for sale. John Davenport remembered Christie Mitchell saying, during her annual Christmas party address to the staff, that the station wasn't for sale and related this to Mr. Schmid.

His attitude was, "Anything is for sale for enough money." He then asked where he could find Christie Mitchell. After obtaining the information, he disappeared up the stairs, onto the street, with the gait of a racehorse, a pace that would earn for him the name "Rapid Robert." I don't know if Bob Schmid ever knew that we called him "Rapid Robert." We used the nickname only in interoffice conversation as a term of endearment.

In a few weeks, Bob Schmid arrived to tell the staff that he had purchased WESC AM/FM. The trade magazines announced the sales price in the $301,000 range. Thirty years later, he agreed to sell the station for an amount in the FIFTEEN TO EIGHTEEN MILLION DOLLAR range! I never knew the exact figure, nor do I know why the sale did not close. As the story goes, the two parties wrote a letter of intent late one night on a paper sack and later proceeded with the sale through their attorneys, but for whatever reason — perhaps the economy of the late '80s — the sale did not take place. Between 1958 and 1988, as Country Earl would have said: "Hang on, chillins, and stay tuned, neighbors. Y'all are in for a wild ride!"

Robert A. Schmid was a tough competitor, a New Yorker who earned his stripes on Madison Avenue! Some of his character traits were probably instilled at Princeton University. He expected superior performance, insisted upon excellence and generously rewarded extra effort. Mr. Schmid did unusual things to help staff members feel "special," usually to reward achievement. Once he called John Davenport from a helicopter between downtown Chicago and the airport. He wanted to congratulate Davenport on a good profit month. A congratulatory call from the boss was appreciated but to have it come while the boss was in the air — in a helicopter — made it special.

In l968, WESC had a very good sales year. Bob rewarded Helen and me with a trip to New York City. He reserved our rooms at the Plaza Hotel and went to the hotel before our arrival to be sure we'd have a good view of Central Park. That made the trip special; however, the date he selected for us to be in New York reflected his attention to detail. He knew of my interest in government so he selected a special time for us to be in New York. President Lyndon Johnson and the New York Democrats would be having a party at the Plaza Hotel, and President-elect Richard Nixon was scheduled to be there the same weekend, staying at the Plaza. We were able to see Ladybird and the daughters at very close range when they left the hotel. The President was whisked out the back door through the kitchen while the post-midnight crowd waited for him at the main entrance.

On Sunday morning we attended a church service at the Marble Collegiate Church where Dr. Norman Vincent Peale was pastor. Before entering the church we waited in line for President-elect Richard Nixon, Mrs. Nixon and the other early worshipers to leave. We were so close to the Nixons, we could have reached out and touched them.

Bob Schmid, of course, couldn't have foreseen all of that but he had the foresight to reserve our room at the Plaza Hotel, knowing it was the place to be on that particular weekend. Incidentally, he lived a few blocks from the Plaza in a brownstone at 450 East 58th Street.

During the trip we ate lunch in the United Nations Ambassador's dining room. I never quite understood how Bob or Heidi, his daughter, arranged it; however, we picked up our credentials at the South Korean Ambassador's office. In the fall of 1968, the people of Greenville County had elected me to be a member of the first Greenville County Council; perhaps Bob convinced the South Koreans Fort Knox was in Greenville County.

Bob Schmid believed in the power of imaging to reach goals. On his very first day as WESC owner he had a mental picture of what he wanted the station to become. He told us he wanted it to be Greenville's radio leader! He wanted it to be THE BEST! His definition of the best was to attract the most listeners and make the most money. In pursuit of these goals he immediately set out to make WESC #1 in the ratings. In the ratings race he raised the stakes: increasing the power of WESC to 10,000 watts, making improvements in WESC FM and investing in programming. He also introduced station consultants to the market. The first was Lester Atlas, a member of a Chicago radio family that had attracted national attention with their success at WIND in Chicago. Les had a sister, "Sis Kaplan," who helped make BIG WAYS (540 KC) a rock hit in Charlotte.

After Atlas, consultants would come and go with each ratings book, the programming changed with each audience survey, and just as often, and for the same reasons, the nameplate changed on the program director's door.

Anybody with an idea was given a chance to see if it would work. Among the innovations was **Greenville Calling,** a mostly talk show from 8:00 to 9:00 a.m. weekdays. People in the news were called on the phone and asked to elaborate on the story. On at least one occasion **Greenville Calling** broke a big story.

I was the first reporter in the world to talk to the first person to return from the edge of space. Lieutenant Clifton M. "Demi" McClure of Anderson, S.C., talked to me in October 1958 about cabin conditions and what the earth looked like, strapped in a gondola 98,000 feet above the earth. Lt. McClure had just returned to earth after participating in "Project Manhigh." This was a pre-NASA program designed to gather information for space flight. Lt. McClure talked to me from his hospital room where he was being examined and debriefed. He said it was hot up there. Otherwise he was in good spirits and did not have any ill effects from the flight. That was about the extent of the conversation.

While I talked to Lt. McClure, a lot of news organizations were holding a vigil outside his room. We had an inside track for the interview because Lt. McClure's family in Anderson had provided us with the telephone number to his room. The story appeared in the afternoon **GREENVILLE PIEDMONT** and the next day in the **NEW YORK TIMES.**

We also talked to numerous political figures on impromptu and unrehearsed broadcasts. We interviewed Governor Orville Faubus in Little Rock during the time the public schools were integrated in Arkansas. Martial law had been declared in Little Rock and federal troops occupied the city. Federal troops were outside the governor's office when we talked to him.

One morning we rang former South Carolina Governor James F. Byrnes. He answered the phone while shaving. That was a short call!

On another broadcast we called Cuban dictator Fidel Castro, considered at this time to be a liberator of the Cuban people. Mr. Castro was visiting New York and was reported to have plucked chickens and eaten them in his hotel room. We wanted to know why he didn't call room service. Castro was not in his room but the Cuban Ambassador returned the call. He said the hotel didn't have room service.

We tried to make the show humorous and not too serious. It was to be newsy but light. The news was a fuse in those turbulent days that could, when lit, have sparked bloodshed if the interviews had not been handled responsibly.

Greenville Calling created "street talk" for the station but was not the blockbuster morning show the station needed and therefore was cancelled when I was promoted to sales manager in 1959.

An effort to build a morning show with "live" musicians failed, and about that time Herb Johnson, an ex-newspaper reporter, came aboard to do local news. This introduced "on the scene reporting" in Greenville. A radio reporter broadcasting news from a news car parked in front of a burning house was rather unusual in Greenville at the time. Herb Johnson had the contacts and experience to get the news and WESC gave him the tools to air it. The " in car transmitter" came in handy one icy morning when Herb Johnson skidded the WESC NEWSMOBILE into a ditch! The radio equipment wasn't damaged, so Johnson went on the air warning motorists about the hazardous streets. Mr. Johnson had just completed Greenville's first mobile traffic report. Not from the sky but from a ditch! The winter of 1960 was a very cold one. It snowed and sleeted almost every Wednesday for about two months so we all got plenty of experience slipping and sliding around town.

The distinction of giving the first "sky traffic" report probably goes to WHYZ (1070 KC) and the Fleet brothers, who used a single engine Cessna for a few weeks to report from the air over Greenville, Anderson and Spartanburg when WHYZ (1070 KC) came on the air in 1964. WFBC (1330 KC) or WMRC (1440 KC) may have covered some special event from the air before 1964 but the WHYZ "sign on" promotion was Greenville's first regular sky report.

Contests! Contests! Contests! WESC made random calls to local telephone numbers, awarding cash when the telephone was answered with the words "WESC Money Street"! Throughout the morning we announced which street was being called and then selected random residents to phone. Presumably, listeners would call residents living on the street to tell them to turn on WESC and if the telephone rang, they should say "WESC Money Street."

136

In another promotion we hid a thousand dollar treasure and held a "treasure hunt." Clues about where the treasure could be found were announced on the radio several times a day. The contest was designed to build interest during the spring ratings period. This contest was *too* successful. The station received complaints from listeners saying their flowers and shrubbery were damaged. Although these calls may have been crank calls or generated by those with selfish motives, the contest was not repeated. WESC did not want anyone's property to be damaged.

Bob Schmid had a network of friends all over America and through them learned about their successful ideas. Any contest offering the listener a chance to win money interested him. Schmid believed the best way to attract listeners was to give 'em money. He also knew it is human nature for people to want to take a chance to win something. So, ignoring the detractors who accused us of attempting to buy the audience, WESC offered cash prizes on most contests. It's hard to believe now but some of the pioneer broadcasters thought it wasn't good radio practice to "buy an audience."

When WESC AM increased its power to 10,000 watts in 1960, 10,000 pounds of ice were placed in a parking lot on Wade Hampton Boulevard near the Church Street entrance. WESC offered 660 dollars to the listener guessing the day, hour and minute the ice would be melted. We expected the contest to last several days. To everyone's surprise, a warm front came through during the first night bringing warm rain, and the ice was almost gone the next morning. The weatherman must have used the **Farmer's Almanac** to forecast the weather. There were no weather satellites, weather maps or TV meteorologists with special radar equipment to inform us of unexpected changes in the weather.

The promotion was important to Bob Schmid because it

announced to the world that WESC 660 in Dixie was now 10,000 watts — South Carolina's most powerful station. If Schmid was disappointed at the turn of events he didn't show it. In fact, he used the picture he had taken of Miss Greenville sitting on the ice, in station promotion material. He sent stories to trade magazines about the promotion that didn't happen. The story was picked up by publications all over the country. The winner of the contest was paid the money. One wag remarked that Bob Schmid would give you the shirt off his back, if he didn't lose it in a horse race.

WESC experimented with Masters golf reports from Augusta during the early '60s but didn't get much of a bang nor a buck. However, we all were proud of our golf pro in residence, Wayne Sumner, for his participation on the CBS radio broadcast crew in the '70s. About 30 CBS radio stations in the Southeast aired that network's coverage of the Masters that began about 1:00 p.m. Thursday, Friday, Saturday and Sunday during the tournament. Wayne Sumner of WESC (660 KC), Bob Shelly or WMRB (1490 KC) and Ken Bostic of WSPA (950 KC) were the local voices on the event. Bostic reported the 11th, 12th and 13th hole, Wayne the 15th and 16th and Bob Shelly the 18th. These reports, as far as I know, were the beginning of the CBS coverage of the Masters. Wayne Sumner downplays his role explaining that he "just did what he was told to do." But we all know if people do what they are told to do, **well,** good things happen.

In the early days of the Masters, stations originated their own reports or joined a pool. The network Wayne Sumner assisted ended its coverage when CBS Television coverage began about 1975.

In 1960, Clemson and the University of South Carolina played their first football game at Memorial Stadium in Clemson. It was also the first Clemson/Carolina game to be played on Saturday. Prior to that year, the game was played on Big Thursday: State Fair Week in Columbia, about the third week in October. Clemson President Dr. Robert C. Edwards and Athletics Director Frank Howard lobbied the state legislature to change the date of the game and play it at the end of the football season because the October date disrupted the school term. Obviously, playing it in Columbia at Williams-Brice Stadium gave Carolina home field advantage every year. There was so much opposition to moving the game that special legislation was passed by the South Carolina General Assembly requiring the game to be played on a home and home basis, usually at the end of the regular season.

Since WESC-FM was the flagship station for the Clemson Network we wanted to do something special to begin the series at Clemson. So, we decided to broadcast an entire day from Clemson. It was a novel idea and one that had never been done before: telling the story of the university, and broadcasting the first Clemson/Carolina game from Clemson while the attention of the state's citizens was on the Upstate.

The Clemson administration supported the idea and provided taped segments from the various departments of the university for insertion in the program. Dr. Edwards held several special meetings to plan the day. Participating in these planning sessions were: Joe Sherman, head of the Clemson News Bureau; Bob Bradley, the Clemson sports information director, who administered the football network; other Clemson department heads; WESC program director Buddy Womack; engineer Harold White; and me.

Most of the segments were written, pre-recorded and timed to the second. We were ready for the FIRST BIG SATURDAY. The program was produced at WSBF (88.1 FM), the campus radio station, and fed to WESC, where it was networked to all the stations wishing to carry it. As I recall, about 15 of the 75 stations on the network took advantage of the opportunity. Selling the program was like fishing in a barrel — WESC sold all its availabilities, inserting the commercials at the WESC studios. The special day went off without a hitch.

We ran newspaper ads promoting the day, advertised it on WESC and erected a sign near the Pendleton Street/Old Easley Bridge Road intersection, which was the main road to Clemson. The sign advertised Clemson Day on WESC 660 in Dixie. The WESC morning show with Johnny Wright went on the road broadcasting from Clemson. This was the first time in Greenville that I remember an entire morning show being broadcast on location. Buddy Womack, WESC program director, picked a spot east of the campus — at the intersection of the Greenville and Anderson highways — to set up the mobile unit for the broadcast. This was before the four lane highways leading to Greenville and Anderson were constructed. Highways 123/93 and 76 formed a fork east of the Clemson campus providing the ideal spot for the remote unit to be seen by fans entering Clemson from the east and south. As planned, the WESC van and Clemson Day programming greeted both Clemson and Carolina fans on this historic BIG SATURDAY, THE FIRST CLEMSON TIGER/SOUTH CAROLINA GAMECOCK FOOTBALL GAME EVER PLAYED AT CLEMSON.

After Johnny Wright completed his morning show, about 9:00 a.m., we switched the origination point to WSBF and fed WESC and the network from the campus station. Buddy Womack, Johnny Wright and I introduced the taped segments, did some live interviews, and Buddy and Johnny took turns roaming the campus with a remote transmitter. These reports were inserted into the show throughout the morning.

One highlight of the day came when Johnny and Buddy used a pack transmitter to interview VIPs sitting in a special

140

section at the stadium during the pre-game show. Among the dignitaries were: Governor James F. Byrnes; Senator Olin D. Johnson; Speaker of the S.C. House Sol Blatt; and Senator Edgar Brown. As I recall, we were able to get all of them on the broadcast. That might have been a first in itself but the "around the stadium coverage" surely was a "first" for local networks. Today's football broadcasters report from the sidelines, taking you into the locker rooms and reporting from wherever there's interest; however, in 1960 it was unique.

Local radio stations did not invest in expensive equipment like this to use a few times a year. WESC chief engineer Harold White was continually looking for something unusual with which to promote the station and had bought the pack transmitter at a bargain price for this occasion. This is just one example of how all the members of the staff were encouraged to share their ideas to help the station succeed. We continued to remind the staff that: "Others have it made — We have it to make, so keep your eyes open for the unusual."

After the Clemson program we used the transmitter for coverage on the sidelines at the Parker/Greenville High School football games on Thanksgiving. I don't believe this was the first sideline coverage at the big Turkey Day event; however, we did use the pack transmitter to get the coach's comments at halftime and after the game. That probably was the first time it had been done locally. As I remember, the coaches nixed the idea of locker room interviews, requiring Johnny Wright to stop at the locker room door. It was interesting to hear the sounds from the locker room after the players had come face to face with reality on the field. The WESC pack transmitter was donated to the South Carolina Museum and is on display in the radio exhibit. The museum is on Gervais Street in Columbia.

WESC was fortunate to have Johnny Wright and Buddy Womack, two experienced broadcasters who were exceptionally gifted for announcing and producing special events. Johnny Wright had been a television personality at Channel 4 in the 1950's and was recognized by the public wherever he went. So, when the VIPs were asked to go on the air with him during that first Clemson/Carolina game at Clemson, they probably thought he was on television.

The success of the Clemson Day program was assured given the support we received from the university and having the advantage of the skills of Johnny Wright and Buddy Womack. They were really special on special events. Clemson wanted us to repeat "Clemson Day" when the game was played at Clemson in 1962. We declined because WESC AM had switched to rock and we did not want to interrupt the format. We considered using WESC FM but Wright, Womack and White had left the station. I had concerns that we didn't have the program skills to pull it off. All our guys in 1962 were great rock jocks but lacked special events experience. Also, we were going through a transition on the sales staff and I was apprehensive about losing the focus of our sales effort. We were striving to make the rock programming successful. In retrospect, perhaps we should have brought in a freelance crew and continued what most certainly would have become a tradition, given the success of the **Tiger Tailgate Show.**

When Johnny Wright left Greenville, he operated a station in Florida before going into educational TV in the St. Petersburg area. He is now deceased.

Buddy Womack eventually accepted a public relations position with the City of Spartanburg and remained with the city until retirement.

After purchasing WESC in 1958, Bob Schmid looked all over the nation for successful promotional ideas. He simultaneously searched for a program format that would excite Greenville. Buddy Womack commuted from Spartanburg for several years and gave it his best shot, taking what was already on the air and improving it. His instructions were to improve the programming but do it with the same people. This limited him. He was further handicapped because religious programs were off limits. He wasn't allowed to move them. Mr. Womack did an excellent job, given the restrictions placed upon him. He introduced the NEWSMOBILE with Herb Johnson. He also employed D.J.'s Mal Harrison and Perry Woods. Buddy's deep voice and his ability to read the news enhanced WESC's programming during his tenure but all the promotional ideas that Bob Schmid found and implemented, the improved news service and the program facelift that Buddy gave the station didn't produce the ratings.

WQOK (1440 KC) had the rock music audience and WFBC (1330 KC) was the established news leader.

WESC's improved news service and hot rock jocks — Harrison and Woods — failed to attract new listeners. We were playing on our competitor's turf! WESC needed to do something different but WHAT? Bob Schmid knew he had the basic staff; however, he needed a rock 'em sock 'em format. So he continued to search for a miracle man.

The office support staff in the early '60s included: Edna Taylor, Ann Jones, Maryanne Taylor, Evelyn Tillotson and Haskell Shumate.

In February of 1962, WESC (660 KC) began a religious series that continues on 660 KC. *The International Sunday School Lesson* has a simple roundtable format. It was suggested by Hub Terry (Blankenship), then general manager of WJOT in Lake City, S.C. — a WESC alumnus. It was successful in Lake City serving listeners in Florence, S.C. Attracting listeners in Florence to a Lake City station was quite an achievement because WJOT was not a super powerful station.

In Greenville on WESC with 10,000 watts, this would be a real public service to churches in northwestern South Carolina, northeast Georgia and western North Carolina, if we could duplicate what was done at Lake City.

At 660 KC, *The International Sunday School Lesson* has a regular panel of lay teachers who discuss the material they use in teaching the lesson at some of Greenville's churches. The program is recorded early in the week; now it is recorded in the McAlister Square studios of WROQ (101.1 FM) and released on Sunday morning on 660 KC, hopefully in time to reach Sunday school teachers before they go to church. We appreciate general manager John Shay at WROQ/WPTP for allowing us to use those studios for recording and general manager Allen Henderson of WLFJ for continuing to broadcast the program.

Among the regular panelists during the 30 minute discussion are Betty Orders (Mrs. James B. Orders, Jr.) and Demi Thompson-Grier. I moderate the program. After a brief introduction and prayer, the panel is introduced for the discussion of the lesson. Through the years, the following people, who are now deceased, have served as panelists: Betty Walker (Mrs. G. Herman Walker), George Lathem, James B. Orders, Jr., and Preston S. "Pete" Marchant.

The panelists have always been some of Greenville's best lay teachers and fill a definite need in the upstate. Here's an example: A lady telephoned Betty Orders to get more information about a lesson. She ended the conversation with an expression of thanks for the program and said the radio program helped her prepare to teach the lesson in her church. The lady said she was BLIND!

Since the *International Sunday School Lesson* is a public service program, the hour has been changed a few times This has caused some confusion among the listeners, but at this writing it is still on the air Sunday mornings at 8:00. The quality and longevity of the program is a testimony. **Since 1962, these volunteer lay people have taken the time to prepare the Sunday School Lesson material, dress for the occasion and come to the station to record it. They have planned their schedules, vacations and family responsibilities around the day and time scheduled for taping: THAT'S COMMITMENT, FOLKS.**

Chapter 10

A Rocking Idea: The WEE-CEE Tiger!

In September 1962, Bob Schmid found his miracle man. A panacea for all the station's ills! Bob Chase was employed as program director of WESC AM/FM. Bob Chase had all the tools of the trade: great voice, terrific production skills, a bright mind and was a creative, tireless worker. He had earned a reputation for producing ratings at WQXI (790 KC), Atlanta's rock station.

Chase was given total control over programming and in the next 60 days reprogrammed the station with a new staff. The new WESC or WEE-CEE TIGER had all new voices, custom made jingles, sharp production with split-second timing, and a top 40 play list. The program switch, counting the expenses of recruiting a new staff, jingles and lost revenue, must have cost several hundred thousand dollars.

Many loyal religious listeners were upset when their favorite programs were cancelled. I was upset because the revenue was lost forever! Some people no doubt blamed me for the change, since I was considered by many to be Mr. WESC. These folks need to know that approval for the change came from a management level higher than I. Perhaps I could have walked out in protest but that would not have accomplished anything. Bob Schmid wanted ratings, and Chase promised ratings. One of the hard and fast rules of selling is "Show a man what he wants and he will move heaven and earth to get it." I knew that rule but played by the other rule of business: "The boss may be wrong but he is still the boss."

Most of us did not agree with the decision to cancel the religious programs but as it turned out that was a blessing in disguise. When the station switched to country in 1965 that bridge had been crossed, thanks to Bob Chase. So, credit Mr. Chase for playing a part in WESC's country music success.

Chase believed if a station is to compete in the ratings race the listeners should not be more than 90 seconds away from the music of the format. After spending several weeks collecting auditions, interviewing and making plans — which included taking all recognizable voices off the air — Chase launched the NEW WESC complete with a mascot he called the WEE-CEE-TIGER. The daily air staff included Bob Chase, Ron Block and Tony Brooks.

It was a great sounding rock radio station; however, in spite of the fact that Bob Chase and the others — in my opinion — produced a better sounding product than its crosstown rival, Greenville's teens didn't listen to WESC. The WEE-CEE TIGER had paper claws. It bombed out in spite of a high-powered newspaper and billboard campaign. In six months the "all out" effort to win or lose had LOST. The problem? Greenville already had a rock station and those listeners were comfortable with it.

By February 1963, the financial losses were mounting up. Although I do not have access to the profit and loss statement, my guess is the station was losing about $8,000 a month. Something had to be done!

Chapter 11

An Affordable Idea

After the ratings were released in the winter of 1962-'63, a distraught Bob and Jarrett Schmid visited me while I was sick in bed with the flu on a Sunday afternoon in February 1963. They were upset with John Davenport because he had not been at the station when they called, and he had not returned calls promptly. They had decided to replace John and wanted to know if I would accept the job as general manager.

I explained to them that John was sick with mononucleosis and in spite of this illness — which requires bed rest and several weeks to recover — he had worked a limited schedule. I told them that I wasn't interested in administration and told them John Davenport was one of the best young administrators in Greenville. I also said we needed to get WESC back on track, change programming to something more acceptable to the potential advertisers and drastically cut the payroll. They asked if I would accept the assignment. After being assured

John would be retained as general manager, I accepted a plan to work with John and make the station profitable.

Basically the station would become an adult contemporary station except in the early mornings, when we programmed country music 'til 7:30. We retained Ron Block, promoting him to program director, and as an emergency move to generate revenue without increasing overhead I took an air shift from 7:30 to 9:00 a.m. We started looking for salesmen with announcing skills and luckily Wayne Sumner applied for a job. Wayne and I developed a David and Jonathan relationship that continues today.

Wayne Sumner was a successful announcer/salesman in Toccoa, Ga. He wanted to relocate to Greenville because he had family in the Hendersonville area. That same week, before I had a chance to talk to Wayne, Bob Nations, a Furman student and part-time billboard salesman, accepted our job offer at WESC. I asked Mr. Davenport to fund both positions. It was a bold step considering the station was broke and we were borrowing money to make the payroll. Had Sumner and Nations known that there wasn't enough money in the bank to pay them, I doubt if this book would have ever seen the light of day.

Bringing two new people aboard at the same time was a demonstration of John Davenport's courage. Nations and Sumner became important links in the chain of events leading to 30 years of solid growth. The sales team of Nations, Sumner and Mullinax set an April sales record in 1963. As we will see later, Schmid and Davenport proved to be risk takers in a risky business. A couple of decades later, Palmer Greer, our consulting engineer, observed: "The radio business isn't for the faint hearted." WESC continued to need a different and potentially popular format but with our strong sales force and prudent management, WESC made a huge financial comeback in 1963.

In the summer of 1963, I was asked to be campaign director for the upcoming March of Dimes Campaign. After checking with some close friends including Gordon Fitts, advertising director for Winn Dixie Inc., Jack Trusdale, display advertising manager at the **Greenville News,** and Cooper Patrick, my pastor at the Overbrook Baptist Church, and others, I accepted the challenge. Our goal was to educate the public about the new goals of The National Foundation, which were birth defects and arthritis. We were asked to raise the same amount of money raised in the county the year before, $15,000. As morning personality, I got most of the credit for the campaign but it was a WESC team effort. We organized the community, raised about $30,000 and spent several weeks talking about The National Foundation's victory over polio and its new goals. We saturated the air with the new message: Help find a cure for birth defects and arthritis. The WESC staff gave 125%.

For its effort in this cause WESC won the **South Carolina School Bell Award** in 1964. Incredible! One year after the station was broke, it won a prestigious statewide award. To use a Theodore Roosevelt expression, Bob Schmid was DE — LIGHTED!

The March of Dimes Campaign established many valuable friendships for WESC. Caroline Crain, the executive director for the March of Dimes, was a tireless worker and helped us promote something for everybody: The school district distributed canisters to all the elementary schools in the county, the bowlers bowled to stamp out birth defects, buckets were passed around at movie houses and at the Memorial Auditorium, members of the Barber's Association gave all the tips received on a "Clipping Day" for the March of Dimes, a Mother's March was held throughout the county, there was a teenage canteen and an amateur show. Coin canisters were distributed at most of the bars and taverns. The chairman of that committee, W.T. Kellett, said he put out canisters to collect "conscience money." We received support from many sectors of the community. Dr. Bob Jones III hosted a dinner at the university helping us to organize the media. There was a chairman for newspaper, radio and television.

Since a preventive for polio had been discovered, the Greenville media turned the spotlight on birth defects and arthritis. To help us do this, Senator J. Strom Thurmond came to Greenville and gave an address at a dinner held in his honor at the Poinsett Hotel, which was broadcast on WESC FM. Several other stations in the state carried the speech. I remember WCSC AM/FM, the John Rivers stations in Charleston, aired the program. Its general manager, Jim Whitaker, and program director, Russ Long, were campaigning for the March of Dimes in Charleston County and used the senator's speech in their campaign.

The volunteers in the March of Dimes campaign in 1964, as they have before and since, gave outstanding service to our community. It's impossible to list them all, but I do want to mention my candidate for a special award, maybe at the Baseball Hall of Fame. If not the Hall of Fame for Lou Brissie, then some special award to be placed at Cooperstown, New York. Lou and his family were members at the Overbrook Baptist Church of Greenville and we were close friends, so he volunteered to help in the March of Dimes campaign.

For those who haven't heard of Lou Brissie, here's a brief review. Lou pitched for the Philadelphia A's and Cleveland Indians after serving his country in the 88th Division in Italy in 1942. His left shinbone was shattered into 30 pieces by enemy artillery fire on December 7, 1944. They said his leg and foot were just about blown off, requiring 23 operations to patch it up. He beat the odds so they didn't have to amputate. After the war, Lou Brissie returned to baseball and pitched through the A's minor league system and into the majors, where he stayed 7 years. He was a member of the major league All Rookie team in 1948 and a member of the American League All Star team in 1949. When his playing days were over, Lou Brissie served for 7 years as director of American Legion Baseball. Also, Lou represented our country in Australia, Central and South America giving baseball clinics.

Lou's service to our country on the battlefield, the baseball field and the fields of life uniquely qualifies him to be a person baseball can point to with pride. When enshrined at Cooperstown little kids could look up at that 6'4" statue of a big ole southpaw pitcher weighing about 210 pounds and their eyes would just about pop out when told about how he made the big leagues — staying there 7 years — on sheer will and determination. After they learned that Lou Brissie stayed in a game after taking a line drive off of Red Sox slugger Ted Williams' bat hitting him on that bum leg, the kids would know that Lou Brissie typifies the great American Spirit.

The March of Dimes campaign developed other new friends for WESC; among them was Dick Riley, a young Greenville attorney who had just been elected to the South Carolina legislature. Mr. Riley, an arthritis victim himself, took time from his law practice to help with the campaign. He believed it was just as important to educate the public about birth defects and arthritis as to raise money. Working closely with Dick Riley we learned about his interest in public education in South Carolina. On the MOD campaign trail, I picked up Mr. Riley at his law office several times a week to make personal calls seeking March of Dimes support. As we rode to our appointments he solicited my support for the public schools, and we became close friends.

After learning our wedding anniversaries were on the same day — August 23rd — our wives, Helen and Tunky, became friends. For several years we celebrated our wedding anniversaries at some of Greenville's best restaurants and talked about his political future. I supported him for governor, writing letters to broadcaster friends around the state and politicking with him in counties where I had name recognition. I believed strongly that Dick Riley would be a great governor.

He did not disappoint me. He was truly South Carolina's education governor. Richard W. Riley was the first South Carolinian to be elected by the people to serve two terms as governor. I worked hard to get the governor's term changed to eight years. I called my broadcaster friends around the state asking them to contact their state representatives and ask them to support the bill to change the governor's term to eight years. Dick Riley was a great governor for eight years and Carroll Campbell also served two four-year terms with distinction. So, I'm proud I was in a position to help with this change, a change that benefited two fine Greenville political figures. Their service to our state was worth the effort.

The change in tenure for the governor also kept Dick Riley in the spotlight. It cemented his political relationships around the country. After leaving the governor's office Mr. Riley served eight years as the U.S. Secretary of Education in President Clinton's cabinet. Only a few South Carolinians have served in the cabinet of a United States President.

In the early '60s, the Downtown Greenville Association became very active in an effort to rebuild interest in downtown. In a drive to drum up support for the association, a committee was formed to canvass merchants in the downtown area to enlarge the membership. Guess who I was assigned to solicit? The answer: businessman Carroll Campbell, who operated parking lots in the downtown area of Greenville and other cities. I did not know Carroll personally, nor was he active in politics at the time. However, when I called him to solicit his membership in the association, he immediately agreed, saying he would send the check to my office. Thinking this was a stall to get me off the phone, I protested that I would come after the check but he insisted that he would send an employee with the check immediately! To me, that spoke volumes about Carroll Campbell. I appreciated his attitude. He went out of his way to assist volunteers who were trying to do something for downtown, an area in which he had an economic interest.

In the 1980's when Carroll Campbell was a congressman representing the 4th district of South Carolina I called on him many times in Washington about South Carolina broadcasters' problems. He was always concerned about their needs and actively supportive of the daytime broadcasters' efforts to get longer broadcast hours. On one of my visits to Washington, he confided that he had plans to run for governor but he did not ask for my support because we were in opposing parties. He said he just wanted me to know of his plans. Carroll Campbell was a great supporter of WESC and I could always count on him to help me get political business for the station.

Incidentally, all of the members of the South Carolina Washington delegation were friends of broadcasting. South Carolina broadcasters could count on them to serve their constituents by supporting SCBA on the issues. Sometimes they told us what their constituents were saying to them about the broadcast industry. This gave us an opportunity to go back to our members and correct whatever had caused the public to complain to their legislator. Unfortunately, as local origination and ownership diminished it became difficult to influence program content.

Now back to 1963 and the recovery following the Wee-Cee Tiger that didn't grow fangs. As the station's business improved — I suppose it was a reward for a job performance — I was assigned to represent the station at the South Carolina Broadcasters meetings.

In 1964 the summer convention was held at Hilton Head Island. This convention was a big deal for us; John Davenport would soon be president of the association, the wolf was away from the WESC door, Bob and Jarrett were enjoying "station owner status" and their dream of commuting from New York to Tryon to train horses was a reality. Convention week, they came from New York to Saxon Woods Farms in Tryon planning to drive Sunday afternoon to Hilton Head for the meetings. John Davenport went to Hilton Head on Saturday to attend to some pre-convention duties. Helen and I left Greenville for the convention early on Sunday morning, so that we could be settled in our room before the Schmids' arrival late that afternoon.

Bob and Jarrett, along with Clarence W. Whippet, a breed of dog in the greyhound family, drove to the resort Sunday afternoon in their new Lincoln Continental. When the Schmids stopped for gas about 30 miles out of Hilton Head Island, unbeknownst to them, Clarence decided to chase a cat into the woods in back of the service station. So the Schmids drove off without him. His absence was not discovered until they arrived at the hotel. A hasty phone call to the gas station located Clarence but it was PARTY TIME AT THE CONVENTION. Since meeting other broadcasters in South Carolina was the most important item on the Schmid agenda, Bob Schmid sent a taxicab back to the gas station to pick up Clarence. It's unconfirmed but Clarence W. Whippet claims to be the FIRST DOG ever to arrive at the William Hilton Inn on Hilton Head Island by special taxi.

Incidentally, Clarence had another claim to fame. He had a stock portfolio! Jarrett and Bob's daughter, Heidi Schmid Powers, does not know how her mother arranged it but Sir Clarence W. Whippet owned a share of stock in the Greyhound Bus Company. The stock was registered in the name of Clarence W. Whippet!

Clarence W. Whippet — Greyhound stock! Only Jarrett Schmid would think of that!

My assignment at the Christmas party each year was to find out from Jarrett what she wanted as a Christmas gift from the staff and buy it, usually with her money. I developed ingenious ways to get the information without her discovering what I was doing. In 1963 she wanted a manure spreader for the farm. Can you imagine eavesdropping on our party talk and hearing Jarrett Schmid describe to me, in detail, just what kind of manure spreader she wanted, how much manure it would spread, etc.? I wasn't an expert on manure spreaders, so Jarrett had to tell me exactly what the machine did and how it did it. Armed with my cram course on spreading manure, and the equipment needed to do it efficiently, I went shopping the very next week and bought the manure spreader she wanted, after extracting a promise from the dealer that if the spreader didn't spread the manure just the way Jarrett thought it should be spread they would accept a return.

In 1964 she wanted a kid goat. The goat was to ride in the horse trailer with her horses to calm them while traveling. John Davenport thought it would be neat, and also give her something to talk about at the "horse circuit" cocktail parties, if the goat was purchased from Carl Sandburg. The internationally known poet lived near Hendersonville and raised prized goats. I spent the entire week before Christmas trying to get in touch with the Sandburgs at their home in North Carolina. Finally, I reached Mrs. Sandburg — I think he was in Europe — and in spite of all my charm she would not sell me a goat.

So, Christmas Day 1964, I purchased a kid from a south Greenville County goat farmer for about $6.00 and took it to Saxon Woods Farms in Tryon, N.C. I delivered the goat in Helen's new Chevy Malibu station wagon. I don't think a

Carl Sandburg goat would have pleased her more, but guess what happened to the station wagon. Oh well, a little soap and water cleaned everything up. Incidentally, the goat grew up and pounced on Heidi's new car. It ruined the top of a 1964 Chevrolet convertible. The goat survived the convertible episode but when it chewed the curtains on Jarrett's VW Rabbit, it had to go.

Max Mace returned to WESC from WFBC in 1964. Secretary Edna Taylor provided office support, Nancy Teague replaced Vickie Hougland at the copy desk, and bookkeeper Gladys Taylor replaced Lib McKinney. At various times during the '60s Don Gowens, Ken Patton and Perry Childers were the technical gurus. Roger Davis joined the announcing staff in 1964 but left Greenville for a TV news position in Atlanta in 1965. Barbara Gibson, bookkeeper; Wendy Gaillard, traffic; and announcers Floyd Edge and Jim McCallister were on the staff as the '60s got into high gear.

In 1963, WESC re-affiliated with the Mutual Broadcasting System, airing MBS news on the half hour. We supplemented the MBS coverage with the AP wire. In fact, WESC was always a member of the Associated Press. In these number crunching days, when a lot of station officials think about expenses, the newswire is one of the first things to get unplugged. At WESC, the Associated Press news service was always given a top priority. I don't know of a single instance when the Associated Press contract was in jeopardy.

WESC listeners followed the story of the assassination of President John F. Kennedy on Mutual news. I was in the studio that Friday afternoon in November 1963 when the news broke. WESC cancelled all regular programs and carried continuous coverage from the Mutual Broadcasting System. That night WESC FM cancelled a Wade Hampton High School football game to continue the coverage. As I remember, one of the sponsors was very unhappy about the cancellation and subsequent make-good effort. Apparently his dislike for President Kennedy caused him to disregard our public service responsibility. After that incident, I don't think any of us ever solicited his business. I never went into his store again.

Clemson football continued to be a fall programming staple. Bill Goodrich, the voice of the Ole Miss Rebels, was employed by Clemson to broadcast the games in the middle sixties. Mr. Goodrich offered WESC the opportunity to continue to be the flagship station for Clemson on the condition that we provide him with full-time employment. Goodrich said Clemson Athletic Director Frank Howard had instructed him to give WESC first refusal, since WESC had such a long history of broadcasting the Clemson football games. We turned him down because the proposition amounted to us hiring a full-time employee and assigning him to Clemson University. Also, in the absence of any notification from Clemson that a change was in the wind we were not thoroughly convinced a final decision had been made. We believed we owed Jimmy Coggins and Ed Osborne our loyalty.

During the early '60s, WESC FM added Georgia Tech to its football schedule and when time permitted aired some of the Wofford College games. We also picked up some games from the Citadel Network. Several new high schools were built to serve the families moving into the suburbs. Since the WESC FM signal could be heard in several counties, we decided it was in the public interest to drop high school football and play music. Wayne Sumner opened the station at 6:00 a.m. with country and gospel, I relieved him at 7:30, Max Mace took the air at 9:00 a.m. and Bob Hooper came on at 3:00 p.m. Each evening, a part-time person — usually a Bob Jones University student — played easy listening music albums from the transmitter.

161

I recall two promotional ideas from 1963 to 1965 that may be worth noting. WESC was the first station that I know about in the country that was allowed to give away S&H Green Stamps. Sperry and Hutchison, the S&H Green Stamp company, franchised the distribution of the stamps through retail merchants such as department stores, supermarkets and other selected retailers. Green Stamps were given to the franchised retailer's customers based on the dollar amount of the customer's purchase. The stamps were then redeemed at S&H premium stores for coffee makers, toasters, vacuum cleaners — hundreds of items — almost everything a family needed.

Just about everybody saved S&H Green Stamps. Competing stores gave other brands of stamps but the public wanted S&H stamps. They were the brand of choice! S&H Green Stamps had a tremendous influence on Upstate purchasing power in the '50s and early '60s. Belk-Simpson and Winn Dixie were WESC customers during these years and the station was granted permission to purchase S&H Green Stamps from the downtown Belk-Simpson store for use as prizes. As I remember, there was a restriction on the number of stamps we could give away during any one contest. We were indebted to John Ellison, general manager of the Belk-Simpson downtown store, and to Gordon Fitts, division advertising manager of the Winn Dixie stores, for their assistance.

Belk-Simpson and Winn Dixie had great acceptance in the Greenville business community and to be associated with them in a promotion helped WESC. This radio promotion was good for Belk-Simpson and Winn Dixie because we announced their stores as S&H Green Stamp outlets. The idea proved to be good for S&H Green Stamps because in a few months other stations across America were giving Green Stamps too.

Another promotion in the early '60s was the WESC Flying Saucer, a vehicle that traveled on a cushion of air. Kids could ride the WESC Flying Saucer around reserved areas in shopping center parking lots while the WESC remote unit was on the air. We packaged airtime on remotes with the Flying Saucer and included a package of commercials in a promotion for a store or shopping center sales event. Of course, a WESC D.J. — usually the last hire — was dressed as an astronaut to assist the kids on their space flight. The Flying Saucer was a money-making idea; however, it was not very popular with the staff members. The spring and summer sun on hot asphalt in a spacesuit wasn't much fun! Max Mace said he and Don Gowens found their introduction to the space age especially distasteful. Flying Saucer duty wasn't fun and radio is supposed to be fun, so John Davenport gave the contraption to charity.

Thereafter, he enjoyed telling new employees about "Wally's Folly," a reference to the fact that I had recommended we buy it.

In the early '60s, Don Dudley (Floyd Edge) offered up country rock, but after a few years left WESC to join Allen Riddle, Bill Ingram and Bill Kirby in establishing WBBR (1580 KC) at Travelers Rest. Among the replacements were K.C. Jones and Ray Beale. Jones left WESC to take a job with the Greater Greenville Chamber of Commerce. He eventually joined the staff of WNOE (1060 KC) in New Orleans.

After about a year, Ray Beale returned to the Orlando, Fla., area where he continued to report the space shots for ABC and other networks from Cape Kennedy. Bob Hooper joined the staff as an announcer/salesman when Ray Beale departed. Mr. Hooper remains with WESC after more than 35 years. He was a key player in WESC's success. There will be more about the Hooper career later but an interesting fact about his first visit to the station was that I interviewed him in the parking lot of the Wade Hampton Shopping Center. He accepted the job and we then went to WESC on College Street to look it over.

Two of the new D.J.'s in the last half of the '60s were Dave Hutchinson and Lonnie MacIntosh. MacIntosh was the first country music overnight D.J. after WESC FM started remaining on the air all night in 1966. In the early '70s, Fred Nabors and Bill Hines held down this spot. Both Nabors and Hines are deceased.

Fred Nabors, a wrestling fan, hit upon an idea that gave WESC a big boost. He interviewed the wrestlers on tape during Monday Night Wrestling at Memorial Auditorium and played the interviews on his show that began at midnight. The wrestling promoters gave him tickets to use as contest prizes on his show and Fred had access to the wrestling stars throughout the night. It was a great tie-in with the wrestling crowd. Most of them were country music fans and I'm betting Fred Nabors kept the fans' car radios on WESC.

During the late '50s, WESC FM programmed easy listening music. A Greenville businessman, Angus Davis, operated the first "in store" music service in Greenville. Mr. Davis used WESC FM to distribute his music service to Bi-Lo supermarkets and other clients. Sometimes, WESC FM originated its programming from Mr. Davis' office and gift shop located in the Lake Forest Shopping Center. The Angus Davis/WESC FM alliance was a win-win situation. It helped the FM station provide an economical quality music program and helped Mr. Davis affordably syndicate his service. When Bob Schmid purchased the station he invested in new equipment and programming; therefore, in a few months after Schmid arrived the arrangement was terminated. Mr. Davis' friends and family need to know that his interest in WESC FM — even though the music he provided had a small audience — helped keep the station on the air during a time when other FM stations were returning their licenses to the FCC. Angus Davis died in 2000 in Naples, Fla.

In the late '50s and early '60s, the WESC FM daytime programs originated from a rather crude automation system devised by engineer Harold White. This early entry into automation consisted of two store bought record players. Mr. White installed a switch that would transfer the music from one machine to a second record player after the last selection on the first album finished playing. This apparatus was wired into a switch connected to another machine to play commercials. All of it was installed in the bookkeeper's office.

It was the duty — and joy — of the bookkeeper, Maryanne Taylor, to keep the albums stacked, insert the commercials and play station breaks. On weekends, announcers performed this task. The system could be transferred by the announcer into the main control room enabling news and weather bulletins to be simulcast on AM and FM with the flick of a switch. It was an improvised system but it worked! Well, most of the time, partly because the commercial load was light, partly because of the love and care it received from Maryanne Taylor, who listened to the music while she attended to her bookkeeping duties. Sometimes when Ms. Taylor wasn't in her office, a machine would release an album prematurely, jamming the system and stopping the music. Although the announcers were cautioned to keep an eye and ear on the FM machines, I don't think they were very diligent in doing it. So, the music stopped! The audience usually was quick to react and get the music back on the air.

When radio equipment manufacturers came up with reliable automation systems, WESC purchased a Harris automation system, complete with reel-to-reel tape machines to play music and carousels to play commercials, weather and time signals. The brain of that first automation system stored the information on tape. WESC was among the first to automate FM, and was among the first to employ and assign a full-time staff member to FM. The first operator of the Harris automation system was a lady I remember only as Tabitha, who operated from a studio-office area in what was formerly studio A. Bob Schmid, John Davenport and the other staff members who worked in FM were committed to FM and its future. It would have been much more profitable and a lot less trouble just to turn the license back to the FCC, as others had done. But WESC hung on and the persistence eventually paid off.

By the summer of 1965, WESC had recovered from its all out effort to "win with rock." Programming settled into a safe haven with a middle of the road format. The station aired Clemson football, NASCAR races and programmed a country and gospel mixture in the early mornings. There was still hope that someday a successful format could be found that would put the station at the top of the rating charts.

It has been said that luck happens when preparation meets opportunity. In retrospect, the staff, management and owner of WESC had been preparing for a long time for some overdue luck. The opportunity presented itself the summer of 1965. While reading trade magazines — and quite by accident — I stumbled upon an article in the Country Music Association Newsletter reporting that a daytime station in Orlando, Fla., had topped the 1965 Spring Pulse survey by playing country music all day. I immediately made plans to check it out. Having read the article late Friday afternoon, I did not have time to make an appointment in Orlando. My wife, Helen, and I put Wally Jr. and Christie, then nine and seven years old, in the car and drove to Daytona Beach early on Saturday morning. As the sun came up Monday morning, I was driving on Interstate 4, going to Orlando. I was at the station when the doors opened.

While I waited for the general manager of radio station WHYI to arrive, I read a story on the front page of the Orlando Sunday newspaper announcing plans for a theme park to be built in the Orlando area by Walt Disney. Engaging a staff member in conversation, I learned that a radio station with a tower site at the proposed entrance to the theme park was for sale. I think they mentioned an asking price of $60,000. Will somebody please figure out how much five acres of land — roughly the size of the tower site — at the entrance to Disney World, if you could buy it, would be worth today?

When the general manager of WHYI came into the office about 9:00 he asked what he could do for me. I showed him the story about WHYI in the Country Music Association Newsletter — he had not seen it. I asked to see the survey, explaining I was sales manager at WESC, a 10,000 watt AM daytime station in Greenville, South Carolina. I added that I did not believe a daytime 1000-watt station in a market the size of Orlando could be #1. I told him I had come all the way from South Carolina to check it out! The GM, perhaps impressed with my honesty and maybe defensive because of my candor, invited me into his office to look at the book. He was honest and forthright, saying he did not know anything about radio; he described himself as "a siding salesman," saying it was a truthful article and handed me the survey. To my surprise it was true! I asked him how they attracted those numbers and he obligingly introduced me to his program director, Jack Gardner.

Briefly, this was their story. Jack Gardner was a "rock jock" who, after reaching adulthood, had become a country music fan. WHYI had switched to country music a few months before the spring rating period. The station didn't do anything special to promote its country music programs except to tie into a couple of country music concerts in the Orlando area. They hadn't changed the call letters. WHYI was supposed to tie into dog racing, horse racing or something. I believe they said a staple of the previous format was announcing racing results. The WHYI call letters were supposed to remind listeners to tune in for racing results.

Since Jack was the morning D.J. on Orlando's only country music station, he was asked to introduce the stars at the concerts. It seems WHYI had been successful the old fashioned way. They earned it by identifying an audience and serving it.

Gardner selected the music from the **Billboard Magazine** charts and the WHYI presentation was like any good rock radio station, except the station played country music hits. Although identifying WHYI as a top forty station would have confused the agency time buyers, that's what it was: A TOP FORTY COUNTRY STATION. I struck a deal with Jack Gardner. "Show me how to do it and if we're successful I'll recommend you to other stations."

Jack Gardner helped WESC to succeed and I kept that promise.

In the years that followed, I recommended Jack Gardner to several broadcasters and sang his praises to everybody who asked how WESC achieved success. Mr. Gardner became a key person in the success of country music stations in Atlanta; Charleston, West Virginia; Mobile, Alabama; Dallas, Texas and some other major cities, mostly jobs that were landed as a result of the WESC success.

I remember one station in particular. Bob Schmid had a friend from his Mutual Broadcasting System days, Pete

Johnson, who owned a station in Charleston, West Virginia. WCAW was underperforming with a rock format and Bob set up an appointment for Pete to come to Greenville and check out how we did the country format. Pete flew into Greenville in his private plane, accompanied by Paul Howard and Paul Miles. I picked them up at the downtown airport and to my surprise they had brought along a tape recorder. They wanted to record every word of our conversation. On the way downtown when I started to tell them how we did it, they stopped me, saying they didn't have power for the tape machine in the car. I was amused and amazed. Amused at how much **importance** they placed on every detail of the conversation and amazed at how much they considered **me** an authority. It had all come naturally at WESC. When I visited Orlando Jack Gardner drew us the picture and we just colored in the blocks.

The WCAW people were very thorough. They wanted to know exactly how the records were chosen and in what sequence they were played. Someone said KISS: "Keep it simple, stupid." They were making a difficult job out of it. After several hours, we got into a discussion about playing songs that were hits by country artists but recorded by pop singers. Wouldn't or couldn't these records be substituted for the original records? I saw that I wasn't getting anywhere convincing them that Bing Crosby wasn't country even if he was singing *Don't Fence Me In*. So, I suggested they hire Jack Gardner. Pete Johnson took my advice and hired Jack Gardner when he returned to Charleston. The team of Johnson, Howard, Miles and Gardner was a big influence in the success of the format in several cities.

For those who have lost their way, I'll review the Gardner formula: A good country music station is like any good radio station, except it plays country music. Two hit country records were selected from the **Billboard Magazine** charts and scheduled with one other country record to make up a quarter hour of programming. The "other record" in the quarter hour might be: (1) a record just off the charts, (2) a country gold, (3) a bluegrass, (4) country-gospel. I learned the hard way the country-gospel song should be performed by a country artist. It's important to insist that all music be records by country artists. Speech was limited to song titles, time, temperature, weather word and station call letters. Call letters were announced three times between every record, i.e.: WESC time, WESC temperature, WESC weather. Gardner wanted the listener to remember the call letters. I called this brainwashing the listeners.

Gardner wanted to establish WESC – 660 in Dixie — as the place to find country music even if the listener had tuned in for just one record. Of course this became an issue. Some said it was annoying, others just plain dumb, but in the '60s the more times the D.J.'s spoke the call letters the higher the ratings. It was the irritation technique. Most of us in the World War II generation succumbed to the Lucky Strike auctioneer's chant. He took us to an imaginary tobacco warehouse and the announcer said: "With men who know tobacco best — it's Luckies Two to One." We chain-smoked Luckies because we were repeatedly told they were *Toasted.*

In the Gardner format, newscasts were no more than five minutes — preferably 90 seconds — scheduled at the top of the hour.

I remember, I got the bright idea to put a five-minute newscast at the top of the hour and another at the bottom of the hour at a time when it seemed everybody wanted news of the Vietnam War. The ratings dropped off. I met Jack Gardner on a street in Nashville. His first question was about ratings. I explained that WESC must have peaked because our ratings dropped off. We talked a little about what WESC was doing on the air and when he discovered that I had added five minutes of news he simply said, "Take off the news on the half hour." We did and the people came back to "660 in Dixie."

Today, I hear older country artists complain on TV talk shows that radio stations, for whatever reason, do not play the records of artists not on the charts. <u>If these complaints are true — this is wrong!</u> I believe all these artists are part of the country music family and their records should be played. A country music station derives its revenue through the loyalty of country music fans. Country radio stations must return that loyalty. If you haven't learned that lesson — learn it! Then you can send me a royalty check because you're gonna be rich.

Perhaps today's play lists are limited to younger artists in order to attract a younger demographic, the "likeness attracts" theory. To these experts — and I believe they are experts — I would pass along the advice given to me by Roy Acuff. I asked Mr. Acuff HOW I should choose WHICH record to play when there were so many good records available. The "King of Country Music" advised me to listen to the lyrics. If the story "grabs you in the heart" play it! Now, think about it. Does an artist have to be young or old, male or female, rich or poor, black or white, Latino or Anglo-Saxon to create something that "grabs you"?

Further, does a record have to be hot on the charts to stimulate emotion? I think not! Some day — and I hope soon — somebody is going to make a fortune playing country music regardless of when the songs were written or recorded. There's a station in Hickory, North Carolina, at 630 KC on the AM dial that plays country hits without much regard to when the records were popular. I don't know how many listeners they have but they sure have me when I'm traveling on I-85 within earshot of their signal.

171

As long as I'm handing out free programming advice, I want to address one of my pet peeves, that of not announcing the title or artist except at the beginning or end of a "set." My take on this is: Radio is a theatre of the mind; if the tunes are announced separately from the artist, casual listeners — unfamiliar with the music — cannot visualize who is singing. Segueing music neutralizes one of radio's unique strengths — listener involvement through the power of imagination. This is not just my opinion. I have had many people tell me they listen to the radio and listen to the country stations but they say, "It just seems like I'm not involved anymore." That's right! They are not involved. They are just listening with half an ear. Suppose the sports announcers called the ball games using glowing terms and descriptive phrases but didn't say who was in the ball game. It wouldn't be much fun to listen, right? But when we're told that our favorite players are in the ball game and we have an exciting announcer tell us what they are doing, we get involved.

Having said this and remembering most people don't value free advice, I'll return to my story of how WESC became a country giant.

Armed with the Jack Gardner two hour cram course on "How to succeed with country music programming," I returned to Greenville from Orlando, convinced John Davenport it was the thing to do, wrote a report to Bob Schmid and waited. We didn't have to wait long!

Chapter 12

The Best Idea: All Country Music!

Bob Schmid called just as soon as he read the report and told John Davenport to switch WESC AM to country music. I was placed in charge of the project. We kept the same announcers and air shifts. Wayne Sumner continued to sign on FM at 6:00 a.m. and WESC AM joined at daylight. I relieved Wayne at 7:30 a.m. WESC FM separated from WESC AM at 8:00 a.m. Max Mace came on at 9:00 a.m. and ran 'til 2:00 p.m., then Bob Hooper was heard 'til sign-off.

For the first six months the FM station continued to program pop concert music from 8:00 a.m. until 11:00 p.m. After that, the public demanded a nighttime country music service. Playing country music on FM until midnight was a "no brainer" because we had a substantial increase in ratings when the fall Pulse survey was released. In fact, WESC was **number one** in some demographics. Spring of 1966, we decided to provide twenty-four hour service. By February of 1966, WESC was promoting live country music shows at

Greenville Memorial Auditorium. The shows were billed as **WESC Country Shindigs.** So, we announced to a Friday night Shindig audience that beginning the first of March, WESC FM would remain on the air and play country music all night. The audience received the news with a standing ovation. It completed the "round the clock" service. Country music fans within 60 miles of Greenville could listen to WESC or WESC FM and hear their favorite music all day and all night. We did not switchWESC FM during the day. FM had a loyal daytime audience with easy listening music, heard mostly in businesses and offices, and we wanted to continue it even if the numbers were small.

Some may ask **WHY**? Why wasn't WESC FM switched to country music in August 1965 when WESC AM started the all-country music format? Why was it done piecemeal? The answer is, it had not been done before in Greenville. A decade before, an all country music station was not successful in Charlotte. Radio stations in several cities such as Spartanburg, Columbia and Atlanta had dabbled with country programming in the past without overwhelming success. When WESC switched to C&W, there were about 230 all-country music stations in America but if any of them were as successful as WHYI, their story had not been reported. So, WESC cautiously started playing country music all day, everyday, and responded to public demand.

WESC's switch to country music was given a big boost by local auto racing fans. As has been said, the NASCAR races were heard on WESC FM; therefore, a lot of race fans listened to the FM station. It was a perfect fit. We established a "cross promotion" relationship with the tracks. We advertised their events on the NASCAR broadcasts and they advertised WESC at the tracks. WESC D.J.'s Max Mace and Jerry Howard were already working at local racetracks as public address announcers. So, we encouraged Bob Hooper and Rod Ramsey to get involved at the other tracks. These four D.J.'s made a lot of friends for WESC at the racetracks. The station call letters were painted on the fences and also on some of the cars. The public address announcers invited fans at the track to tune to WESC. This strategy was especially helpful when the afternoon thunderclouds threatened. Race fans were told to listen to WESC to learn if the races were rained out. It boosted our Saturday audience as well as giving us credibility with race fans.

Several of the drivers painted the names of the WESC D.J.'s on their cars. It was a good arrangement for the track promoters, the car owners, the drivers, WESC and its D.J.'s. We were indebted to Pete and Tom Blackwell of the Greenville Pickens Speedway, Charlie Mize of the Anderson Speedway, Luke Cannon at Riverside, Wade Ashley at Laurens and Jack Suttles at the Fountain Inn Speedway for their support.

Another promotional opportunity was the county fairs. The Upper S.C. State Fair, Anderson County Fair, Greenville County American Legion Fair, the Elbert County Fair in Elberton, Georgia, and some of the others were promoted by WESC and in return the fairs promoted the station. A.H. "Pete" Blackwell, Tom Blackwell, I.V. Hulme, Carl Nusener and Cecil Buchanan were the principal fair promoters. We developed a plan to cross plug each other. WESC provided live local country acts, gospel singers and remotes to boost the station at the fairs. The D.J.'s were assigned "extra duty" during fair week. It was a great team effort. Everybody at WESC welcomed the opportunity to do "extra duty" to build their name so they would be more marketable. All promotions were planned to attract fans to country music. We knew our success depended on building the fan base. When young people stopped movin' and groovin' to rock music and just

175

wanted to listen to lyrics, they "crossed over the bridge" from rock to country.

The TV networks did not program much country music in those days. The country music broadcasters were encouraged to lobby for the country shows shown on TV. We suggested that sponsors use country music in their TV commercials and we generally promoted the country music industry. It worked. Stars such as Jimmy Dean, Glen Campbell and Johnny Cash were seen on TV at various times in the '60s. Country music radio stations were urged by the Country Music Association to advertise the TV shows. When the TV shows came up for renewal, WESC listeners were asked to write to the TV sponsors to keep the artist on the air. Radio stations across America pitched in to help do the selling job at all levels of the advertising community. It was the **What's good for you is good for me** philosophy.

Once I was in New York talking to an ad agency. The young female buyer with whom I was discussing WESC placed millions of ad dollars on radio and TV but she didn't know anything about country music because she was a native New Yorker. When she asked me what type of music WESC played, I responded country music. She didn't know much about country music stations and asked whose records were played on the station. I named several of the artists on the play list including Glen Campbell. Since she watched Glen Campbell on television she could **now** relate to a station playing country music; it was a Glen Campbell station. You should have heard my pitch to her. It sounded like we didn't play anybody else but Glen Campbell.

It took about ten years for TV stations and the networks to see the value of programming regular country music programs. Some knew the power of country music and included a country flavor in their commercials but for the most part the large media companies — for whatever reason — shied away from regular country and western programming. By the way, a lot of country acts were not comfortable in front of the cameras and it showed! Tennessee Ernie Ford, Jimmy Dean, Glen Campbell, Kenny Rogers, the Oak Ridge Boys, the Statler Brothers, Dolly Parton and Loretta Lynn are just a few of the country music television pioneers showing personality and poise on camera. They paved the way for country music television.

WESC's commitment to country music was strong. We cancelled all speech programs more than five minutes in length, Monday through Saturday. This included the Clemson football schedule beginning in 1966. A delayed Grand Ole Opry program was available by transcription, so WESC programmed 5 hours of the Grand Ole Opry on Saturday afternoon. Throughout the late '60s and into the '70s, WESC sent all the D.J.'s to Nashville in October and originated programs from the Country Music Association convention. Also, the Grand Ole Opry celebrated its birthday at the convention. Most of the country music artists attended the convention and appeared on the Grand Ole Opry as well as other shows originating in Nashville during convention week. It was a great opportunity to meet and interview the stars.

Since WESC was one of just a few stations in the nation to originate its programming from Nashville during convention week, the stars lined up to be interviewed by Bob Hooper, Wayne Sumner, Jerry Howard, Rod Ramsey and me. The country stars with hit records were interviewed several times during the Thursday through Saturday broadcasts. It was a special thrill to talk with cowboy singing stars Gene Autry and Tex Ritter. Also the tailor who made the performers' costumes, Mr. "Nudie," came by to talk about his clients, many of whom appeared in western movies, at the Opry and in country music venues across America.

One year, Wayne Sumner negotiated with a Nashville policeman and reserved a broadcast site — curbside — between the Andrew Jackson Hotel and the Hermitage Hotel in Nashville. That's where the action was. It was convenient for the stars to stop by the WESC remote unit as they walked between the Andrew Jackson and Hermitage Hotels. Incidentally, the remote unit was in front of a liquor store and the storeowner generously cooperated. This probably promoted his business or perhaps they were going to see him in the first place. Location! Location! Location!

Bob Hooper and Wayne Sumner deserve a tip of the ole country hat for these Nashville trips; Bob Hooper because he drove the remote unit all the way to Nashville and Wayne Sumner for sleeping in a bathtub to escape Jerry Howard's snoring.

In 1967 Wayne and I hit the jackpot! The CMA awards were being taped for Network TV at the Ryman Auditorium. It was sold out. I don't remember how I got tickets; perhaps Jack Gardner promoted them. Whoever was to deliver the tickets to our motel did so after work and we were almost late for the show. When Wayne and I entered the Grand Ole Opry House, we were asked to sit on the front row because the Opry did not want the "no show" empty seats seen on television. Seated in the front rows were the country music legends, the movers and shakers of the music industry and the powerful of the TV industry — **all of them had on black tie and tux**. On the front row were Wayne and Wally on national television in street clothes. I think I wore a black and white glen plaid suit, white shirt and a black tie. Wayne wore a multi-colored sport coat with a loud shirt and tie — almost a Spec Rhodes outfit. You might say we created some attention.

During one visit to Nashville — I think it was 1969 — a writer named Al visited the remote unit. He declined to be interviewed but said he was gathering material for a book and wanted to know if any of the D.J.'s or artists would speak out against the Vietnam War. Nobody talked to him. I wasn't present at the remote unit when he came by and hoped he would return because I had some definite opinions about the war. I supported our troops in Vietnam, and I thought anyone who spoke out against the war aided the enemy. I believed then, and now, it was a just cause. The soldiers who came back should have been given a hero's welcome because they stopped the spread of communism in southeast Asia. Perhaps the reason they were not given parades and such wasn't because the vast silent majority of Americans didn't appreciate them. It was because America was tired of the divisiveness brought on by the war. Responsible citizens wanted a time of healing.

The peaceniks would have probably spoiled the homecoming. It was better to just tell these guys personally how much their service was appreciated.

When we went to Nashville, I paid special attention to the advertising to get ideas for commercials and WESC promotions. One year a billboard picked up a line used by a Grand Ole Opry star — I believe it was Oswald — to advertise a product. I couldn't wait to get home to implement the phrase, **How Sweet It Is,** to describe WESC's country music. To my knowledge it was used on the Opry years before Jackie Gleason used it.

One year a billboard proclaimed Oprah Winfrey as news anchor for a UHF TV station. In those pre-cable days UHF TV stations were struggling. Having never heard of Oprah, I inquired about the chances of success for an African-American woman to anchor a TV news program. I was told that Oprah had a great TV personality. Charlie Pride was coming on strong and with this African-American female doing news, it caused me to wonder if a black female country music D.J. would get attention. If I could have foreseen the success of Oprah, I might have sought out some African-American women and given the idea a shot.

On September 12, 1969, WESC was granted 500 watts standard sign-on. The magician in this sleight of hand trick was Sam Slaughter, an attorney with the Pearson, Ball and Doud law firm in Washington. Mr. Slaughter was also proficient in electronics and he or somebody convinced somebody somewhere at the FCC and someone else at WNBC in New York that WNBC would gain listeners in Virginia by having WESC protect the New York station with a directional antenna system during critical hours. The move limited WESC's service in the early morning and late afternoon towards New York, but strengthened its signal to the south. This improved WESC's reception before sunrise in south Greenville and Anderson counties.

In the mid '60s, WESC retained Palmer A. Greer as an engineering consultant. The addition of Mr. Greer to assist chief engineer Don Gowens helped the station to have the expertise necessary to build WESC into a super station. After Palmer Greer was retained as engineering consultant he started improving the AM and FM signals. He replaced the ten year old ground system, added AM stereo and a new AM and FM transmitter. He increased the FM tower height on Farr's Bridge Road and gained permission to transmit the AM from the 600+ foot FM tower.

Now those of you with engineering know-how may want to explain just why transmitting AM from 600+ feet is better than 365 feet. I never did quite understand why the FCC would permit it. Perhaps Mr. Greer had a magic wand similar to Sam Slaughter's. In the old days an AM tower height was determined by the frequency. Stations on the low end of the

AM band had high towers and those around 1600 KC had much shorter towers. Transmitting AM from taller towers wasn't done much around the Carolinas and Georgia until Mr. Greer did it for WESC.

By the 1980's, WESC increased FM power to 100,000 watts, eventually moving the FM transmitter and tower to Caesar's Head Mountain — A SUPER STATION! Maximum power! Maximum tower height! WOW! WESC's 1,225-foot tower on a 3,000 foot mountain topped any station in the state. Bob Schmid was ecstatic. He hired a helicopter to take pictures of the awesome thing...and remembering the Jolly Green Giant on the bean can as well as the story of Jack and the beanstalk, he inquired if the FCC would allow him to paint the tower GREEN! Although that idea didn't fly he had his super station and he was DEE-LIGHTED! But not for long; a winter ice storm at the end of January 1983 caused the tower on Caesars Head Mountain to fall under the weight of 55 tons of ice.

WESC was not alone; several towers around the country toppled because of unexpected strong winds and ice. Broadcasters got some expensive experience in the construction and maintenance of tall towers in the '80s. LeRoy Hamilton of Simpsonville, South Carolina, was given a contract to remove the twisted steel and pave the way for a new tower to be erected.

The Kline Construction Company of Columbia, S.C., a company with a national reputation for tall tower construction, was granted the contract for the second tower. It was equipped with emergency generators, heaters and whatever else was needed to assure country music fans dependable service.

Although not a staff member, Palmer Greer provided WESC with excellent engineering service. His office was conveniently located at the WESC AM transmitter site, making him available when needed. Palmer Greer and his successor, William Culpepper, who bought the Greer Consulting firm, assisted WESC engineer Don Gowens to build a facility second to none.

A drive up Caesar's Head Mountain on any clear day will help the reader to appreciate the accomplishment of erecting a 1,225 foot steel tower on a 3,000-foot mountain. The tower property is the last piece of land in Greenville County, South Carolina. The road to the tower turns off of Highway 276 in North Carolina and curves around a mountain peak winding back into South Carolina. Now, you try explaining that to electric power and telephone people who cannot cross state boundaries to install lines and poles. Messrs. Greer and Gowens coordinated the subcontractor's work schedules with the arrival of building supplies. When the tower was completed, they successfully received the program signal by microwave from the studio located on Stone Avenue in Greenville. It was an enormous task and country music fans everywhere need to know that Don Gowens and Palmer Greer accomplished it not once but twice, without injury or loss of life.

After Palmer Greer's retirement, William Culpepper did the engineering work for 50,000 watts on 660 KC. The WESC AM power was raised to 50,000 watts/10,000 watts directional during critical hours on August 1, 1984. At last, Bob Schmid had his maximum power stations — 100,000 watts FM with maximum tower height and 50,000 watts AM on a dream frequency, 660 KC. Country was king!

"Greenville is growing and Greenville is fair...there's room for more stations to come on the air."

WESC's tall towers were not only country music beacons, but beacons for airplanes. Several pilots over the years told us about using the WESC transmitting towers as navigational aids. Mr. John Hamilton, for many years the executive director of the South Carolina Aeronautics Commission, told me the WESC towers and the signals they transmitted were especially helpful to him to safely fly state officials in and out of small airports in the upstate. The WESC signals were his navigational aids since the rural airports did not have such equipment.

The '70s and '80s were good times for WESC. Among those who helped the station succeed were Frances Jamison, Penny Gaines, Barbara Goldsmith, Ginger Case, Lowell Fletcher, Barbara Jackson Powers, Allan Power, John Landrum, B.J. and Dan Nash, Jim Neubau, Charlie Munson and Ken Dockins, just to mention a few of the crew. John Landrum has the distinction of having a town named after his family. B.J. Nash left WESC for a position with Greenville Tech. She can be seen almost any time on cable channel 14. Way to go, B.J.!

WESC always gave wannabes a boost. Stevie Coggins a nine year old lad was presented on a Shindig and Loretta Lynn immediately took him on her tour and opened doors in Nashville.

Tennessee Ralph wanted to be a song-writer. He wrote several songs and after they were recorded we included them in the format, calling them "Carolina Country picks." One song *Wally the DJ Man* was played on stations around the country. WOLA in Jackson, Michigan listed it number 18 on its play list April 25, 1971. Another local hit was *Where the Radar Are.*

Charlie Craig and Clyde law recorded some of Tennessee Ralph's music. The band was called *Clyde Law and The Lawmen.* The guys in the band were from Laurens County. In addition to Clyde and Charlie the boys in the band were: Donnie Wilson, sax; Wester Todd, steel guitar; Carroll Bagwell, standup bass; and Clyde Pennington, bass.

183

Charlie Craig sought my advice on how to succeed in the country music field. I told him to go to Nashville — get a job doing anything to support himself and knock on doors 'til he got a break. Charlie Craig went to Nashville and has succeeded.

There have been several other locals that made it in Nashville but time, space and my memory prohibits their stories being told here.

During the last half of the seventies, and there after, the program and sales departments were separated both in duties and studio locale. We had a young D.J. that was gaining some attention with his style and sports reports. The new kid on the block was Charlie Munson. I heard he had resigned to enter Greenville Tech. to study computers, so I looked him up. Catching him in a hallway, I said something like this: "Charlie, I hear you are leaving us — are you crazy?" He defended himself by saying that he was disillusioned with the radio business and had come to the conclusion that he didn't have a future in radio. I responded that what he was doing was a dumb thing since he would probably replace Bob Hooper on the morning show. I said, "Hooper ain't getting any younger, you know. Radio is like baseball: the young guys play it and the old guys run it." This ole guy from the front office probably scared Charlie Munson half to death charging him like that but I really, really thought he had the makings of a GREAT morning man.

As this goes to press Charlie Munson IS a great morning man. The first thing my wife, Helen, does when she wakes up every morning is to turn on Charlie Munson and Roger Davis for the news, weather and sports. We both wonder what Charlie looks like without the beard. Maybe he could have a contest to shave it off. Say, a fundraiser for the John I. Smith Scottish Rite Center for Children with Language Disorders located on Cleveland Street in Greenville.

The major promotional efforts in the '60s and '70s were the country music shindigs. Country music promoters Keith Fowler and Carlton Haynie teamed up to book Grand Ole Opry acts into Greenville Memorial Auditorium. After a couple of years, Mr. Haynie went his way and Keith Fowler promoted the shows in Greenville. Haynie concentrated in another town, I think, somewhere in Virginia. WESC advertised the Greenville shows extensively and was given credit for presenting the concerts. This promotional tie-in with the concerts and resulting relationship with the artists were strong promotional tools.

Throughout the country the station/concert tie-ins were so effective the FCC wrote new guidelines for presenting the shows. The new notice prohibited stations from advertising that they sponsored the concert, unless the station actually contracted for the performances. We could say "WESC invites you to" or "WESC welcomes," but not that the show was sponsored by WESC. It was a fine line and in my opinion was perpetrated by competitors who lost millions of dollars in advertising to new country-formatted stations.

In Greenville, WESC was fortunate to have good competitors — they would beat you with resources, not political shenanigans. However, some stations across America with politically powerful ownership were slow to adapt to change. So, I was told they engaged in some mischief — if you can't lick 'em, pass a law agin' 'em! If it's true, the strategy didn't work. The public didn't care who sponsored or presented the shows; they just wanted to see the country stars sing the songs they listened to on the radio.

Wayne Sumner was the WESC salesman assigned to the Greenville Memorial Auditorium account. Although Wayne was the liaison with the auditorium management and promoters, all of the D.J.'s and most of the staff were involved

185

in one way or another. Everybody, including Wayne, did a great job! Wayne administered the details of the concerts and edited a "Shindig Program Book" which was given to the fans as they entered the door for the concert.

The WESC D.J.'s took turns introducing the stars. Usually, five artists were booked for each show. This enabled every personality to be seen on stage at least once. The D.J.'s greeted the fans as they entered the building, thanking them for attending the show and giving them a complimentary "Shindig" program book. These "Shindig" books contained pictures of the artists, the D.J.'s, advertising about the participating businesses, plus photographs and stories of past Shindigs. Some of the pictures from these books appear in Part III of this book through the courtesy of the South Carolina Broadcasters Association Archives located at the University of South Carolina in Columbia.

Incidentally, the SCBA Archives houses historical materials from many radio and television stations in the state. Students upon request may examine these materials. One day — soon we hope, people from all over the world may be able to log on to an SCBA Archives web site and pull up this material. For now, my readers may visit the archives by appointment and explore this treasure.

Some of these old radio programs are really good and reflect some of the best air talent of their time. There is a program that Cliff "Farmer" Gray, the morning man on WSPA AM (950 KC) in Spartanburg in the '30s, '40s and '50s, aired on WSPA AM and the CBS radio network. The site of the broadcast was the Southern Railroad Station in Spartanburg. The occasion was the passing through Spartanburg of the funeral train of President Franklin D. Roosevelt in 1945. Farmer Gray said before he went on the air he had been walking the streets of Spartanburg looking at the faces of the people. He said this is a cotton mill town and the people on the streets are mill workers, some are farmers, others work and live in town — all are good Americans. They were led out of the Depression by Mr. Roosevelt, they sent their sons off to war under his leadership, now they have lost him. THEIR PRESIDENT IS DEAD and they are grieving!

Although these words are not a direct quote, they are close enough to demonstrate to you that Farmer Gray could move an audience. He was a master wordsmith.

WESC's chief engineer, Don Gowens, was a control operator for Cliff Gray in the days when Don commuted to Gastonia, N.C., to study electronics at Gaston TEC. Don says Cliff Gray was close to his audience. He visited farms in Spartanburg County, going into the fields to talk with the farmers who listened each morning. Mr. Gray wanted people to tell him what was on their minds. His programs reflected Spartanburg County. Now you know why Spartanburg ran on "Cliff Gray Time." Although we were able to make some inroads into Spartanburg County we were never able to dominate Spartanburg County like we did the counties to the west and south of Greenville.

WSPA AM was a pioneer news station; WESC was a pioneer country music station.

The country stars endorsed WESC while on the concert stage, the WESC banner hung over the stage during concerts, and while the shows were in progress, WESC was broadcasting from its remote unit backstage. We interviewed the stars and beamed the interviews back to the station by microwave. That was something! When country music fans couldn't come to the shows they kept up with their favorite star's performance in Greenville on WESC. The "Shindigs" soon became a community event, a place where country music fans went to see and be seen. Many friendships were established and business deals struck at the "WESC Country Shindigs."

Radio stations, TV stations, country music promoters and dozens of other industry people came to Greenville to learn why country music concerts were having so much success in Greenville. They wanted to know how we managed to sell out the shows. Record producers came to Greenville to watch the audience react to new songs and new faces. Greenville was considered a premier stop on the country music tour. WESC cooperated with everybody interested in promoting country music. The attitude throughout the country music industry was: "We're all in this together, so let's help each other."

The Greenville Memorial Auditorium staff and its executive manager, Leslie Timms, were always cooperative and helpful. In return, WESC promoted the building. Mr. Timms expressed his appreciation to me many times for WESC's support of the Greenville Memorial Auditorium. The building was built in the late '50s but country music shows had not been very successful until the "Shindigs" came to town. The timing was right: a strong local country music station selling the right talent mix and a community hungry for country music. Keith Fowler and his associates booked acts the public wanted to see and WESC was successful in promoting the shows. The movers and shakers of Greenville wanted the fans to come to town. Greenville was just getting a taste of the tourist dollar.

Incidentally, WESC was paid to promote the shows. The events were a regular business transaction for the station. WESC received cash for promoting the shows and some tickets to be used for promotional purposes.

After providing tickets for the D.J.'s, we packaged the rest of the tickets with commercials and advertising space in the program booklet, giving WESC another income stream. So, if there's anybody out there trading airtime and receiving only a few promotional tickets for the concerts, remember: "You can't sell it IF you give it away."

In addition to Mr. Timms, the auditorium staff included box office personnel Fritz Capell, Ida Holtzclaw, Barbara Shaw and Jean Poole; the concessions and facilities manager, Bill Turner; lighting, Lewis Machen; and sound, Hubert Brown. Festus Hawkins of the Greenville Police Department headed up security and assigned Policeman Horace Copeland to the back door. Mr. Timms' assistant managers at various times were Bill Luther, Jack Shands and Cliff Wallace. Mr. Timms recommended all of them for bigger and better jobs at public buildings around the country. Bill Luther went to Huntsville, Alabama; Jack Shands to Fayetteville, North Carolina; and Cliff Wallace to the Superdome in New Orleans.

WESC supported efforts to build a new 12,000 seat building. But the referendum was defeated in 1973. Some people speculate what might have happened in downtown Greenville if the referendum had passed. Of course, the building with its 12,000 plus seats would have been paid for but antiquated by the 1990's. The Bi-Lo Center would probably have been built much earlier than the '90s. It might have been built in Greer, making that city the hub of the Greenville/ Spartanburg Metroplex. In spite of all the doomsday economic speculating, taxes would likely have been lowered. Tickets for small attractions in Greenville would be cheaper because the 12,000 seat building would have been debt free in the 1990's. Who knows, Greenville/Spartanburg may have attracted major professional sports and Greer would have become the hub. By the way, did you know Greer once was known as **Greers?** About the time WESC took to the airwaves many listeners called the station wanting songs played for folks who lived in **Greers.** When the name was changed to Greer, I don't know.

Among the auditorium trustees during the time of the Shindigs were: car dealer Paul Carter; Dan Joyner, realtor; Leon Campbell, realtor; "Doodle" Thomas, textile executive; Sam Hunt, banker; Waldo Leslie, real estate developer; and Wally Mullinax, broadcaster. The trustees supported Mr. Timms' management of the auditorium. Therefore, WESC had strong support selling country music to the community.

Two examples of the friendships made at Country Music Shindigs, in which lives were changed, are the careers of Dale Morris and Governor John West of South Carolina. Dale Morris was a pharmaceutical salesman living in Inman, S.C. Morris aspired to become the manager of a country music star, and requested that he be allowed to go backstage during performances to make contacts. As a result of Dale Morris' people skills and the opportunity to meet the "right" people at the Country Music Shindigs, he eventually landed a job in Nashville with the Morris Talent Agency. Later, he became the personal manager of Billy "Crash" Craddock.

Always on the lookout for fresh talent, Morris discovered a virtually unknown group that became known as **ALABAMA**! When opportunity knocked, Dale Morris was ready! WESC Country Music Shindigs gave Morris an opportunity to meet the stars. By the way, although Myrtle Beach gets the credit for nurturing the **ALABAMA** band, it appeared at a local Greenville establishment for a year or two before coming to the attention of Morris. I believe they called themselves *Wild Country* in those days.

The Country Music Shindigs played a large part in changing the life of Lt. Governor John West. Mr. West was a candidate for governor in 1970 when he was introduced to Loretta Lynn at a WESC Country Music Shindig. Thereafter, when Loretta Lynn appeared in South Carolina, John West was present. Loretta Lynn always introduced Mr. West as "My friend — and the next governor of South Carolina." Some political observers credit Loretta Lynn's endorsement of Governor West with turning the tide in his successful campaign against Albert Watson.

After the election, Governor-elect John West appreciated the boost he received from Loretta Lynn and invited her to entertain at his inaugural. Until this time a country music act had never appeared at such a formal state function in South Carolina. It was a thrill for me to have been asked to contact Loretta and arrange for the appearance. She accepted and was a big hit at the governor's inaugural. Exposure such as this helped country music stations attract new listeners, new sponsors and make friends in high places. After all, if Loretta Lynn entertained at the governor's inaugural, some of the large companies began to see the value of placing commercials on country music stations. The relationship probably boosted Loretta Lynn's career too, because about this time, her picture began appearing in national news magazines. It's not known if her appearance at the inauguration attracted some of this attention. My guess is it did.

These are just two examples of how WESC helped win acceptance for country music. The challenge was not to attract country music listeners; WESC was the upstate's exclusive country music station, and the ratings were good. The challenge was to sell large advertising agencies on the buying power of this audience. Agency executives needed to know — and accept the fact — that the interstate highways had changed the way America traveled, they changed our distribution system from trains to trucks, and air conditioning brought northern companies south...the way to reach untapped markets was to advertise on country music stations. Although country music was getting more exposure on radio, TV and records, some advertising time buyers were slow to see its value as an advertising tool. So we invited the skeptics to the Shindigs. When these admen saw the crowd's reaction to the stars, their sales resistance evaporated.

The Country Music Shindigs had some anxious nights. The first night Charlie Pride was on the Shindig stage there was concern for his safety. As far as I know, there were no threats but we were concerned because he was the first black man to entertain the all-white country crowd. Although there were about 30 plainclothes law enforcement people in the crowd there wasn't even a racial slur from the capacity crowd that came to hear Charlie sing.

I introduced Charlie Pride that night. Before he came to Greenville I had read stories in the trade magazines about Charlie Pride filling the big indoor arena in Detroit, as well as other large buildings. But when we were standing behind the curtain, just before going on stage, Charlie peeked around the curtain at the crowd and told me it was the most people he had ever seen in one place.

Conway Twitty's secretary, Lou Manley, contacted me in the late '70s or early '80s with her concern about some of the mail Conway had received from a fan in Greenville. So, when Conway came to town we again had tight security; however, the show went off without incident. None of this ever saw the light of day because some things are better if they are not publicized.

While Wayne Sumner was working to promote WESC through the Country Music Shindigs, Bob Hooper was promoting the station by contacting the artists, record companies and local country music groups. Bob Hooper emceed the summer shows at the Shoal Creek Country Music Park near Lavonia, Ga. He drove the WESC remote unit each week to Georgia and emceed the Friday or Saturday night shows, sometimes sharing these duties with Billy Dilworth, a northeast Georgia country music newspaper writer, D.J. and emcee. The owner of the Shoal Creek Park was Alton Walters, now deceased. Alton Walters is remembered as a staunch fan and supporter of WESC and a valuable station client.

On one trip to Shoal Creek, Bob Hooper lost control of the remote unit while rounding a curve on a Georgia country road. He wrecked the van and if I'm not mistaken it was totaled. I'm told Hooper was lucky to have escaped serious injury. It probably wasn't Hooper's fault because the console, desk and other heavy equipment were installed on the left side of the vehicle, so the weight shifted and he lost control. When Bob returned to South Carolina he had to face general manager John Davenport. To Bob's relief, John dismissed the incident with the statement "You won't let that happen again, will you?" John always probed a subject by saying to a staff member, "Tell me about it."

We wondered what Bob's answer would have been.

After the accident we teased Hooper saying the Georgia cop had given him a break or he would have spent the weekend in a Georgia jail. Sounds like the makings of a country song to me but we'll leave it to Tennessee Ralph or Country Earl to tell the story.

Bob Hooper was named program director in 1965, serving in that capacity until he became morning personality in 1975. As program director, Hooper selected the music list, circulated it to music shops, assembled the records for airing, made contacts with local country music acts and worked with them to promote WESC. In turn we promoted the local talent. Bob also secured public service "tie-in" opportunities and supervised quality control. Bob Hooper did a great job as program director and established a reputation for doing whatever needed to be done. Sometimes he worked overnights after performing his duties the previous day. He did this without complaint. Bob's willingness to go the extra mile earned him an opportunity to move into the morning show in 1975 when it became apparent we needed a change. He was ready when the opportunity came. The name **BOB HOOPER** was a household word in the late '70s and '80s.

There are many good Hooper stories. One of the best happened at a Country Shindig. To create "street talk" in the '60s the D.J.'s — especially Max Mace — built Hooper up as a ladies' man. Hooper explained all this to his wife, Kay, by saying it was "all just D.J. talk."

During the days leading up to the shindig, we all told our audience that our wives would be introduced at the next show. We always "cross plugged" — that is, we talked about how pretty our wife was and how much we wanted our listeners to come to the show and see her, ending with "and Hooper's wife will be there and we want you to see how pretty she is, too." At the appointed time Max introduced the D.J.'s wives, one by one, leaving Kay Hooper until last. Then Max said something like, "Now ladies and gentlemen, I know you have all come to see Bob Hooper's wife." While the spotlight panned the auditorium, 20 women who had been asked in advance to do so stood up all over the place.

Everybody except Bob and Kay enjoyed the joke; however, they were good sports about it. No doubt Hooper got even with Max. Some say Hooper hid the little bottle of "cough syrup" that Max kept on the console table while he was on the air.

After WESC became a country music giant in the late '60s, the staff positions remained about the same as before. My title was station manager; however, my principal duty was managing local sales. I also worked an account list, supervised the format and did the morning show. The morning show speech content was not changed when WESC started programming country music full time. It was a program of controversy, mostly political, reflecting the times and information.

Chapter 13

Another Idea: Run For Public Office

In 1968, Greenville County installed Home Rule. Previously, the county had been governed by members of the Greenville County Delegation assisted by an appointed board of commissioners. By the '60s, the state was growing rapidly and the state legislature needed to spend its time on state matters. The legislature relinquished local governing responsibilities to a local county council elected by the people. Since I was having so much to say on the radio about the poor planning, the improvements needed in education, Sunday selling laws, the deplorable jail conditions, and most especially about Democrats defecting to the Republican party — I called them turncoats — several people suggested that I run for the new governing body and straighten it out. So, I ran for the first Greenville County Council as a Democrat. I called myself a "DO MORE CRAT." In a countywide election I was elected to represent District #2, which was roughly the Wade Hampton area between Pleasantburg Drive and Greer.

After the election, we used the morning show to inform citizens of whatever the council thought would benefit Greenville County: zoning, better roads, consolidation of health services, construction of a new art museum (to house the Andrew Wyeth collection), a new law enforcement center, a technical high school, more deputies, school crossing guards, punch card voting machines, and funding county recreation were some of the issues producing fireworks.

Some political observers credit my candidacy with increasing voter registration for the 1968 elections since many citizens registered to vote in this election. At Marietta, S.C., a lady and her blind son came to vote. The box manager asked if she needed assistance. She responded, "Yes. We came to vote for two people: Franklin D. Roosevelt, who gave us social security, and Wally Mullinax, who gave us country music."

There must have been many more like this dear lady because I led the county council ticket and placed third or fourth among all of the candidates for public office. The Presidential race between Richard Nixon and Hubert Humphrey was very close in 1968, so I think that enabled me to get more votes in the county than either of them.

I have had some people — mostly broadcasters — ask how I was able to stay on the air and run for public office at the same time. The answer is, I had a very good and decent opponent in Willard Metcalf. WESC gave Mr. Metcalf some free commercials and I agreed not to mention my candidacy on the radio. Willard and I ran our campaigns free of "mudslinging." In those days candidates respected each other. In return the public respected both winners and losers. Some people listened to candidates and eliminated the mudslingers. Wouldn't that be great! It would clean up campaigns in a hurry if the public voted against the mudslingers.

By the next election, times had changed. The FCC had

mandated that if a radio/TV personality ran for public office then all his opponents must receive "equal time." I support equal time in theory but the devil is always in the details. To my knowledge the issue was never litigated before the FCC but the strictest interpretation at the time I was to run for reelection was that all opponents of a personality **must receive exactly as much time as the personality's voice was heard on the air.** In other words, if I introduced a record and it took 20 seconds to say the title, etc., then my opponents — no matter how many were in the race — should receive 20 seconds of free advertising. Oddly enough, if my voice was on a commercial, those seconds didn't count. The FCC took the position that I couldn't be deprived of a means of making a living.

None of the above ever applied to me because I suffered a serious illness in the spring of 1970 and was advised by my doctors to cut back on my schedule. Dr. J.I. Converse said he wasn't going to tell me **what** I could do but **how much** I could do.

The first Greenville County Council was elected countywide and therefore answered to all the citizens of the county, not just a small minority in a single district. We were able to do things for all the people of Greenville County without being concerned about the objections of a small group. One of the first issues we tackled upon taking office was to update the voting system. A study committee was appointed by the state legislature; since much of the confusion and long lines had occurred in Greenville County, where paper ballots were used, I was appointed to represent all of the counties in the state on the study committee. After studying all the available options and considering the cost of each system we recommended the "punch card" voting system. Also, we recommended that election day be a school holiday and that election workers be paid. Previously, the election workers had been volunteers. Most of the study committee's recommendations were later passed into state law.

The first Greenville County Council also tackled countywide zoning. We decided to begin by zoning part of my district, District #2. This was the "hot spot" for Greenville County development. I suppose the planners thought that since a lot of the people were moving in from states where the cities and towns had zoning laws we would have less opposition. If that's true, they were wrong! The people really got upset. The area to be zoned was the area between Pleasantburg Drive and Greer bounded by Wade Hampton Blvd. and Interstate 85. In 1970, much of this area was rural and the uncertainty that always comes with change upset some residents, but today, property values continue to appreciate and home values are protected from unplanned development. Most voters appreciate this safeguard for their homes.

The year 1970 taught me a lesson in human nature. Some people were really upset with me and I learned the three most frequent things the people forget. They are: past favors, childbirth and hangovers. I don't know if it was zoning, my prolonged absence from the air due to a serious illness, or what, but Monty DuPuy of WFBC really clobbered me in the spring ratings. Bob Schmid probably would have replaced me were it not for the outpouring of flowers, cards and get-well wishes from my supporters. While I was in the hospital, I received enough flowers to place bouquets at the bedside of every patient in the Greenville General Hospital. We had some left over for the nurses too!

An example of how the first council worked with other branches of government to serve the people is this: We needed a traffic light at Edwards Road and 291. The Highway Department said it couldn't be done. It would create a bottleneck and was a bad idea. A garden club in the area contacted me about their unsuccessful efforts to get a traffic light. I mentioned it to then State Senator Dick Riley and dismissed it from my mind. In a few days a Highway Department engineer phoned, saying he was instructed to contact me about the traffic signal Senator Riley wanted at Edwards Road and 291. Now thirty years later there's no REAL traffic jam at this red light. That experience leads me to believe that the RIGHT politicians — working together — can cut through the bureaucratic red tape.

The members of the first Greenville County Council were: Ralph Blakely from the Moonville area, Joe Earle from Greenville City, Bill Hunter from Greenville City, W.M. Kay, Jr., of the Welcome area, John Jarrard of Marietta, Ed Green of Fountain Inn, Don Owens from Greer, Bob Vaughn of Greenville, and I represented the Wade Hampton area. The staff included: Bill Bolin, Director of Fiscal Affairs; E.P. "Ted" Riley, legal counsel; and Louise Moore, secretary. Also, Cecil Buchanan, assistant fiscal affairs director; Sam Bagwell, purchasing agent; and Bert Winterbothem, county planning director.

This first Greenville County Council spent most of every day and usually an evening or so a week working for the people. We cooperated with the legislative delegation to change laws and bring Greenville County government into the 20th century. It may surprise you to learn that Greenville County did not provide life or health insurance for its employees until the first council was installed. If a county employee or a family member got sick or died, they were treated as charity. One of the first accomplishments of the council, after organization, was to provide insurance coverage for county employees. Raising taxes isn't politically popular anytime and to do it so soon after the election was risky, but the first council raised taxes a few months after taking office to provide insurance for county employees. Thereafter, when county employees or their families were ill or died, all of the councilmen felt a sense of pride for having addressed this issue so soon after the election. In fact, a key county executive, Bill Bolin, died a few days after the policy went into force. The Liberty Life Insurance Company paid the claim promptly without question. This may have defused the outcry from the anti-tax crowd.

My participation on the Greenville County Council would not have been possible without the full support of Bob Schmid, John Davenport and the WESC staff. My fellow staffers covered my station duties when I was off on county business. Their support was greatly appreciated.

The first council was proud of its accomplishments but there was one disappointment. A year or so before the election of 1968, the planning commission, delegation and highway department prepared a "GRATS" master plan for a system of freeways through the city of Greenville. Motorists would have been able to go to or from Greer, Travelers Rest, Fountain Inn or Easley without stopping for a red light. All members of the council were excited about the plan and passed an ordinance — on first reading — designed to fund it. We proposed a $10 annual windshield sticker for all cars registered in the county. This caused an outcry! I tried to sell the idea each morning on WESC, saying gas — then thirty cents a gallon — would someday be seventy-five cents a gallon and commuters could save enough gas in a year to pay for the sticker. The "aginners" didn't buy it. They shouted me down! They wouldn't believe gasoline would ever be seventy-five cents a gallon. Governor Robert E. McNair asked the council to come to Columbia, where he told us we were starting a taxpayer's rebellion. At his request we promptly abandoned the project. Folks, when you are tied up in traffic, burning $1.50 per gallon gas, near Haywood Mall, the East North Street/ Pleasantburg intersection, at the intersections near Bob Jones University or anywhere else in the county, remember those freeways could have been paid for in 1980 and under our proposal the windshield sticker removed.

"Greenville is growing and Greenville is fair...There's room for more stations to come on the air."

In 1966, my Furman University classmate Harold "Mule" Lollis, then a schoolteacher and coach at Wade Hampton High, dropped by WESC to inform me that he was going to run for the city magistrate's post, which was being vacated. He showed me a savings and loan passbook containing his life's savings and said he planned to spend it all to get the job. He asked me to plan and place his advertising. Now folks, this will cause a conscientious advertising salesman to search his soul. We selected time on all the stations, mostly on news programs in AM and PM drive, and allocated some monies for newspaper space. I suggested he spend one-fourth of the money in the first race and reserve a fourth for the second race. I suggested he keep one-half of his saving account as a family nest egg, just in case he was defeated.

We worked with Harold "Mule" Lollis to create a commercial, and since he had such a beautiful singing voice we suggested he record it. The announcement was great! He left for an appointment before the commercial was produced. Sometime later, we discovered it was about five seconds too long. In order to meet the time requirements for a network insert, the tape was speeded up and sounded a little like Donald Duck. We tried to get Mr. Lollis to come to the station to redo it but he was too busy politicking. When the commercial was aired on all the Greenville stations it sounded just like ole Donald Duck, which, by the way, was playing in a lot of the theatres at the time. Mr. Lollis polled enough votes in the three-man race to get into a run-off election. When we met to make plans for the second race, I suggested that we redo the commercial. The future judge wouldn't hear of it. He said people were teasing him saying he sounded like Donald Duck. Harold "Mule" Lollis WAS elected and served the people of Greenville as a summary judge until his retirement. He died in 2000.

In 1970, the Greenville Junior Chamber of Commerce decided to discontinue sponsoring the annual Christmas parade. Their reason for doing so was that the Downtown Merchants wanted to move the parade to Sunday afternoon but some ministers objected. I lambasted the idea: "What? No parade in Greenville? The most progressive city in the state and we don't have a Christmas parade? Would Santa Claus come to see our kids? Poor kids!! No Santa Claus!" Instantly, the phones started ringing. WESC listeners demanded WESC sponsor the parade and insisted that I lead an independent campaign to stage it. Mayor Max Heller gave it a name. He called it "The People's Parade."

Greenville responded in a remarkable way. Mayor Heller, the Clemson University ROTC, the Hejaz Temple, about 17 high school bands, church youth groups and hundreds of interested citizens pitched in to stage the "People's Parade" held on a Saturday morning. The *Greenville News* reported a crowd of 90,000 attended. The parade was taped for television and shown on WGGS TV Channel 16. We appreciated the strong support of Channel 16 President Jimmy Thompson. That station was rapidly growing by identifying an audience and serving it. The next year, 1971, the merchants took a more active role in staging the parade. WESC continued to support it but gave the leadership role back to the business community.

WESC involvement in the Christmas parades demonstrates how a station can listen to its listeners and accomplish big things with almost no budget. The project brought WESC newspaper exposure and coverage on the evening news programs on all the local TV stations. WE COULDN'T BUY THIS KIND OF ADVERTISING.

About 17 high school bands, from all over the upstate, came to Greenville to participate. We were especially indebted to Mr. Loy Wagoner, band director at Ware Shoals High School, who by the way had been my classmate at Furman, for enlisting and organizing the participation of the bands. The Burger King franchisee in Greenville, Mr. Lawrence G. Stokes, furnished food for the bands. Considering there may have been 1000 hungry people to feed, this was an important undertaking and a key to having the bands participate.

Several years later, I asked Mr. Stokes why he volunteered without solicitation to feed the bands. He said WESC was doing something for the community and he wanted to have a part in it. Mr. Stokes then told me WESC had successfully promoted his first restaurant. That Burger King was one of the first, if not the first Burger King Franchise in the nation. The original owner operated restaurants under another name in Miami, Fla. Mr. Stokes told me he suggested that the name "Burger King" be bought from an independent restaurant and used by the fledging chain.

Mr. Stokes' store was on Laurens Road near the Pleasantburg Shopping Center; he told me he opened the restaurant but nobody came. The franchise office of Burger King in Florida advised him to place a saturation radio spot campaign on the most popular radio station in town and circulate coupons within a two-mile radius of the restaurant. The message was "Buy one, get one free." He said he didn't know which station to use, so he asked some friends at the airport and they advised him to call me. The promotion was a huge success and it relieved all his fears concerning the success of his new enterprise. Mr. Stokes' son Larry is still active in community projects. Jacks Tingle, an "adopted son," became a franchisee and was a very successful businessman, continuing Mr. Stokes' attitude of community service.

The support we received from Shriners and Masons during the Christmas parade project encouraged several staff members to become Masons and Shriners. In those days Masons did not "rush" prospects but whenever a potential candidate asked a Mason about the organization, the questions were usually answered and a petition for membership forthcoming. WESC staff members who were Masons, some joining before they came to the station, included: Max Mace, Jerry Howard, George Clement, Ken Dockins, Gordon Anderson, Sterling Wright, Jim Brownell, Fred Nabors, Bob Hooper, Don Pearson, Earl Baughman and me. Most of us became Shriners and supported the work for the Shriners Hospital by advertising and participating in fund-raisers.

The WESC nobles were pleased when George Clement was elected Oriental Guide. I made his nomination speech at the annual meeting. His election to Oriental Guide almost assured us that one of our own would eventually be Potentate. George, however, had other ideas and to our disappointment left WESC before he became Potentate. George purchased WCCP AM in Clemson. He eventually received an FM grant and presumably has done well with a sports format.

Our participation in Masonic organizations was helpful to WESC because many Masons are country music and auto racing fans. It was a bond of friendship and helpful to all parties. I met many outstanding people as they progressed in Masonry. Two of them rose to the top of the class. G. Kent Elkins, who participated in my Blue Lodge degrees, rose to be Grand Master of Masons in South Carolina, and H. Wallace Reid, whom I met while "politickin'" for Dick Riley, had a distinguished career as Grand Master of Masons in South Carolina and later was the head of the Scottish Rite Masons in South Carolina. Brother Reid died in 2002.

WESC staff members were encouraged to join civic clubs and become active in the community. Here are some of the affiliations: Wayne Sumner represented WESC in the Pleasantburg Lions Club; Bob Hooper, a Wade Hampton-Taylors Jaycee and Crimestopper; John Davenport, a member of the Greenville Rotary Club; Bob Nations, a Civitan; Allan Jenkins, Advertising Federation; Wally Mullinax, Greenville Sales and Marketing Executives, the Waldon Blue Lodge, Scottish Rite and Shrine; and Van McClenaghan, Sertoma. Through the years, WESC was represented in the Greenville Jaycees, the Touchdown Club, the Greenville Country Club and the Poinsett Club. Staff members held memberships in the Pebble Creek Country Club, the Hejaz Recreation Club, the Green Valley Country Club, and the Botany Woods Golf and Tennis Club.

WESC also supported the National Association of Broadcasters, the South Carolina Broadcasters Association, the Society of Broadcast Engineers, the Greenville Chamber of Commerce and the Downtown Greenville Association. During some of those years, depending on the level of activity, the station supported the Daytime Broadcasters Association and the FM Radio Association. Some big radio corporations may feel that having their staff involved in the community is a waste of time, but believe me, it pays to build community relationships. Then the huff and puff from the big bad wolf doesn't blow your house down.

We encouraged the staff to participate in **one** service organization and to be active in the church of their choice. We warned them to keep a healthy balance between their responsibilities at the radio station and all outside affiliations.

As the sizzling '60s closed and WESC rolled into the '70s, the people loved WESC and WESC loved serving them. Ratings were good and business boomed! Americans believed the prosperity would last forever but they soon got an oil shock.

Chapter 14

Another Idea:
Change the Show

In 1974, the nation's economy almost collapsed! That's how South Carolina Congressman Butler Derrick described it. OPEC, the cartel controlling oil prices, caused the price of fuel to skyrocket. Many small businesses closed, lots of people lost their jobs and the ripple effect hit their cars and homes. When the people were forced to reduce their standard of living, entertainment was the first to go. A spring country music show drew only a few hundred people. One artist on that show — I believe it was Carl Smith — told of driving up I-95 from Florida and seeing just a few cars and trucks on the road. Motorists waited in lines for hours to get a few gallons of gas, and according to audience surveys fewer radios were tuned to WESC. Perhaps they were listening to news stations for word about the economy or obsessed with President Nixon's Watergate quagmire or maybe they were tired of the whole stinking mess and turned their radios off — but for whatever reason, WESC listening declined. The gurus called it a "cyclical decline."

This dip in audience along with the crisis in the economy caused revenues at WESC to tumble! In the radio business a decline in ratings and a drop in sales is double jeopardy. It was time for change. Bob Hooper was moved into the morning time slot and I was named general sales manager. My mandate was to hire more sales people and get the sales up. Dale Gilbert, who at the time of this writing is a meteorologist at WYFF Channel 4, was hired as program director. In an effort to broaden the WESC customer base, WESC FM programmed an oldies format called **The Great Ones** twenty-four hours a day.

"Greenville is growing and Greenville is fair...there's room for more stations to come on the air."

In August 1975, WQOK (1440 KC) made Bob Nations the offer he "couldn't refuse." Bob had developed a large customer base at WESC and produced a lot of business. To say that I was devastated would be an understatement. Bob took a week's vacation to "think it over" after telling us about the possibility of his leaving. During that week, I thought about a future without Bob Nations and decided that although we would be inconvenienced, WESC would survive without him. After all, it was the radio station that was producing sales results for the clients. I figured if we distributed his accounts to the other salesmen and hit the streets running before he got to the accounts to tell them about a change, we should be OK.

It worked! The pruning made the sales staff healthier. I asked them to work a little harder; they did so, and with the addition of Johnny Salter, former general manager of WEAB (800 KC), sales increased! Perhaps the sales increases came from a combination of a fresh morning personality, the economic recovery, a resolution of Watergate and hard work, but for whatever reason, advertising revenues started a 12 year climb.

In a few years Bob Nations left WQOK radio (1440 KC) to organize his own company, purchasing WAIM AM/TV and WCAC FM in Anderson, S.C., stations that were owned by Anderson newspaper publisher Wilton E. Hall and managed by Betty K. Black.

I recommended Bob as a prospective buyer for these stations to a representative who was quietly working with Mr. Hall to find a purchaser. Bob Nations and his associates improved the radio stations and sold the TV station, Channel 40, for more than enough money to pay for the radio stations. Mr. Nations changed the programming of WAIM AM to all country and cancelled the CBS contract. I thought it was a great compliment because WAIM had been on the air since 1935 and was South Carolina's first CBS station. I couldn't believe that we had introduced a format into the market that caused such a great change in such a pioneer station. *Dan the Melody Man* on WAIM (1230 KC) had supplied all the Hit Parade songs of the big band era for my high school generation and the Clemson Cadets in the late '30s and early '40s. And the western part of South Carolina listened as the CBS news teams trotted the globe to report the war. It was unbelievable! WESC and country music had forced a dramatic change in a truly great pioneer CBS station. The FM station (WCAC 101.1 FM) became WCKN-Rock 101, and was operated from Anderson under Nations' management. When the FCC rules permitted, Rock 101 was sold and the call letters changed to WROQ-Rock 101. The new owners moved it to Greenville.

I appreciated the good job Bob Nations did for WESC. His strong sales support certainly contributed to the early success of full-time country music programming in Greenville. In addition to his sales ability, Bob Nations also recommended that we hire Allan Jenkins as a sales rep. Suggesting Allan Jenkins as a potential salesman may have been Bob Nations' greatest legacy for WESC because Allan Jenkins contributed to the company for over 30 years.

A Greenville native, Allan Jenkins had a lot of retail contacts. He also represented WESC in the Greenville Advertising Federation, where he made a lot of friends for the station. His work in the GAF prepared him for positions on the regional and national boards of that trade group. Among the awards earned by Jenkins were the Silver Medal Award from the Greenville Advertising Federation and the Legion of Excellence from the 3rd district of AAF. The Legion of Excellence award reflects the confidence the advertising community places in Allan Jenkins. Only four people received that honor before Jenkins. Allan Jenkins avoided the limelight but he was a real unsung hero in WESC's rise to prominence among the nation's great radio stations. I am proud of Allan and glad to have had a part in bringing him into the advertising business. We all benefited from his service.

Another standout — among a staff of outstanding people, was Nancy Teague, who came to WESC in 1964 from WFBC. Nancy's creative ability, her organizational skills and downright hard work helped WESC sales reps to please their clients and increase budgets. Nancy Teague was WESC's secret weapon. One observer said of Nancy Teague, "If I wanted to dismantle WESC, I would start with Nancy Teague."

What Nancy Teague provided in copy skills, Judy Camp matched in people skills and patience. As bookkeeper Judy Camp was responsible for billing, recording payments and general bookkeeping procedures. She did it with efficiency and grace, even when the customer "didn't receive the bill" or "the check was in the mail" but never received, or as one advertiser explained, he had sent his secretary to the station with the cash but she must have gotten lost. Judy kept a straight face, empathized and did not laugh even when she **knew** some of the excuses to be just plain lies.

Some of the WESC staff dreamed of a beautiful studio building on the transmitter property on White Horse Road at Farr's Bridge Road. We envisioned white columns on a two story colonial building. That dream would have been a nightmare! In January 1974, the Greenville Fire Department used about 3 million gallons of water to extinguish a blaze on the third floor of the Prevost building. The WESC studios, located in the basement, were flooded.

The next day, John Davenport waded in water up to his waist to retrieve the financial records and collect enough music to keep going. I broadcast the morning show from a remote unit at the transmitter on White Horse Road. While the copy files were being reconstructed, all the commercials were ad-libbed. Later, WESC staff members fished out most of the phonograph records, cleaned them up, and adjusted to change. My explanation of the next few weeks was: the boat capsized, we swam through a swift river to the first rock, then another and another until we reached the shore.

We lost all the photographs taken at the Country Music Shindigs. They were action shots from the stage and backstage of WESC D.J.'s and almost all of the stars appearing in the shows. I have tried to locate the professional journalist who made those pictures, without success. His name was Alan D. Whitman. Alan came to the shows, made the pictures, and delivered them to us at the next show without charge. In return he was able to shoot pictures of the stars hoping to get the **one shot** the artist would pay big bucks to get. The only information I have on Alan is that he was from Spartanburg and as I recall he graduated from the University of Georgia. I have checked with UGA and followed up on the leads they gave me without success. Perhaps my readers will help me locate him. A selected number of these pictures appear in Part III.

213

In Part III you will find pictures made by Joe Jordon, Henry Elrod, Bill Cox and other professional photographers. Most of these pictures are deposited in the SCBA archives at the University of South Carolina; however, some are from private collections.

A day or so after the fire WESC began construction of temporary studios in the Berea Shopping Center. The 18 months spent three miles west of town — while Greenville was booming on the east side of town — showed us we needed a central downtown location. So, WESC purchased a building at 223 West Stone Avenue, added several rooms and in August 1975 moved in. Gone was the dream of a Southern colonial mansion with the white columns.

The entire staff adjusted quickly to the change of the studio site. Don Gowens, Palmer Greer and their assistant engineers put together the temporary studios in Berea and also new studios on Stone Avenue, in record time. The manufacturers were very cooperative to help us recover from the fire. They delivered equipment soon after WESC purchased it, probably pulling gear off their production lines intended for somebody else, to meet WESC's emergency. This was a testimony to their respect for Palmer Greer and WESC's reputation for paying bills promptly. There was a lesson in this experience: personal relationships and a good credit rating solve problems.

The WESC staff had a new look when it moved back to town. John Davenport was named president and general manager of the Broadcasting Company of the Carolinas; I was named general sales manager with a mandate to build a larger sales staff. Johnny Salter and Tom Bright joined the staff to help beef up sales. The nation was recovering from the 1974 recession and our priority was increasing revenues. Bob Hooper gave the morning show a new sound. More music, less talk, no controversy! He used contacts developed during

Shindig days to get interviews with stars and acquire concert participation. Hooper handled hundreds of requests from WESC advertisers and cemented relations with them. Bob Hooper spent his waking hours serving WESC listeners. His big promotion was the annual "War on Cancer." Eventually, the TV stations and newspapers took up the cause. The focus of the campaign was an all-out war to defeat cancer. Bob raised about a million dollars during six "War on Cancer" campaigns. That is a record that may never be broken!

Radio stations today do not normally pre-empt sold out programs to wage an "all-out" public service campaign. WESC did it from its earliest days in the 1940's with radiothons for the March of Dimes, again in the '60s for the National Foundation's educational effort on birth defects, in the '70s for Technical Education Days, in the 1980's for the War on Cancer and many more. It's impossible to put a price tag on the public service projects in which WESC invested time and financial resources. The station could afford to do it because it was family owned, financially successful and committed to public service. Thousands of citizens joined the WESC public service campaigns, the most successful of which was Hooper's Army to fight cancer. At the risk of offending those who contributed many hours to this cause, four people need to be mentioned: Willis Smith, Tony Austin, Larry Jones and David Robinson. These guys spent weeks fighting cancer. Smith and Austin worked the mikes and phones with Bob while Jones secured prizes and Robinson enlisted the National Guard. Bob Hooper created "radio personalities" out of these volunteers, making them a part of his show.

Almost always when the War on Cancer took WESC to a remote broadcast that might potentially cause a traffic hazard, Greenville policeman "Fuzz" Reese would show up to direct traffic. Reese stood at intersections whirling his arms like a windmill and pointing his white gloved hands and fingers like a weather vane. Brother Reese must have been the city's good will ambassador for media events because he could be seen just about anywhere, anytime, if his services were needed. I'm sure he contributed greatly to the success of Hooper's War on Cancer because the people loved his street show.

Hooper was perhaps the only radio personality in Greenville who could announce a citizen's name on the air as not having given to the cause, and not get sued. Usually these not so subtle solicitations resulted in $100 donations. Such a fund-raising tactic for the "War on Cancer" got Bob in hot water, at least once. The offended businessman threatened to sue! It took some "fast talking" by WESC salesman Steve Brown to soothe the hurt feelings. To this day nobody has thought to ask if Bob got the $100 from the guy. Bob Hooper has received the Richard G. Shafto Award from the University of South Carolina College of Journalism and the SCBA Life Membership Award for his public service and industry achievements.

In 1975, WESC FM programmed **The Great Ones**, a Peters Production. In doing so, it strayed from the programming that was successful. It moved away from the image embraced by the public. Some of the same mistakes of 1950 and 1962 were repeated. After a few weeks, it was obvious the **Great Ones** were not so greatly received in Greenville. I called Bob Schmid in New York and reported to him that I was getting complaints from listeners who missed the nighttime country music service. To his credit he immediately had it changed.

By the way, even though he always solicited my input, I did not discuss the operation of WESC with Bob Schmid after we recovered from the 1962-'63 fiasco; however, I broke this self-imposed silence twice. That was when **The Great Ones** replaced country music on FM in 1975 and when the Washington Avenue Baptist Church service was taken off the air in the '80s. Since John Davenport was general manager of the station, I thought Mr. Schmid should speak through him in operating the station and we should communicate with Mr. Schmid through John.

I don't know why we took the detour with **The Great Ones**. Perhaps other stations were having a lot of success splitting FM and attracting another audience. Possibly **The Great Ones** were successful in other markets, or maybe some consultant advised the change. For whatever the reason, it was wrong for WESC FM and I applauded Schmid for promptly correcting the mistake. After **The Great Ones** episode, WESC and WESC FM began simulcasting country music programs. This proved to be a good move because it provided country music service on both AM and FM. The ratings bounced back.

"Greenville is growing and Greenville is fair...There's room for more stations to come on the air."

In 1976, WESC FM rejoined the University of South Carolina Gamecock Network. Bob Fulton, Tommy Suggs and Don Williams were the sportscasters for the Gamecock Network. The winning tradition of Head Football Coach Jim Carlen, Head Basketball Coach Frank McGuire, the loyalty of the Carolina fans, the popularity of the sportscasters and the network quality made the Gamecocks especially attractive to advertisers. I was really proud of our station and its staff when I attended my first Gamecock affiliates meeting at the roundhouse in 1976. Coach Carlen introduced me to the group and said that WESC FM was the network's newest affiliate; he said he listened to the station when he was in the upstate and he wanted the entire network to sound like WESC. He never explained why he liked WESC; however, I took it to mean he liked country music.

217

The winning of the Heisman Trophy by running back George Rogers brought some attention to WESC from outside the United States. After Mr. Rogers was announced as the winner of the Heisman, we had a phone call from a news outlet in Australia wanting information to write a story for their paper. I referred the caller to the proper person at the university.

The time buyers accepted the Gamecock broadcasts as a plus for the station. The 100,000 watts power, a state university, the name recognition of Carlen and McGuire, the reputation of Bob Fulton, Tommy Suggs' knowledge of the game and the professionalism of Don Williams combined to make South Carolina Sports an attractive advertising package for WESC.

Eventually Don Williams was replaced on the sidelines by former Gamecock quarterback Todd Ellis and upon the retirement of Bob Fulton, Charlie Mac Alexander was named the Gamecock play-by-play announcer. WESC enjoyed a pleasant relationship with the University of South Carolina Athletic Department during the years I represented the station. I negotiated the network contracts and followed up to see that all parties fulfilled the agreement. As vice president of sales, I planned the sale of WESC's local commercials on the broadcasts and the promotion of the games. We used two main sources for promoting the games.

We ran a lot of WESC promotion spots and a "game day" ad on the sports page of the **GREENVILLE NEWS.** Sometimes we purchased ads in the **Independent-Mail** in Anderson and **Spartanburg Herald.** However, our experience taught us that people listened to their local station if it carried the game. If my readers want to make a note of what I consider to be very important in the promotion of any sports event, write on your daily reminder: **Game day ad on** the sports page of the local daily newspaper and have all the station D.J.'s plug game. Talk about the game, and get involved. Treat the sports event like a country music event. Now, if you sell more advertising on your sports event, send me a check. By the way, you newspaper guys can help me sell a book for that plug.

I found the University of South Carolina to be loyal to their stations and very cooperative when called upon to provide extra services for our advertisers. Three network executives were very helpful: Clark Newsome and Don Williams with the South Carolina Network and Liz McMillan with Host Communications. During some of the years in the '70s the Gamecocks were networked by WIS radio (560 KC) in Columbia. Their quality and service was always excellent. I would recommend that any station in South Carolina looking for a sports package give the USC network a call. They run a first class operation.

We kept a contest going among WESC sales reps to boost sales. Usually we gave cash to the winners. We ran small contests for a week or two in length to boost whatever we wanted to push. Contest goals were new contacts, collections, calling on old accounts that may have stopped advertising or selling some special promotion — these sorts of things. We awarded the money in sales meetings to excite the troops.

In 1981, we decided to do a contest for the entire year. The goal was to sell a million dollars of local advertising. WESC sales representatives who reached their goal would receive a trip, along with their wives, to Hawaii when the Gamecocks played the University of Hawaii in December 1981. The winners also received spending money for the trip. If you think we were just being generous by including the wives, you are wrong! Wives were included so they would cheer, nag or whatever to get their guy to meet his goal. The goal of a million dollars in local sales was reached! Steve and Mary Ella Brown, George and Faye Clement, and Helen and I went to Hawaii for the game. We observed the 40th anniversary of the Japanese attack on Pearl Harbor and spent 10 days seeing the sights on the island of Oahu and the big island of Hawaii. Wayne Sumner also won the trip but he and Nancy Sumner elected to go at a later time with their family.

"Greenville is growing and Greenville is fair...There's room for more stations to come on the air."

I'll always remember the trip to Hawaii. It was satisfying to achieve the sales goal by selling a million dollars in local advertising for the first time. We enjoyed the game with friends from South Carolina, it was a delight to visit what was then the largest shopping center in the world at Christmas time, but the most moving experience was being at Pearl Harbor at 8 O'CLOCK on the morning of December 7, 1981 — exactly forty years after the Japanese sneak attack. I'll never forget the pride I felt watching the American flag fluttering victoriously in the wind at Pearl Harbor. There were hundreds at Pearl Harbor and later at the Punch Bowl Cemetery honoring their dead at this special time. I will always remember seeing them throw flowers into the harbor as oil seeped from the watery graves at the Arizona Memorial, and later the people of all faiths praying at the Punch Bowl Cemetery. It was a touching reminder of the price of freedom. **Remember Pearl Harbor** was a cry for **WAR.** The memory of the suffering — by people on both sides of that war — should remind us to keep the peace.

Chapter 15

A Nonstop Idea

In the late '70s, I received a phone call from a program salesman who outlined a new country format that was enjoying success in some markets across the country: "Twelve in a Row," a syndicated service. After hearing the salesman's telephone pitch, I declined to give him an appointment, explaining that WESC was built on public service, produced its own programs and served local needs with local D.J.'s. The salesman completed the call with the threat that if WESC did not buy the "Twelve in a Row" service he would put another country music station in Greenville. At that time WESC was the only country station in the upstate. I considered his comment just a business bluff and dismissed the remark as poor manners from an obnoxious salesman; however, in a few months Greenville had its second country music station, WSSL-100.5. As it turned out it would have been a smart move to have bought the service and "put it on the shelf."

"Greenville is growing and Greenville is fair...There's room for more stations to come on the air."

Bob Schmid loved it! He was almost overcome with joy. The thrill of competition charged his batteries! He vowed to outspend, outpromote and outperform the new kid on the block, WSSL. WESC began offering listeners hundreds of thousands of dollars IF they had the right birth date. Imagine, free money by reason of birth. Country was king and the listeners were to get the spoils of the radio wars. General manager John Davenport joined in "The Giveaway Spirit." Actually, Davenport and Schmid had a contest between them. The sales department jokingly called it "The Great Money Giveaway." Or, how much money can we give away today? If you are now working for a large group and agonizing over sales and expenses, close your eyes and dream about a time when promotions were planned with almost no restraints.

John Davenport, who always had an open door policy, might call a meeting of whoever was available at the time to plan a promotion. He might open with the question "How much shall we give away this time?" He usually answered his own question with $50,000 or $100,000. "How shall we promote it?" Again he answered with saturation TV, a 100% billboard showing, direct mail and perhaps a supporting country show. That was it! Conference completed. If you hung around to discuss it, you might sit through a morning or afternoon of telephone calls because John loved to chit-chat on the phone while staff members waited in his office to complete a conference. I don't mean to imply the ideas of others were not solicited or heard. They were! However, we didn't have to go before a super committee or wait for corporate to give its approval. Meetings were not all day, every day occurrences. Nor were they placed in an appointment book. We just did it. It's said of Abraham Lincoln that he detested generals who made plans and asked his permission to carry them out. He loved General Grant's way of waging war. Just do it! Then tell him.

That was mostly the Schmid/Davenport management style.

Although WESC was presenting most of the country acts that came to town and Bob Hooper was handing out donuts to the crowds that waited in line all night for tickets at the auditorium, when WSSL became a competitive factor, we decided to return to the Shindig concept and book our own shows. This helped to establish a close relationship with the fans and the artists. We called these concerts the **WESC Family Reunion**. Program Director Allen Power and Glenn Reeves of Jacksonville, Florida, worked together to book the talent, stage the shows and attend to the details. Our sales department packaged the program advertising and tickets, selling them to area businesses.

Most of the WESC staff turned out on show day, usually at Greenville Municipal baseball stadium, to greet the fans and give them a **Family Reunion** program book. The WESC D.J.'s appeared on stage and introduced the acts. It worked! WESC stayed at the top of the ratings. This was an expensive, time-consuming promotion that proved once again that country music fans want to see their favorite D.J.'s on stage with the artists. The fans also appreciate a handshake from the D.J.'s and an autograph from the stars. After these shows Bob Hooper shook every hand and the stars signed autographs 'til everybody was gone. If you are taking notes, have an understanding when you contract for a show that the performer will sign autographs.

Why are the shows important? As we have said, radio is a theatre of the mind; listeners have a mental image of the people they hear on the radio and want to see them. The listeners want to talk with their favorite D.J.

223

D.J.'s must get out among the people and artists must sign autographs! It takes promotion minded management to understand this. The most successful country music program on radio is the **Grand Ole Opry** on WSM (650 KC) in Nashville, Tennessee. One of the strengths of the show is the tie-in between the radio station, the stars and the audience. They complement each other.

In the '70s, Doris Turner left the bookkeeping spot and Gladys Taylor returned to keep tabs on the money. Evelyn Roper, who had replaced Edna Taylor as secretary, left the station while it was located in the Berea Plaza. Millard Adams, a newsman returned from the Vietnam War, worked for a while as a WESC newsperson, then departed for Milton, Florida, where he purchased a station, ran for county council and eventually devoted full time to politics. Paul Brown served as a WESC newsman for a few months before leaving to freelance TV news in Anderson County. Paul Brown also continued to be WESC's reporter in Anderson and is one of the reasons WESC was so popular in Anderson County.

On November 6, 1977, 176 million gallons of water swept through the campus at Toccoa Falls College, Toccoa Falls, Georgia, when an earthen dam above the campus broke. WESC's Paul Brown, an alumnus of the school, was the first news reporter on the scene. For the next 36 hours Paul provided WESC — and numerous other news outlets — coverage of this tragedy that claimed 33 lives and caused **America** to grieve for them.

You can read about it in **Dam Break in Georgia** by K. Neill Foster with Eric Mills, published by Horizon House Publishers of Camp Hill, Pennsylvania.

True to its tradition WESC kept its listeners informed but it didn't stop with reporting the news. In the true Davenport tradition, WESC did something about it. Bob Hooper and the rest of the WESC crew raised tens of thousands of dollars, as did other media outlets, supporting a drive to soften this awful blow to the small northeast Georgia Christian school.

WESC had some other good reporters in the '70s and '80s. Bob Rightsell, a product of the USC College of Journalism, served as a newsman before leaving to join the news team at WIS AM (560 KC) in Columbia. Lowell Fletcher, who had earned a good reputation as a news anchor at WSPA TV Channel 7 and WLOS TV Channel 13, came over to do news and manage the FM station's daytime automation programming. Soon Mr. Fletcher entered the real estate field in Easley, S.C. Beth Kelly served as a newsperson for a time before taking a position with the South Carolina Network in Columbia. Beth eventually married Jack Jones, a reporter with the S.C. Network. At this writing, Beth is director of South Carolina Radio for the Blind, a part of the South Carolina Commission for the Blind, and Jack is running the AP bureau in Columbia.

Allen Bookout came aboard as news director when Beth left and quickly established himself as a key man with the **Bob Hooper Show**. Mr. Bookout was a seasoned newsman who also had a flair for public service, promotion and comedy. A graduate of the University of North Carolina School of Mass Communications, Allen Bookout wrote and voiced a newscast that in the words of Ben Avery, the Associated Press vice president at the time, sounded like radio news should sound. Some broadcasters have that gift. They can make a radio newscast sound the way listeners **think** it should sound. In my opinion, Allen Bookout's departure loosened the grip Bob Hooper had on the upstate morning audience but the change did not become evident for several years. Bookout retired as news director of WSSL (100.5 FM).

When Bookout left WESC his assistant, Kim Deal, a USC College of Journalism grad, moved into the news desk. Kim

225

had good writing and reporting skills and soon attracted the attention of Channel 4 News. Kim accepted a job as assignments editor at WYFF. Upon the departure of Kim Deal, Roger Davis returned to WESC. This is the same Roger Davis who left WESC in the early '60s for an opportunity to do TV news in Atlanta. Mr. Davis' career path took him into Georgia politics. Jody Powell, whom the reader will remember as President Jimmy Carter's press secretary, for a time was Roger's boss in Georgia.

While on the subject of names it should not be overlooked that WESC affiliated with the ABC Radio Network to get the Paul Harvey news programs in the late '60s or early '70s and this became a magnet to attract listeners. Also ABC paid WESC a tidy sum to air its news. Now you know the rest of the story.

Chapter 16

Ideas Refined and Executed

Connie Glennon served as the executives' secretary and later as promotions director before establishing her own firm. Becky Clement replaced Ms. Glennon. Ms. Clement remained until the early '90s. In every organization some of the unsung heroes are the secretaries who administer a thousand details while the boss is doing whatever bosses do. Four were standouts at WESC: Edna Taylor, Evelyn Roper, Connie Glennon and Becky Clement. Edna Taylor held the position when John Davenport was president of the South Carolina Broadcasters Association and I was president of the Greenville Sales and Marketing Association. Mrs. Taylor's support was very helpful in the 1964 March of Dimes campaign for which WESC won the S.C. School Bell Award. Edna Taylor made us a better radio station. Ms. Taylor is now deceased.

Evelyn Roper was secretary while WESC was recovering from the fire. Mrs. Roper supported the Christmas parade effort and a public service campaign for the Boys Home of the South, which won for WESC and me the prestigious G. Richard Shafto Award from the College of Journalism at the University of South Carolina. When I ran my race for public office it was almost impossible to get elected without the support of Piedmont, S.C. Since Evelyn was the queen of Piedmont she lined me up with the powers of Piedmont, Shorty Smith and M.J. "Dolly" Cooper. They made Piedmont "Wally Country."

Connie Glennon brought to the executive secretary's desk her valuable promotional skills. Her ability to take the thoughts of "ordinary folks" and turn out extraordinary sales letters and proposals helped WESC climb to the top. Connie Glennon would be a great asset on any station's management team. If there's anyone out there looking for promotional or PR help, CONNIE IS A PRO. However, I'm sorry to say she will not have her favorite typewriter; it was scrapped after John's retirement.

Becky Clements' ability to write legible letters from quickly scribbled notes helped us stay on top. All of our secretaries were loyal and efficient. We are indebted to them for their good work.

In 1987, the exciting career of Robert A. Schmid came to an end. Gone were the infectious laugh, the deep voice, and the blue eyes that sparkled with excitement about a coming radio battle. His enthusiastic spirit vanished into eternity! Bob Schmid's goals were met. His victory won!

Robert A. Schmid provided the leadership to move WESC from a 5000-watt daytime station with an FM antenna on top of the AM tower, to a full power FM station with a mountaintop antenna. WESC AM was developed to its maximum under the rules of the 1980's — 50,000 watts daytime. Schmid took a good local station with limited advertiser acceptance and moved it to a nationally recognized primary radio buy. WESC documented its audience in the hundreds of thousands. Bob Schmid identified his goal, dreamed the dream and supported his staff to make it happen. His daughter, Heidi, succeeded him as chairperson.

In the Heidi Schmid Powers administration, the station was operated as in the past. John Davenport continued as president and general manager. Heidi Schmid Powers provided creative leadership. Audience ratings soared, business boomed and as the '80s came to a close, WESC AM/FM enjoyed billings in the millions of dollars. Public acceptance was at an all time high. In spite of a downturn in business during the 1989 recession, WESC was still enjoying substantial profits and its #1 position.

Chapter 17

An Old Idea: Public Service

Public service was an important factor in the development of WESC. What is public service? Is it a newscast in which the station informs the public about imminent bad weather? A commercial telling a family living on a tight budget where they can save some money? Or should public service be confined to material broadcast without charge to benefit a nonprofit organization? I submit that public service is all of the above and lots more.

One of the most effective public service efforts for WESC was to air school, industry and business closings during snow days. All WESC personnel were required to be available to work the phones during weather emergencies: gathering information, airing the special announcements, changing commercial copy, selling special weather related promotions and whatever else was needed to serve WESC listeners and sponsors during ice and snow storms. New hires were informed when they joined the company that WESC was a service organization and they were expected to contribute.

Bob Hooper jokingly tells about the first upstate snow after he came aboard. It was perhaps January 1965; Greenville woke up with several inches of snow on the ground and Bob called the station to inform us that he couldn't get out of his driveway. He says my comment was "Where are you going to work tomorrow?" Bob walked in the front door in about an hour. This was what I was told the first winter after I went to work for WFBC. My boss was Hubert Brown, the guy who gave me my first job in radio. When I called in with the excuse that I was visiting my grandmother, who lived near Norris, South Carolina, about 30 miles from Greenville, and couldn't get back to work, Hubert said the buses and trains were operating and I was expected to come to work — on time.

WESC opened some new accounts because we were available to give customers service during snow days. So, it's a good idea to work when you can be of service to the public. If you give more service than you're getting paid for, soon you'll get more pay than for which you give service.

WESC tied public service into special events. A project started in the late '80s: a golf tournament for North Greenville College. WESC's golf pro in residence, Wayne Sumner, teamed up with a strong committee of businessmen and the North Greenville College Director of Development, Mike Carlton, to stage what has become an annual spring event. At the time of this writing about a million dollars has been raised in these tournaments. Larry Stokes has chaired the committee from its beginning. Jacks Tingle, John Gregory, Judy Shirley, Roy Dooley, Dan Bowling, Jim Snyder, Rick Snyder, Dean Anderson, Bill Wheless, myself and other friends of the college worked together to establish the event. Through the years faces have changed but other people have stepped up to continue working for this good cause. Many Greenville businesses support North Greenville College in numerous ways to make the NGC golf tournament a success.

In the early '90s, WESC learned that bluegrass artist Charlie Moore was buried in an unmarked grave in Greenville Memorial Gardens on Augusta Road near Moonville. Led by bluegrass musician Carl Story, who was airing his weekly show on WESC, and with the help of morning personality Bob Hooper, we persuaded WESC listeners to give enough money to install a grave marker reflecting Charlie Moore's stature as a bluegrass music star. Country musician Ernest Harvey donated the use of his Powdersville Opry House for the fund-raiser; the Bluegrass Express and many other bluegrass musicians donated their time. This project was a reflection of the "family spirit" prevailing among country music listeners, musicians and D.J.'s. All of us felt obligated to mark Charlie Moore's grave appropriately.

Guess who is a former member of the Ernest Harvey Band? Our good ole buddy Billy Rainey of WGGS-TV Channel 16 in Greenville. Billy Rainey has a popular program, **Down Home Gospel,** which is shown on Channel 16 Saturday nights at 8:30. Tune him in and hopefully he will tell his viewers to buy this book.

Chapter 18

A Revolting Idea

The first of June 1990, General Manager John Davenport surprised the staff by announcing his retirement. I don't know if Heidi Schmid Powers was informed earlier but he didn't give the staff much notice. The resignation was effective at the end of June, 1990. This should not have been a surprise to us because Davenport always said he would retire at age sixty-five. I guess the 1989 recession and the added workload of the "sale that failed" must have reaffirmed his resolve to enjoy his remaining years. It proved to be a good decision because John Davenport died in 1998.

John Davenport was an organized, intelligent, articulate and shrewd executive. He had the ability to work through others to accomplish the company objectives that were defined by President Bob Schmid and his advisors. Mr. Davenport was very skillful at "fine tuning" ideas proposed by the staff, and supervised their successful execution. A man of patience, empathy and people skills, John Davenport left some big shoes to fill and Program Director Allen Power, whom John had been grooming for the general manager's post, vowed to fill them. Many saw Allen Power as a carbon copy of John Davenport and predicted that he would take WESC into the next millenium with insight and vigor. Unfortunately, the consolidations occurring in the industry would prohibit Allen from fulfilling that prophecy. After a few years at the helm he left WESC to manage a group of religious stations in Atlanta.

John Davenport served the South Carolina Broadcasters Association as its president in 1965. He was inducted into the South Carolina Broadcasters Hall of Fame in 1983. He was also the recipient of the Greenville Chamber of Commerce Small Businessman of the Year award and many other honors. Active in the Greenville Little Theater and the Anderson Theater, John Davenport won many awards for his acting and support of the arts. He served on the South Carolina Arts Commission. Although a modest man Davenport was very proud to have played opposite actress Joanne Woodward in a Greenville Little Theatre production of **The Glass Menagerie**.

Davenport loved a practical joke. One still lives. April Fool's day 1970 — while I was recovering from an illness that had kept me from work for three months, he had me do a telephone report announcing to the world that WESC would switch its programming to rock and roll the next morning at 6:00 o'clock. To make it convincing I denounced Country Music programming as a curse on the universe and praised rock and roll as the salvation of radio. They say the phones went wild; some people came to the station to protest. The Reverend Bill Bryant — who at this writing is a Chaplain at Perry Correctional Institute in South Greenville County, remembers that he was very upset. He went to the radio station to give me a piece of his mind. Lucky for me, I was not there.

After John Davenport's retirement, the WESC management team consisted of: Heidi Schmid Powers, president and CEO; Allen Power, general manager; Wally Mullinax, vice president of sales; and Jeff Blake, program director.

Among those added to the sales staff in the period from 1976 to 1991 were: Johnny Salter, George Clement, Bobby Long, Jo Quinn Murphy, Jim Ball, Steve Brown, Tom Bright, Martha Malone, Sarah Jane Roddy, Van McClenaghan, Peggy Van Dyke and Myra Crocker. They were very good sales representatives. I'm pleased to have been associated with them and proud of their accomplishments. I hear that they are all doing well. One of my radio sales protégées, Steve Brown, is now a novelist and has published four books. Way to go, Steve! Remember your ole WESC buddies when you hit the jackpot.

In 1991, after passing my sixty-fourth birthday, I retired, ending a 42 year career with WESC. They say we humans are motivated by three basic desires: the desire for financial security, the desire for recognition and the desire to help others. If this is true, and it probably is, then my career at WESC was successful. The first desire: I was fortunate to have provided a good standard of living for my family, educating my children and preparing for retirement. The second desire: I was properly recognized for my efforts. Among my awards: I received the Silver Medal Award, the Greenville Advertising Federation highest honor; the Abe Lincoln Merit award, a national honor from the Southern Baptist Radio/TV Commission; and in 1990, I was inducted into the South Carolina Broadcasters Hall of Fame, the 14th broadcaster in the state to be so honored.

My years at WESC provided opportunities for service to others through the Greenville County Council, the Greenville Memorial Auditorium Board, the S.C. Aeronautics Commission and the Board of Trustees at North Greenville College. WESC supported me as president of the Greenville Sales and Marketing Association, Crimestoppers of Greenville and the South Carolina Broadcasters Association. The station supported me in other areas of service: the Overbrook Baptist Church of Greenville, the National Foundation for the March of Dimes, the Downtown Greenville Association, the Salvation Army and various other service organizations. Basically, I was told to go do the job.

When I said good-bye to 42 years with the company, WESC sponsored a breakfast honoring me at the 1991 summer meeting of the South Carolina Broadcasters Association at Myrtle Beach, S.C. In attendance were President Heidi Schmid Powers and her husband, Norman Powers; General Manager Allen Power and his wife, Susan Power; my wife, Helen; and many friends at SCBA. It was certainly a nice touch to close my career. I was grateful to the people who took time to come to Myrtle Beach for the occasion.

The history of WESC's next half century is being written every day in the hearts of its listeners. Perhaps one of these gifted individuals will record WESC's next fifty years.

Postscript

Soon after my retirement at WESC the stations were sold to Benchmark Broadcast Partners, of Baltimore, Maryland. Later, the station was sold to Capstar Communications and still later, to Clear Channel Communications, of Austin, Texas. When Clear Channel Communications purchased the SFX stations, WESC and WSSL were consolidated. By the time this book was ready for the printers, as I have said, Allen Power had departed, Allan Jenkins left to run his Altamont Advertising, Jim Ball had joined the WFBC/WSPA group, Bob Hooper was made sales manager of WESC, Wayne Sumner was still producing big bucks as a WESC senior account executive, John Landrum and Jerry Howard were still spinning records at the station, Don Gowens had retired, Ken Dockins had left the station. Craig Debolt, Judy Camp, Jim Neubau and Michael "Shot Gun" Hunt were assigned to WROQ/WPTP in a merger spin-off. Nancy Teague had retired. Finally, Perry Childers, a wonderful staff member who had supported all of us with friendship, words of encouragement and loyal service, had died. The studios on College Street and Stone Avenue were closed. Times do change.

At press time the community is remembering the life of veteran WFBC Radio, Television newsman and television executive Norvin C. Duncan, Jr. Although Norvin never worked at WESC, this radio legend had a profound influence on all of us who aspired to do news. Norvin Duncan was a true professional and good friend. We'll all miss him.

Part II

Who and Where

WESC staff 1947 to 1960 taken from station records obtained from the SCBA Archives at the University of South Carolina.

Name	Job Description	Year of Employment
Anderson, Willie Rachel	N/A	1954
Anderson, Julius C.	Janitor	1954-1956
Anderson, R. Gordon	Sales	1951-1952
Anderson, William Charles	N/A	1953
Ashley, Doris M.	CCA Director	1957-1959
Barnett, Ellen Guest	Copywriter	N/A
Barnett, Marion F.	N/A	N/A
Bennett, Margaret Ann	Secretary/Receptionist	1951-1955
Bryan, E.F. Sr.	N/A	1953
Brock, William	N/A	1956-57
Baehire, John C.	Transmitter Operator	1953
Brown, Irene	N/A	1952
Baldwin, Billy	Transmitter Operator	1951-52
Blankenship, Herbert E.	Announcer	1951
Bochman, William C.	Commercial Manager	1950
Bagwell, Fred Troy	Audio Control Operator	1947-1948
Bailey, Felton B.	Chief Transmitter Operator	1947-1953
Bell, Betty Lee	Music/Traffic	1947-1950
Black, John L.	N/A	1949
Blair, Edward Thayer	News/Announcer	1947-1948
Bowers, Clifford W.	Commercial Manager	1947-1950
Brownell, James L.	Announcer	1949
Byrd, Tom	N/A	1947
Battle, Bette	Women's Director	1951
Bollinger, Gene	Program Director	1951
Briers, Evalena	N/A	1951
Bray, W. Ennis	General Manager	1951-1952
Bump, L.E.	N/A	N/A
Bryan, E. Fred	Transmitter Operator	1951-1953
Bailey, Donald Lee	Copywriter/Announcer	1952-1954
Baughman, Earl T.	Country Music Personality	1953-1960's
Childress, Norma L.	N/A	N/A
Croft, John Morgan	Commercial Manager	1952-1953
Cole, Joe	Announcer	N/A
Carter, Hiram	Janitor	N/A
Clary, Ronald	Announcer	1949

Cline, Caldwell	Program Director	1947
Cowan, Charles	Transmitter Operator	1949
Cox, Dorothy	N/A	1948
Curtis, Peggy	General Office	1951
Cooley, Tamara Maxine	N/A	1954
Clements, Joseph C.	N/A	N/A
Devine, Robert John	Transmitter Operator	1958-1959
Danials, Charles M.	Janitor	1953
Davenport, James A.	Sales	1953
Dale, Harold B.	Announcer	1952
Davis, L. Wayne	News/Announcer/Program Director/Station Manager	1947-50 & 1953-57
Dick, Paul R.	Transmitter Operator	1947-1948
Dickerson, Jessie R.	Audio Control Operator	1949-1950
Duke, William G.	N/A	1947
Davenport, John Y.	Bookkeeper/Station Manager/ General Manager/VP/President	1950-1990
Dubose, Charlie	Sales	1954
Dixon, Harley	N/A	1954
Eckman, Dorthy C	N/A	N/A
Edge, Joseph	Country Music Personality	1955-1960's
Ethington, William George	N/A	1953
Edwards, James M.	N/A	1953
Estep, Willis H.	N/A	1952
Edwards, Robert W.	Audio Control Operator/ Country Music Personality	1948-1950
Elias, Lewis W. Jr.	Chief Transmitter Operator	1947-1950
Evans, John R.	N/A	1948
Fowler, Fredrick	N/A	1959
Fowler, Billie Ann	N/A	N/A
Fabbri, Sylvia	Bookkeeper	N/A
Ferguson, Julie	Copywriter	1951
Farkns, Joy Hamilton	N/A	1947
Fletcher, Charles W.	Janitor	1947
Fox, Vernon Thompson	Announcer/Musician	1948-1949
Freezor, Ann	N/A	N/A
Fuller, Milton	Janitor	N/A
Griggs, John	Janitor	1957-1959
Gordon, Ralph	Audio Control Operator/DJ	1957-1960's
Goldsmith, Fletcher W.	Janitor	1957
Garren, F.O.	Transmitter Operator	1951
Gettis, Ellen D.	Sales	1950
Green, Jack	Transmitter	1950
Garrett, Willie Clinton	Janitor	1949-1951

Griffith, Lawrence E.	N/A	1947
Goller, Harold P.	Audio Control Operator/Announcer	1947-1949
Gregory, William Dallis	Transmitter Operator	1947
Goodyear, Charles B.	Commercial Manager	1952-1953
George, Howard	N/A	1953
Green, Hillard	Janitor	1955
Goldsmith, Coax	Janitor	N/A
Huff, Carlisle T.	Sales	1959
Howard, M. Upsom	Transmitter Operator	N/A
Heatherly, Ken	Announcer	1947
Hammond, Josephine C.	N/A	N/A
Hamil, Alma	Women's Director/CCA Director	1955-1957
Haynes, O.P.	Transmitter Operator	1952-1953
Heard, James	N/A	1954
Hancock, Laverne H.	N/A	1954
Heckman, Fred	Announcer/News Announcer	1952-1953
Henderson, Jack	N/A	1953
Holford, Thomas Jr.	N/A	1952
Healy, Edwin P.	Transmitter Operator	1950-1951
Harwood, Chris	Morning Personality	1950
Harvey, Galen Miller	Entertainer/Musician	1948
Howard, Ben G.	Sales/Announcer	1947-1950
Hunt, Audry	Women's Director	1947-1948
Hutchenson, Sam	Salesman	1947-1948
Ivestor, Agnes F.	CCA Director	N/A
McIntruff, Ray E.	Transmitter Operator	1959
Ingram, John William	Sales Manager	1954-1959
Jackson, Paul	N/A	1956
Jenkins, Louis Byron	Announcer	N/A
Jarrett, Hugh	Announcer	1952
Jackson, Earl B.	N/A	N/A
Jervey, Mary Elizabeth	Copywriter	1948
Jordan, Joe	Free Lance News	N/A
Johnson, Rosemary	N/A	1947
James, Robert Preston	Sales Manager/Sales	1950-1951
Kennedy, Betty Sue	General Office	1955
Kreiger, Bernhard A.	Announcer/Program Director	1954-1957
Keese, Jacquelyn	Program Assistant	1947
Keese, Ken	Music Director/Announcer	1947
Kirkwood, Charles Edward	Transmitter Operator	1948-1951
Klosky, James A.	Sales	1948
Kirksey, Ruth	N/A	N/A
Kirksey, Marvin	N/A	N/A
Kirby, William H.	Sales	1957-1960's

Kuykendall, John Lewis	Sales	1958-1959
Lominick, Nancy Coyle	Bookkeeper	N/A
Lipscombe, Joan	Copywriter	N/A
Lewis, Eddie Jr.	N/A	1954
Little, James Bryson	Commercial Manager	1947
Mobley, Olive W.	Sales Secretary	1959
Meade, James G.	Sales Manager/General Manager	1953-1955
Marr, Joan Lipscombe	Sales	1957
Moore, Willie	Janitor	1951-1953
Moss, Dave	Program Director/Sports Announcer	1951-1953
Mullinax, Wallace A.	Announcer/Personality/Sales Manager/VP Sales	1949-1991
Moody, Francis LeRoy	Janitor	1951
Moore, Judson	Copywriter	1950-1951
Murphy, Joe	Sales	1951
Mack, George	N/A	1947-1948
Martin, Edward Lyle	Sales	1947-1950
Mathews, Paul F.	Transmitter Operator	1950
Moorehead, Doris	Copywriter	1949-1950
Mosley, Harmon Irving	Sales Promotion	1947
Morris, Horace Alexander	Transmitter Operator	1947-1948
Moeller, C.S.	Transmitter Operator	1952-1953
Meeks, Carl	N/A	N/A
Marquis, Dyrell J.E.	Announcer	1955
Moore, J.B.	N/A	1955
Russell-Meade, Christie K.	President/General Manager	1950-1957
Mace, Ernest Max	Announcer/DJ	1959-1960
McMannis, Sylvia	Copywriter	1955
McGuire, Ben F.	Copywriter	1955-1959
McGuire, Betty Jo	Secretary/General Office	1954-1959
McClure, J.R.	Sales	1951-1952
McClure, Clyde J.	Transmitter Operator	1950-1951
McCowan, Betty	Executive Secretary/Bookkeeper	1947-1950
McNeil, Robbie Smith	N/A	1947-1948
McCray, Virginia	N/A	1953
Neal, Jean	Receptionist/DJ	1950-1952
Nielhay, Edwin A.	N/A	1948
Norman, Hal C.	Announcer	1948-1949
Ouelette, Kenneth R.	Transmitter Operator	1952
Pitts, James Milton	Copywriter	1959
Poole, Louis Franklin, Jr.	Sales	N/A
Patton, Kenneth N.	Transmitter Operator	N/A
Peterson, James Donald	Sales	N/A
Poteate, Pete	Sales	1952

Parris, Helen E.	Sales	1950
Presson, Jake T.	Announcer/Transmitter Operator	1948-1950
Petti, Ralph A., Jr.	Program Director/News Announcer	1953
Rollinson, John Earl	N/A	N/A
Riddle, Tommy Henry	Announcer	N/A
Riddle, Luther Allen	Announcer/Program Director	1958-1959
Rabb, Robert	Transmitter Operator	1956-1957
Richards, Richard W.	Sales	1951
Roberts, Arthur H.	Program Director/Morning Personality	1947-1950
Russell, Scott	President/General Manager	1947-1950
Roberts, Helen Wilson	Copywriter	1947
Rayer, Robert H.	N/A	1948
Riggins, Avery Leon	Transmitter Operator	1953-1955
Shelton, Skip	Free Lance DJ	N/A
Storie, Ralph Ed.	Announcer	N/A
Simpkins, Bill	N/A	1956
Simpkins, Charles	N/A	1956
Smith, James H.	N/A	1953
Slothower, Thomas	N/A	N/A
Spears, Charlie	News Announcer	1953
Strong, Jack C.	Used Cactus Jack as Country Personality and Jon Huskey as Announcer	1950-1952
Simpkins, James D. Jr.	Announcer/Entertainer/Sports PxP	1951-1952
Strong, David	N/A	1951
Sarlin, Shirley A.	Free Lance Artist	1947
Seitzer, Marguerite G.	General Office	1947-1948
Slaughter, Dorothy Ellen	General Office	1947-1948
Smith, Dan	Transmitter Operator	1948
Stanfield, Ray Marshall	Announcer/Sports PxP	1948-1950
Staton, Boyd R.	Sales	1949-1950
Shelton, L.C.	N/A	1953
Starcher, Buddy	General Manager/Country Music Singer	1953-1954
Shumate, Haskell	Janitor	1953-1954
Taylor, Marianne M.	Bookkeeper/FM Programmer	1956-1959
Thomas, Jim	Announcer	1956-1959
Tate, George D.	Chief Transmitter Operator WMRC/WESC Emergency Technician	1952
Tallevast, Enistine Anne	N/A	1957
Thomas, Jack B.	Audio Control Operator/Announcer	1948-1949
Thomas, Joe Cleveland	Announcer	1947-1948

Thompson, Louis B.	N/A	1947
Turpin, George R.	Sales	1948
Thornton, Mary Smith	Sales	1958-1959
Vowel, Davis F.	Transmitter Operator	1950
Vogal, Robert James	Transmitter Operator	1947-1949
Ward, Harry	Free Lance Boxing Announcer	N/A
Whitted, Francis Dean	Copywriter	N/A
White, Joseph Harold	Chief Transmitter Operator	1954-1959
Way, Robert R.	Program Director/News Announcer	1952-1953
Whalan, Arthur B.	N/A	1952
Walker, Wilfred J.	Free Lance Football Play By Play	N/A
Wright, Sterling W.	News/Announcer	1953
Woodard, Ray A.	Announcer	1952
Waldrop, James A.	Announcer/News Announcer	1951
Watkins, Margaret	Copywriter/General Office	1948-1950
Walter, Edward L.	N/A	1954
Young, James R.	Sales/Sports Announcer/Country Personality	1954-1956

WESC Staff 1960 to 1991

This list was developed from the memories of those who knew and worked with them. My apology to those who are not listed.

Program Director

Block, Ron

Chase, Bob

Gilbert, Dale

Heidelberg, Dan — Air Name Dan Nash

Hooper, Bobby Lee

Martin, Robert

Power, Allen

Womack, Buddy

News Director

Adams, Millard
Bookout, Allen
Davis, Roger
Deal, Kim
Fletcher, Lowell
Johnson, Herb
Jones, K.C.
Kelly, Beth
Rightsell, Bob

Copywriters

Hougland, Vicki
Teague, Nancy
Tillotson, Evelyn

Office Support

Bridges, Mary Ann
Camp, Judy
Case, Ginger
Clark, Hazel
Clement, Becky
Davenport, Gladys Taylor
Gaillard, Windy
Gibson, Barbara
Glennon, Connie
Goldsmith, Barbara
Jackson, Barbara
Jones, Ann
Lambeth, Penny
McKinney, Lib

McNair, Tersa
Mullinax, Christie
Roper, Evelyn
Taylor, Edna
Taylor, Marianne
Turner, Doris
Waddell, Theresa
Wham, Ann

Sales Representatives

Ball, Jim
Bright, Tom
Brown, Steve
Clement, George
Crocker, Myra
Dockins, Ken
Fletcher, Lowell
Jenkins, Allan
Long, Bobby
Malone, Martha
McClenaghan, Van
Mullinax, Wallace A. Jr.
Murphy, Jo Quinn
Nations, Robert
Roddy, Sarah Ann
Salter, Johnny
Sumner, C. Wayne — Sales/Announcer
Van Dyke, Peggy

Air Personality/Sales Manager/VP Sales

Mullinax, Wally

Announcers/DJ's

Baughman, Country Earl
Beale, Ray
Block, Ron
Brooks, Tony
Cooper, Mays
Floyd Edge (Uncle Dudley)
Garrett, Gregg
Gentry, Tommy
Gilbert, Dale
Gillespie, Chuck
Harrison, Mac
Harrison, Mal
Hines, Bob
Hooper, Bobby Lee
Howard, Jerry
Hunt, Michael
Hutchenson, Dave
Johnson, Joanne
Johnson, Riley
Landrum, John
Mace, Max
Mack, Jimmy
McCantosh, Lonnie
Miller, Terry
Munson, Charlie
Nabors, Fred
Nash, B.J.
Nash, Dan (Heidelberg)
Neubau, Jim
Pearson, Don

Ramsey, Rod
Rogers, Ken
Seal, Wayne
Seegers, Ben
Stubbs, Carl
Tabitha
Woods, Perry
Wright, Johnny — Sales/Announcer

Transmitter Operators

Childers, Perry
Gowens, Don — Chief Operator
Patton, Ken

General Managers

Davenport, John Y.
Power, Allen

Part III

Names
and
Faces

Some People Who Made WESC A Great Radio Station

Thanks For The Memories
The First Team

WESC's First Staff Christmas

Kneeling left to right: Wayne Davis-Announcer, Art Roberts-Emcee of *Breakfast in Bedlam*, Ed Blair-Announcer. Back row left to right: Cliff Bowers-Commercial Manager, Dot Slaughter-Copywriter, Marguerite Seitzer-General Office, Helen Roberts-Program Creator, Robbie McNeal-General Office and Scott Russell-President/General Manager.

Joe Thomas
Announcer

Edward L. Martin
Salesman

Wilfred J. Walker
Sterling High Football
Announcer

Ray Stanfield, Host of
Stanfield's Showcase

WFBC general manager Bevo
Whitmire discovered Ray Stanfield's
voice while Ray was jerking sodas and
singing at Bruce and Doster Drug Store
near Poinsett Hotel on South Main Street.
Ray was on the staff of WFBC, WESC
and WIS before leaving South Carolina.
Eventually, Ray Stanfield became a very
successful radio and television station
broker with offices in Los Angeles and
other major U.S. cities.

Typical Radio Control Room
of '40s and '50s

Bob Poole produced his early
morning "Poole's Party Line" at WMRC
in this studio. In those days, a control
operator operated the controls and the
Personality used another studio. Note the
mike in the adjacent studio. WMRC's Bob
Poole and WESC's Art Roberts enjoyed
playing pranks on Mayor Kenneth Cass
and each other.

~Ginny Bray Collection

Wally and Wayne...
"On the Road Again"

A key to WESC's early success was
remote broadcasting. Here Wally
Mullinax and Wayne Davis take the
"Ebony Swing Club" to Haverty
Furniture Company in the spring of 1950.
The store celebrated its anniversary with
annual graduation parties for female high
school graduates.

~Wayne Davis Scrapbook

Hank Williams, Sr., on WESC
October 8, 1950

Hank Williams, Sr., appeared on
WESC with Bob Edwards and the Blue
Ridge Rangers during a remote broadcast
from Mary's Record Shop. Left to right:
Bob Edwards, Hank Williams, Sr., and
Ms. Mary Mitchell, the shop co-owner.

254

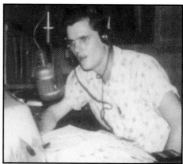

**The Squire on the Wire
Country Earl Spinning
Records in the '50s**

Note the stack of mail. WESC personalities received so much mail 'til some of it went unanswered. It was stored in 4x4 boxes. The flood of unanswered cards and letters became a storage problem, so the fire marshal ordered it trashed.

~Country Earl Collection

**FM Radio Pioneer
W. Ennis Bray**

The WESC General Manager believed the FM audience would surpass AM. Bray served as GM in 1951-53.

Gene Autry and His Greenville Reindeer

WESC freelance personality Skip Shelton and WESC freelance reporter Joe Jordan escorted cowboy singing star Gene Autry around Greenville during his visit in the '50s. Both Shelton and Jordan were Greenville policemen. Where's Rudolph?

~Joe Jordan Collection

WESC's Country Earl with Elvis' First Band

Left to right: Scotty Moore, guitar; Country Earl; and Bill Black, bass. An unidentified member of the Jordanaires is in the background.

Aunt Jemima Garden Show
It's Springtime in Caroline!

WESC broadcast remotes from the Annual Home & Garden Show at Textile Hall on West Washington Street. Aunt Jemima Grits advertised on the Chicken Shack and Country Earl Show. To get attention we sometimes said: "There ain't a bug in a carload of Aunt Jemima Grits." When the national sales manager came to town to find out why the campaign was so successful he stopped the ad-libbing. When he left town, Charles Tumblin, the local salesman, told us to go back to ab-libbing because he wanted to keep selling grits.

~Photo: 1955 USC/SCBA Archives

"660 in DIXIE"

WESC

WESC

WESC
660 AM   5000
92.5 FM   Watts

...AKE
...P
...OLINA"

...p Morning Personality ★

EARL BAUGHMAN

"The Earl of Country Music" DAILY MONDAY THROUGH SATURDAY—5 A.M. TO 9 A.M.

WALLY MULLINAX
"EBONY SWING CLUB"
1:00 - 3:00 P.M.

WAYNE DAVIS
"NEWS & SPORTS"
7:45 - 8:00 A.M.

DON BAILEY
"DINING WITH DON"
12:15 - 1:00 P.M.

The Personalities Make

WESC

The Friendly "Voice" Of Greenville

JIM YOUNG
"MELODY ROUNDUP"
3:00 - 4:00 P.M.

Sunday
JUNE 27, 1954

AUNT MARGARET
"TINY TOT TIME"
4:00 - 4:30 P.M.

BILL KRIEGER
"660 CLUB"
5:15 - 7:00 P.M.

WESC   ★ Ask to See the 1954 Pulse Radio Survey!

ROGER DAVIS, son of Mr. and Mrs. Wayne Davis of Fountain Inn and the grandson of Mr. and Mrs. Lyman Davis of Third Avenue, and a former resident of Greenville has taken a position with station KVII TV in Amarillo, Tex. He was formerly with WSPA-TV in Spartanburg. At one time he was associated with WESC Radio here. 7-26-68

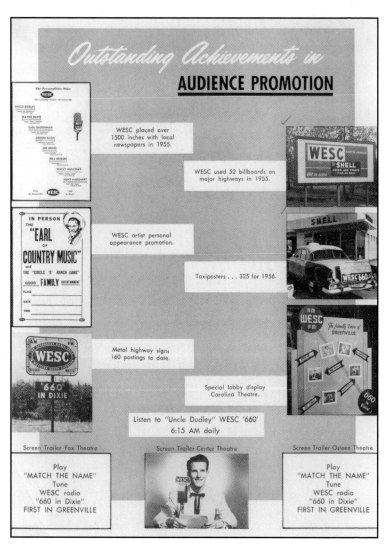

WESC Promotion Was Everywhere

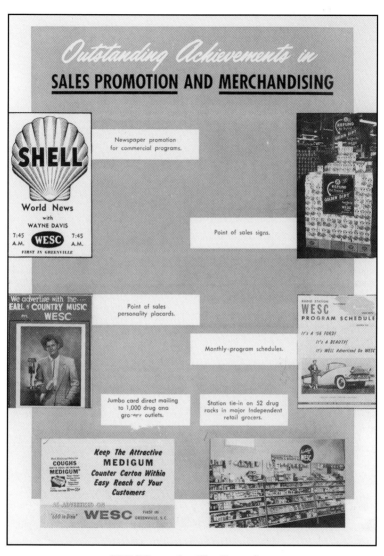

WESC Promotion Was Everywhere

The First Mobile Mike in the Nation

Shown here promoting National Radio Week. It is believed all Greenville radio stations broadcast some of their broadcast day from the studio during National Radio Week. This vehicle was sold to WCOS in Columbia where it was photographed by a LIFE Magazine reporter and later published.

~Photo: 1955, USC/SCBA Archives

Mobile Mike-Ero

The next generation of mobile mike was built on a Ford Ranchero. It could be moved easily from location to location in about an hour. WESC could broadcast several remotes a day. Note the speakers providing public address service during the radio broadcast. WESC engineer Harold White installed the equipment; the studio was built by Rimer Mobile Homes.

~Photo: 1956, USC/SCBA Archives

Fabulous Fifties Team

Top row left to right: Bill Ingram, Sylvia McMannis, Wayne Davis, and Harold White. Second row: Bill Krieger, Marianne Taylor, Betty Jo McGuire, and John Davenport. Bottom row: Floyd "Uncle Dudley" Edge, Ben McGuire, Allen Riddle, W.A. "Bill" Kirby, Wally Mullinax, "Cousin" Alma Hamil and Country Earl Baughman (1957).

Hello America

This is Jim Pitts reporting from your nation's capital. Now a Furman University chaplain, Dr. Pitts sharpened his persuasive talents at WESC while a student at Furman University.

Take A Letter, Ms. Mobley

Olive Mobley was the first sales secretary. She says her qualification for the job was that she made a tasty cup of coffee. All of the secretaries who came after Ms. Mobley knew that she had to have been a good speller, also.

Have A Pepsi...Win A Buick

It may have been Greenville's first big car giveaway. Greenville's principal radio stations combined to promote Pepsi Cola and give away a new 1957 Buick. Left to right: Frank Cope, WMRB; Wayne Davis, WESC; Bob Shelly, WFBC; Tommy Hartness, Pepsi Cola bottler; and Mayor J. Kenneth Cass.

~Photo: 1957, USC/SCBA Archives

Community Club Awards Breakfast

In the late '50s, usually in the fall, WESC held a Community Club Awards promotion. Hundreds of club women earned CCA points that were redeemed for cash. Pictured is an organizational meeting held annually at the Poinsett Hotel. At the head table are seated left to right: Bill Krieger, Marianne Taylor and Doris Ashley. Standing left to right: Alma Hamil, Marty White, John Davenport and Bill Ingram.

263

Community Clubs Awards Produced Results!

WESC general manager John Davenport and Community Clubs director Agnes Ivester are sure to get a renewal of the Bond Bread account showing these wrappers.

WESC Produced Results! So Greenville Was Used As A Test Market

Many advertising agencies tested the power of radio by advertising on WESC to break new campaigns. They saw WESC's format as a means of reaching the blue-collar worker. Rhythm and blues music targeted blacks and teens, country and western music reached the people with a Rural background, and gospel music and Religious programs attracted religious listeners. The 3 R's was considered a results oriented format. Anytime during the day WESC reached 1 person in 4 in a 9 county area.

Hello...This Is Greenville Calling

"Greenville Calling" from 7:30 a.m. until 9:00 a.m. Wally Mullinax called people in the news to talk about their story. This was a pioneer talk show.

~Photo: 1958-59, USC/SCBA Archives

WESC Live In the Mornings

Seated are left to right: Ansel Garrett, Bill Huffman and Bobby Lawson. Standing left to right are: Allen Riddle, Don Dudley (at mike), Harley Cox and Dr. Ralph Polson.

Those Funny Little Foreign Cars

WESC was visible just about everywhere when the foreign car craze hit the upstate. The personalities went rollin'-rollin'-rollin'. They are left to right: Dave Hutchenson, Harold White, Allen Riddle, Country Earl, Bill Kirby and Max Mace.
~Photo: 1959, USC/SCBA Archives

266

Mr. Greenville on Television

Johnny Wright was Mr. Greenville on Channel 4 in the '50s. He left the industry for a few years, coming to WESC as morning personality in 1960. Johnny took his show on the road to Clemson for the first Carolina/Clemson game played in Clemson. This was the first full day of programming outside the station. It is believed to be the first full length morning show produced on the road.

WESC Was at Clemson November 12, 1960

WESC originated a full day of programming from Clemson on the day the first Clemson/Carolina game was played at Clemson. A network of about 16 stations in SC carried the day that showcased the school. Seventy-five or more stations carried the football game on the Clemson Network. Jimmy Coggins and Ed Osborne described the game. WESC's Johnny Wright and Buddy Womack interviewed VIPs in the stands. Wally Mullinax produced the show from the campus radio station, WBSF.

267

A Tower of Power!

Greenville Mayor Dave Traxler symbolically pushes the switch to make WESC AM South Carolina's most powerful station in 1961. Shown left to right are: U.S. Congressman Robert T. Ashmore, Mayor Traxler, State Representative Burnett R. Maybank, Jr., WESC President Robert A. Schmid and General Manager John Davenport.

~Classic Collection of Joe Jordan, Photographer

Greenville's North Main Street Area in 1961

WESC AM increased power to 10,000 watts. The studio was in the basement of the Prevost Building across from the Ottaray Hotel.

~Classic Collection of Joe Jordan, Photographer

The Top Moguls in Town!

WESC celebrated its power increase to 10,000 watts in 1961. WESC president Robert A. Schmid and wife, Jarrett, are flanked by Robert A. Jolley, president of WFBC/AM/FM/TV, on the left and Walter A. Brown, president of WSPA/AM/FM/TV, on the right.

The Ad Men Came

Greenville's top ad men came to the big power increase celebration in 1961. Left to right: Bob Schmid, president of WESC; Bill Leslie, founder of Leslie Advertising; Jim Henderson, founder of Henderson Advertising; Sid Lowe, co-founder of the Lowe and Hall agency; and John Davenport, general manager of WESC.

269

Tower of Ice

The tower of ice was supposed to last several days but a warm front came through and melted it almost overnight. To succeed you must sell your problems. The story of the promotion that just melted away was told and this picture circulated to time buyers all over the country. There's no doubt the promotion was a bigger success than if it had gone off as planned.

~Nov. 1961, USC/SCBA Archives

Singer Sonny James Puts March of Dimes Campaign Over the Top!

Sonny's big hit of the '50s, *Young Love,* had sustained his career but he needed a boost in 1964. At Max Mace's invitation he appeared in Greenville to benefit the March of Dimes and the picture was taken. It appeared in several national publications and Sonny James gives the event a lot of credit for reviving his career. Sonny's singles and albums were always on the charts from 1964 to 1979. This is the air staff that switched WESC to all county music in 1965. Left to right: Bob Hooper, Jim McAlister, Wally Mullinax, Sonny James, Max Mace and Wayne Sumner.

~The Classic Collection of Joe Jordan, Photographer

Up...Up...and Away

Greenville County Sheriff Johnny Mack Brown and WESC personalities Bob Hooper and Allan Bookout pose before the launch. Freedom Weekend was a lofty way to be where the action was in the '80s.

~The Classic Collection of Joe Jordan, Photographer

Clear!

Don Pearson and Wally Mullinax do a walk around check before take off. In the early '70s, the two learned to fly and used the experience to build interest in private aviation. Their talk about hammer head stalls, cross wind landings and getting lost caused WESC listeners to get involved. One lady called Wally to say that she threw 'maters at him every time he buzzed her garden. By the way, Don Pearson flew a Piper Cub owned by his father and Warren Gwinn, manager of a fleet base operation at the downtown airport, provided Wally with Cessna 150's and 172's.

~The Classic Collection of Joe Jordan, Photographer

Turning the Big Guns on Cancer

Bob Hooper and his Cancer Freedom Fighters collected about $1,000,000 for cancer. WESC devoted hundreds of hours of air time every year and assigned staff members during their working hours to the project. Community volunteers were the backbone of the campaign that took weeks to plan and execute.

~1985, The Classic Collection of
Joe Jordan, Photographer

He's Everywhere! He's Everywhere!

Billboards — Television — Cash Contests — Newspapers — Live Country Shows — T-Shirts. Wherever people would go, they were reminded of the *Super Hooper Show.*

40 Years Makes A Big Difference

WSPA Transmitter

The first WSPA transmitter put in service in 1929.

WESC Transmitter

The WESC state of the art transmitter plant in 1969.

273

Crash!!

Around midnight, January 31, 1983, the WESC tower on Caesars Head mountain came crashing down under the weight of about 55 tons of ice. WESC immediately started to rebuild. LeRoy Hamilton of Simpsonville, S.C., was given a contract on February 7, 1983, to remove the damaged equipment, twisted wires, steel, etc., paving the way to rebuild it.

The South Carolina Legislature honors WESC General Manager John Y. Davenport, recognizing his achievements in radio upon his induction into the South Carolina Broadcasters Hall of Fame in 1983. Making the presentation on the *Bob Hooper Show* is State Representative Tom Marchant.

The Grand Old Opry Stars Came to Greenville for WESC Shindigs

About six times a year between 1967 and 1977 the WESC Country Music Shindigs packed the Greenville Memorial Auditorium. Usually there were five acts that played to "sold out" audiences. The auditorium seated about 6,750 people and 2,500 could be seated in the annex. The people came from Georgia, Tennessee, North Carolina and Upstate South Carolina. These shows developed Greenville into an entertainment center.

Running Radials on the Road

Consulting engineer Palmer Greer takes field strength readings to provide the FCC information on the signal strength of WESC and other stations using frequencies close to 660 on the AM dial. Stations were required to take field strength measurements regularly, as well as, when power increases were requested.

And Away We Go To Nashville!

Bob Hooper drove this remote unit to the Country Music Association meetings in Nashville until he wrecked it in Georgia.

Wally's Folly

The WESC Flying Saucer whizzed around shopping centers during remotes in the early '60s. It wasn't very popular with the staff because of the heat, so it was given to charity. Thereafter John Davenport jokingly called it Wally's Folly.

Give Him A Hand!

So many listeners called Wally Mullinax during the morning show that WESC had to provide extra hands to do the work. Wally is playing records, telling where the radar is, answering two phones, giving away green stamps, adjusting his mike, keeping a log, pulling his hair out and saying a prayer.

~Photo 1969, USC/SCBA Archives Collection

Greenville County Councilman Wally Mullinax explains the punch card voting system to Greenville Chamber of Commerce executive Bob Ware. Some were concerned that voters might not clearly punch their choice.

~1969

The Sunday School Lesson has been on 660 KC each Sunday morning about 8:00 since 1962. Left to right: Wally Mullinax, moderator; Betty Orders; Betty Walker; Demmie Thompson-Grier and George Lathem (Walker and Lathem are now deceased).

The 5th String and other area bands were used as "warm up" bands for Family Reunions and other events. Shown here are: Susan Snyder, guitar; Alan Brooker, banjo; David Snyder, mandolin; and Henry Dockery, bass.

278

Dr. Richard Uray, Executive Manager of the South Carolina Broadcasters Association is inducted into the South Carolina Broadcasters Association Hall of Fame at the winter meeting in Columbia in 1995. Helen Mullinax assists in the unveiling of the bronze likeness of Dr. Uray while Emcee Wally Mullinax looks on.

SCBA Board of Directors 1961-1962

President was Louis M. Neal, Jr., of WBEU in Beaufort, South Carolina, seated in the center of the first row. Some others in the picture are: Wilson C. Wearn, WFBC AM/FM/TV, Greenville; W. Frank Harden, WIS, Columbia; Ed Osborne, WBCU, Union; John Davenport, WESC, Greenville; and Cleatus O. Brazzell, WELP, Easley. How many can you identify?

SCBA Awards of Distinction...January 2002

Bob Hooper of Clear Channel-Greenville was recognized for his industry success and his remarkable accomplishment in public service with the SCBA Honorary Life Membership Award. L to R: Sandra Dill, Bruce Logan, Bob Hooper, Roy Costner, Roxanne Walker, Bill McMartin, and Wayne Sumner.

Greenville broadcast pioneer Monty DuPuy received the SCBA distinguished Masters Award, recognizing his lifetime contributions to South Carolina broadcasting. Pictured here L to R: Wally Mullinax (Past President of SCBA), Mr. Monty DuPuy, Roxanne Walker (Clear Channel-Greenville), Mrs. Monty "Miriam" DuPuy.

Good Ole Days — Shindig Nights 1965-1977

Waylon Jennings
Wally Mullinax

Jan Howard
Mayes Cooper
Bill Anderson

Millard Adams

Charlie Pride
Wayne Sumner

Bob Hooper
Colonel Sanders

Rod Ramsey
Jeannie
Shealey

Kenny Price
Lowell
Fletcher

Bob Hooper
Tammy Wynette

Jerry Howard
Merle Haggard
Bonnie Owens

Connie Smith
Max Mace

281

Some More VIP's

John Davenport

Dale Gilbert

Don Gowens

Allan Jenkins

Nancy Teague

Steve Brown

Connie Glennon

Ken Dockins

Barbara Jackson

Virginia Case

WESC Air Staff
1980's

WESC
FM Stereo 92
AM Stereo 66
BIG COUNTRY

PERSONALITIES

BOB HOOPER

ALLEN BOOKOUT
"THE WAKING CREW"

FRANCES

DAN NASH 10-3 FM 92

B.J. NASH 10-3 AM 660

LONG JOHN 3-7 AM/FM

"MUSIC" MUNSON
7-MIDNIGHT FM 92

ANTHONY BAGWELL
MIDNIGHT-5 a.m.
FM 92

KIM DEAL
WESC NEWS

ALLEN POWER
FM 92
SUNDAYS 6-10 a.m.

Hejaz Shriners welcome Wally Mullinax into Hejaz, November 1972, at Myrtle Beach.

WESC wins Station of the Year in 1976.

Greenville County Council Chairman Ralph Blakely, and Vice Chairman Mullinax receive Chamber of Commerce resolution on election improvements from Greenville newspaperman Bill Morris.

WESC promotes gospel singing, 1974.

The WESC main control room, 1976. The station had just moved to Stone Ave. in Greenville. L to R: Wally Mullinax, vice-president, sales; WESC AM/FM; Dale Gilbert, program director; John Davenport, president.

A Half Century of Greenville Morning Radio

Left to right: Bob Hooper, WESC AM/FM; Monty DuPuy, WFBC AM/FM and WGXL; Wally Mullinax, WESC AM/FM; and Bob Poole, WMRC AM/FM, WMRB AM and WFBC AM/FM. A home video of their philosophy is on file at the USC/ SCBA Archives.

The South Carolina Broadcasters Go to Washington
Left to right: Walter T. Brown, president of Spartan Radiocasting (WSPA AM/FM/TV) in Spartanburg; Cleatus O. Brazzell, president of WELP in Easley; the Honorable Ernest F. "Fritz" Hollings, US Senator from South Carolina; and Wally Mullinax, president of the South Carolina Broadcasters Association.

~Photo 1974, USC/SCBA Archives

Bob Nations wins the Distinguished Salesman's Award at the Greenville Sales and Marketing Executive Association's annual event. Bob receives the award with wife, Haley at his side.

1968

WESC Supported All The SCBA Presidents!

WESC actively supported all presidents of the South Carolina Broadcasters Association. At least one representative attended all the winter and summer meetings. Also, when WESC staff members were named to committees they were expected to participate. Shown here are some past presidents and the year they served.

Bottom row left to right: Nick Frangias (86); Bill McElveen (85); Matt Sedota (95); Frank Harden (62); Wally Mullinax (74); Hub Blankenship (65); Tad Forgel (73); Barry Brown (97); Charles Batson (57).

Top row left to right: Jim Whitaker (69); Joe Sessoms (91); Jack West (93); Harold Miller (92); Betty Roper (79); Dick Laughridge (72); Ben Davis (80); Dixon Lovvorn (90); Randy Davidson (58); Gloria Wilson (87); Ken Harmon (82); Wayne Sawyer (70); Beau Sanders (83); Wallace Martin (54); James Coggins (56); Ed Osborne (60); Lou Kirchen (98); Ron Loewen (96).

Dr. Jimmy Epting, president of North Greenville College cites Wally Mullinax for service to the college at the end of his term as a trustee in 1995.

A Million-Dollar-Year in 1981 was rewarded with trips to Hawaii. Left to right: Helen and Wally Mullinax; Mary Ella and Steve Brown; and Faye and George Clement. Wayne and Nancy Sumner chose to go at another time.

Lynn Anderson and Lonnie McIntosh

Wally and Lt. Governor and Mrs. West. Senator Harry Chapman brought Govenor West to the Auditorium.

Loretta Lynn and Wayne Sumner

Conway Twittie and Wayne Sumner

The book wouldn't be complete
without these pictures

Allen Riddle

Les Timms
Auditorium Manager

Evelyn Roper

Nancy Teague

Shriner Bob Hooper

Judy Camp

292

In the fall of 1946 WESC established temporary offices in the Otteray Hotel on North Main Street — where the Hyatt Regency now stands — while WESC studios and offices were under construction across the street in the basement of the Provost building. The hotel was a popular spot for towns folk and travelers. They sat on the porch and rocked in large green rockers to watch the world go by.

At the Christmas party of 1990, I told these guys that we may never be together again. Bob Schmid was dead, John Davenport had retired, so I thought we should take the above photograph; L to R: Bob Hooper, Morning Personality; Don Gowens, Engineer; Paul Brown, Newsman; Wally Mullinax, VP sales and Jerry Howard, D.J. In the car going home Helen said, "They said so many good things about you — look out they may ask you to retire!" It did turn out to be my *Farewell Party*.